Investing
in the
New Europe

Also available from
BLOOMBERG PRESS

Investing in REITs: Real Estate Investment Trusts
by Ralph L. Block

Masstering Microcaps: Strategies, Trends, and Stock Selection
by Daniel P. Coker

Investing in Small-Cap Stocks: Revised Edition
by Christopher Graja and Elizabeth Ungar, Ph.D.

Investing in Latin America: Best Stocks, Best Funds
by Michael Molinski

Investing in Hedge Funds: Strategies for the New Marketplace
by Joseph G. Nicholas

Market-Neutral Investing: The Essential Strategies
by Joseph G. Nicholas

Small-Cap Dynamics
by Satya Dev Pradhuman

Investing in IPOs Version 2.0
by Tom Taulli

A complete list of our titles is available at
www.bloomberg.com/books

ATTENTION CORPORATIONS

Bloomberg Press books are available at quantity discounts with bulk
purchase for sales-promotional use and for corporate education or
other business uses. Special editions or book excerpts can also be
created. For information, please call 609-279-4670 or write to: Special
Sales Dept., Bloomberg Press, P.O. Box 888, Princeton, NJ 08542.

Investing
in the
New Europe

ERIC UHLFELDER

BLOOMBERG PRESS
PRINCETON

First edition published 2001
1 3 5 7 9 10 8 6 4 2

Library of Congress Cataloging-in-Publication Data

Uhlfelder, Eric.
    Investing in the new Europe / by Eric Uhlfelder.
        p. cm.
    Includes bibliographical references and index.
    ISBN 1-57660-028-9 (alk. paper)
    1. Investments--Europe. 2. Securities--Europe. 3. Capital market--Europe. I. Title.

HG5422 .U37 2001
332.67'3'094--dc21

00-046782

Edited by Maris Williams

Book Design by Laurie Lohne / Design It Communications

Dedicated to Professor Rebecca Todd, whose enthusiasm for all things financial proved most infectious;

to Kathleen Price, who provided me access to the most awesome work space in New York; and

to Richard Levin, whose success in business has helped make much of my work possible.

Contents

Investing Approaches and Issues

List of Illustrations & Tables

Acknowledgments

Many people helped to produce this book. Every country description, every sector report, every stock analysis involved discussions with numerous individuals who had nothing in particular to gain and still offered their time graciously: Nick Antrill and Duncan Farr, Morgan Stanley Dean Witter; Khalid Beydown, Steve Turner, and Victoria Maxwell-Snape, HSBC; Eric Biassette, ING Barings; Eric Bleines, Indocam Asset Management European Equity Portfolio Manager; Sam Brothwell, Nicholas Byrne, Richard Coleman, Fay Dodd, Ian Graham, Mal Patel, Chris Rowland, and Marie Owens Thomsen, Merrill Lynch; Richard Burden, Goldman Sachs; Professor Fred Choi, Dean of the undergraduate Stern School of Business, New York University; Michael Cohen, Andrew Light, and Richard Urwick, Schroders SalomonSmithBarney; Pierre Coiffet, BNP Paribas; Gary Klopfensteen, GK Capital; Alberto Montagne, Lehman Brothers; Neil Rackoff, President of Friedberg Mercantile Exchange; Marc Rode, Warburg Dillon Read; Angus Runcimen, J.P. Morgan; and Clive Vaughan, Retail Intelligence.

A variety of institutions provided access to superb sources of data. I'm indebted to Joe Abbott, formerly of IBES International, for hooking me into trapeze.net, and to his successor Joe Kalinowski for continuing that access; Julie Arnold, the *Financial Times;* Alexander Bateman, Economist Intelligence Unit; Carl Beckley, FTSE (I apologize that we didn't have room for your wonderful sidebar); Deborah Ciervo and John Prestbo, Dow Jones Indexes; Adrian Hill, BNP Paribas; Stephen Murphy, Martha Conlon, and Bridget Hughes, Morningstar; and the writers of the *Financial Times* and *The Economist,* who provided a constant flow of news and analysis of the very latest issues right to my doorstep and desktop.

Many thanks to the investor relations specialists at each one of my featured companies and the folks at the Electronic Resource Center at New York University's Bobst Library.

At Bloomberg, many thanks to Emil Efthimides, Barbara Diez Goldenberg, JoAnne Kanaval, Laurie Lohne, Wilson Fan, Jared Kieling, Peter Lederer, James Sannella, Bob Wilson, and my editor, Maris Williams, who deftly managed the transformation of a long manuscript into a book.

And special thanks to Scott Clemons, comanager of the 59 Wall Street European Equity Fund; Michel Fleuriet, chairman of HSBC France; and Jean-Yannick Liatis, head of French equity research at BNP Paribas.

On a personal level, I wish to thank Kathleen Price, for giving me access to her phenomenal library; Stewart Fergus, for his insights on the United Kingdom (nay, Scotland) and on Europe in general; and Dieter Hess, for his unbiased views of the Fatherland, his bearish perspective of the stock market, and his overall support.

Introduction

DOMINATING THE NEWS out of Europe during much of 2000 was the continuous decline of the euro. But Europe's beleaguered currency is by no means the Continent's top story.

The truly big news is government and corporate restructuring that's been going on for nearly a decade. This has created extraordinary investment opportunities as evidenced by European equity performance since the middle of the 1990s. And for U.S. investors, a cheap euro only makes Europe an even better buy for the long term.

There are two basic reasons why investors should be buying European stocks. One, many Continental companies are superb investments. Global powerhouses like mobile phone and network manufacturer Nokia, retail leader Carrefour, and utility giant Suez Lyonnaise des Eaux are aggressively securing huge chunks of their respective markets, enjoying strong profit margins and very bright futures. The second reason: improving corporate and economic fundamentals are driving up European multiples—that is, price-to-earnings ratios—accelerating stock price growth. Even more radical than the U.S. corporate restructurings of the 1980s, these changes are revitalizing European business, just as they did in the States. Profit-driven Anglo-Saxon management techniques are replacing less-bottom-line-oriented agendas and strategies motivated by social agendas, politics, and inefficient "old boy" networks, justifying these reratings.

Labor reform is leading to greater production efficiency and lower costs. Economic and monetary union is forging a slew of broad macroeconomic benefits—low interest rates, privatization, and restructuring topping the list—which are vastly improving the business environment across Europe. These changes are bringing a new focus on shareholder value.

And the introduction of common currency—what Michel Fleuriet, chairman in France of HSBC, the huge global banking and financial services organization, regards as the "mother of all mergers"—has introduced price transparency, access to larger capital markets at lower costs, reduction in foreign exchange costs, and a strong impetus for cross-border mergers and acquisitions.

Although improving fundamentals may justify higher multiples, soaring demand for securities is what's making them a reality. Long-term decline of bond yields and an increasing faith in equities as sound investments are creating a whole new class of investors that never existed before. Workers from all economic classes, from Ireland to Greece, are shifting an increasing percentage of their assets from savings accounts and bonds into stocks and mutual funds. And European pension funds are doing the same thing.

Nowhere else on the globe have conditions aligned themselves in such a potentially explosive manner. And if unions, politicians, and traditional corporate powers don't stand in the way—and they didn't in the creation of the euro—then it's a good bet that Europe will continue its business renaissance, enhancing profitability from the small clothing manufacturer in Lille to the largest multinationals in Frankfurt. And that's what makes investing in the new Europe so compelling.

THIS BOOK METHODICALLY GUIDES you through all the essentials for investing in Europe. Part One lays out the investment thesis, explaining the structural changes in government and corporate operations that together are creating lucrative investment opportunities.

Part Two reveals these changes as they evolve across nineteen major markets of western and central Europe, from the core economies of France, Britain, and Germany to the rapidly expanding tiger economies along the periphery of the Continent—including Ireland, Portugal, and

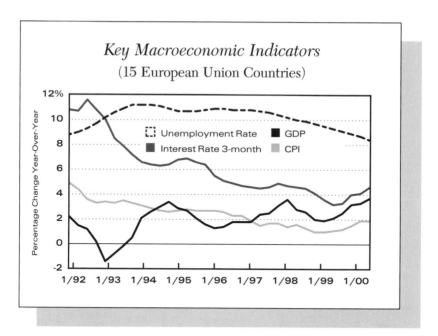

Key Macroeconomic Indicators
(15 European Union Countries)

Legend:
☐ Unemployment Rate   ■ GDP
■ Interest Rate 3-month   ▨ CPI

Source: Merrill Lynch

the Netherlands—through the emerging markets of Hungary, Poland, and the Czech Republic. Here we explore the economic, political, and social influences each nation exerts on its respective equity market.

Part Three gets down to investment specifics, illustrating how fundamental improvements are turbocharging five major sectors. Ten company analyses then provide concrete examples of the promise of Europe, each characterizing the major themes of change discussed at the beginning of the book. Part Three also shows how investors can use mutual funds to profit from the new Europe.

This part then concludes by discussing three important investment issues: fundamental differences between U.S. and Continental accounting and reporting standards, foreign exchange, and equity benchmarks.

Perhaps the most valuable component of the book comes at the end: Resources. The one theme that characterizes investing in the new Europe is change. It is occurring at a cosmic pace, and at any given time, events can turn askew even the most basic investment assumptions. For example, during the three-month period after I completed the sector analysis in spring 2000, telecommunications tumbled by nearly one-third. Several featured stocks have taken hits.

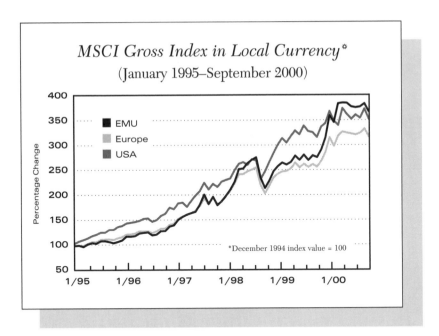

MSCI *Gross Index in Local Currency**
(January 1995–September 2000)

*December 1994 index value = 100

EMU
Europe
USA

Source: MSCI

Does that mean I erred in their inclusion? Not at all.

The featured sectors and stocks tell the story of European economic transformation. But readers need keep in mind that due to the extraordinary volatility of today's markets, at any one moment my picks may or may not be the leading investment opportunities over any twelve-month period. However, over the long term they have proven their worth.

This leads us to a basic premise about investing—good timing. And to help investors determine the most opportune moments to climb into stocks, I've assembled an extensive list of publications and Web sites to enable investors to stay on top of the latest European news. These resources will help you trade and invest more profitably. You must do your homework. Regardless of how diligently I've done mine, there's no such thing as a free lunch, especially if it can be purchased for 25 percent less than the going rate.

As for the bedraggled euro, consider its misfortunes the market's way of keeping the pressure on for further government and corporate reform. In October 2000, nearly all analysts agreed that the euro was significantly undervalued. As corporate and individual investors continue to recognize the metamorphosis going on across the Atlantic, you will see the euro regain parity with the dollar, giving your investments an added boost.

Part One

Today's Europe

Chapter One

The Promise of Europe

IN 1999, SHARES OF THE U.K.-based bank HSBC climbed by 57.4 percent in local currency terms. French retailer Carrefour rose 71 percent. Swedish insurer Skandia more than doubled. And shares of Finland's world-class mobile phone maker Nokia more than tripled.[1]

Just a lucky year? Hardly.

From 1995 through 1999, each one of these stocks generated phenomenal annualized returns: HSBC 34.8 percent, Carrefour 39 percent, and Skandia 61.7 percent, and Nokia nearly doubled each year, averaging gains of 92.2 percent a year.[2]

This is the new Europe. It's the Europe that's attracting America's largest banks and investment houses to shift substantial resources across the Atlantic, that's getting George Soros, Kohlberg Kravis Roberts, and GE Capital Corp. to commit billions in private equity and venture capital into various Continental ventures, financing mergers and acquisitions, and leverage buyouts on a scale resembling the United States in the 1980s when today's bull market started its historic run. The prospect that Europe is poised to track similar success is what the big money is betting on. But to most individual investors, this Europe is as obscure as a panaché.

The irony of all of this is that although Europe has never had a problem attracting airplane-loads of travel dollars to its shores, when it comes to its equity markets, most individual investors just don't seem to think there are a whole lot of Eiffel Towers and Grand Canals trading across the region's various bourses. For Americans in particular, the thousands of miles of ocean does tend to keep us focused more domestically. Also, the big news stories that dominated the 1990s—erratic European growth, perennially high jobless rates, and the euro's out-of-the-block collapse—simply hasn't encouraged shipping capital across the Atlantic when the American economy and markets have been performing so well.

However, systemic change is making European investments not only an effective way to diversify a portfolio but a smart bet for locking in strong returns. Europe has started to shed its government-influenced, border-conscious, structurally rigid style of doing business and is increasingly committed to competing in the global marketplace. For labor, management, consumers, and investors, the implications of this change are dramatic. And the metamorphosis is only in its early stages.

The Continent has a way to go to replicate U.S. market efficiencies, with countries like Germany, Austria, Belgium, Sweden, and Italy still well behind the curve. This is the risk of investing in Europe. But it is also the reason why Europe offers such opportunity.

As crass and unseemly and as profitable as McDonald's on the Champs Elysées, companies are becoming increasingly Americanized. Restructuring, mergers, friendly and hostile buyouts, and privatization are happening with a new, keen attention to enhancing shareholder value while low interest rates, privatized pensions, and an explosion in Continental mutual funds are driving an equity boom from the Scandinavian fjords to the Greek Isles. Fueling all of this change has been adoption of a common currency that has led to improved macroeconomic conditions, market deregulation, and the increased efficiencies of more open competition, which are strengthening the concept and potential of a truly unified European market.

The bottom line is that you can find Microsofts, Baby Bells, and ExxonMobils in bourses across Europe, which in many instances, U.S. investors can buy in the form of American Depositary Receipts (ADRs) listed on our major domestic exchanges. In fact, more than 200 leading European corporations—everything from consumer goods and banks to telecoms and high-tech start-ups—trade every day on the New York and American Stock Exchanges and the Nasdaq. With Asia's emerging markets still trying to recover from the turmoil of the late 1990s, with Russia still unable to figure out what kind of economic and political systems it wishes to embrace, with Latin and South American markets unable to sustain consistent growth, and with our own interminable bull market defying the logic of its own age, the restructuring of European economies and companies offers one of the best risk/return scenarios to be found anywhere.

Some Pretty Heady Numbers

WESTERN EUROPE EQUITY MARKETS have been on a tear. In 1999, they rose collectively by nearly 28 percent in local currency terms, led by Finland (up 193.7 percent), Sweden (up 87.4 percent), and France (up 50 percent).[3]

Stocks within the eleven-nation eurozone (before the entry of Greece) performed even better, rising 37.5 percent. However, the weakness of the euro cut the region's dollar-based gains to 17.4 percent, which was still only 3.5 percentage points below U.S. returns for the year.

Favorable comparison with the U.S. market goes back further. Eurozone returns between 1996 and 1998 virtually matched the astonishing performance U.S. stocks had. During those three years, the Dow rose an annualized 26.24 percent while eurozone stocks appreciated 25.58 percent a year in dollar terms. Half a dozen bourses outperformed the Dow. Belgium stocks ran up an annualized average of 26.52 percent, Irish stocks gained nearly 30 percent, and Italian stocks were up 30.7 percent. Spanish and Portuguese stocks jumped 33.4 percent and 35.32 percent, respectively, while Finnish stocks realized annualized gains of more than 44 percent.[4]

These numbers may be a surprise to some, and for good reason. "For the first time, many European companies are focused on profitability," explains Mark L. Yockey, who manages the $3.6 billion Artisan International Fund, "and as a result, corporate profits are taking off."[5]

Near-term corporate earnings will likely remain strong. A spring 2000 consensus of analyst profits estimates, collected by IBES International for 2000–2001, suggests European corporate profits will compare favorably with those of the United States. Earnings in nine nations—France, Spain, the Netherlands, Italy, Finland, Sweden, Greece, Poland, and Hungary—are expected to outpace U.S. earnings growth over that time.[6]

European Market Returns in Local Currency

COUNTRY	1ST H 2000*	1999	1997–99 †	1995–99 ‡
Austria	(6.20%)	4.88%	4.08%	1.73%
Belgium	(13.16)	(1.33)	24.94	20.84
Czech Republic	8.88	24.33	1.10	0.40
Denmark	8.37	29.31	26.04	22.25
Finland	6.80	193.70	101.74	61.09
France	10.47	49.95	35.65	26.60
Germany	(3.68)	39.05	33.43	24.88
Greece	(21.87)	73.64	66.08	39.27
Hungary	(2.68)	30.74	45.46	48.59
Ireland	(14.79)	0.72	19.90	19.29
Italy	7.97	15.41	36.20	21.21
Netherlands	4.93	23.30	25.38	24.89
Norway	3.91	36.62	5.52	8.01
Poland	6.45	53.95	9.91	18.44
Portugal	1.48	4.43	27.52	21.11
Spain	(2.61)	21.28	34.00	32.48
Sweden	12.07	87.35	40.91	35.55
Switzerland	0.63	7.44	24.49	23.32
United Kingdom	(7.17)	13.28	16.82	16.06
U.S.A.	(2.53)	20.86	27.06	27.36
The World Index	(0.90)	26.27	22.04	19.62
EMU	3.78	37.47	34.85	26.55
Europe	0.89	27.92	27.81	23.04

* Half-year actual price returns   † 3-year annualized price returns   ‡ 5-year annualized price returns

Source: MSCI

The New Europe

IN PROVENCE, FRANCE, in the offices of the world's largest manufacturer of smart cards, Gemplus SCA has made English its spoken language. The company is waging battle against French unions, planning new production facilities in foreign countries where labor is cheap, and working out details for an initial public offering in the States.[7]

Well before Switzerland's primary telecom service provider, Swisscom, went public in 1998—the country's first state-run firm to be pri-

European Market Returns in U.S. Dollars

COUNTRY	1ST H 2000*	1999	1997–99†	1995–99‡
Austria	(10.30%)	(10.47%)	(3.81%)	(2.84%)
Belgium	(16.95)	(15.77)	15.46	15.30
Czech Republic	5.20	3.97	(7.82)	(4.52)
Denmark	3.38	10.85	16.73	17.49
Finland	2.14	150.71	85.45	54.02
France	5.64	28.00	25.62	21.54
Germany	(7.89)	18.70	23.33	19.26
Greece	(26.74)	47.58	50.79	30.79
Hungary	(8.87)	10.81	25.10	26.41
Ireland	(18.51)	(14.02)	9.02	14.77
Italy	3.25	(1.48)	25.75	17.06
Netherlands	0.35	5.25	15.74	19.12
Norway	(2.30)	29.52	(2.27)	4.35
Poland	1.19	30.52	(2.84)	6.54
Portugal	(2.96)	(10.86)	17.18	15.71
Spain	(6.87)	3.53	23.53	26.48
Sweden	9.16	77.76	30.76	31.83
Switzerland	(0.94)	(7.81)	17.40	18.45
United Kingdom	(12.80)	9.74	14.50	16.75
U.S.A.	(2.53)	20.86	27.06	27.36
The World Index	(3.04)	23.56	20.11	18.09
EMU	(0.75)	17.35	24.57	21.14
Europe	(3.74)	14.12	20.65	19.84

* Half-year actual price returns   † 3-year annualized price returns   ‡ 5-year annualized price returns

Source: MSCI

vatized—the company installed new management and consolidated Swisscom's seventeen units into four. Annual capital expenditures were cut nearly in half, and the workforce was slimmed down from 22,000 to 18,000. The company's $5.6 billion IPO was Europe's largest for the year.[8]

After seeing its venerable reputation sullied by forty years of state management, Skoda, the Czech Republic's leading carmaker, sold off a majority stake to Volkswagen. After investing $1.6 billion into the company, VW has created a fully modernized production facility, replaced

most of management, designed new models that share a common manufacturing platform with other VWs, and with almost 20 percent fewer
workers, has nearly doubled production.[9] In the spring of 2000, Volkswagen bought the state's remaining 30 percent stake in the company
for $301 million.[10]

Europe is realizing its traditional economic formulas can't be sustained, because the global marketplace in which it's competing plays by
a far less restrictive set of rules. High labor costs, inflexible work rules,
cumbersome taxation, budget-breaking social spending, and corporate
nationalism (which had kept governments running airlines and utilities,
avoiding deregulation, and restricting competition) have handicapped
operations. In the worst instances, they have perpetuated corporate
flight—especially out of Germany and Sweden—to countries with lower overall costs. Ericsson, Sweden's leading telecom manufacturer and
one of the country's best-known exports, is constantly threatening to
uproot its corporate headquarters to London.

These structural deficiencies have contributed to erratic growth,
double-digit unemployment, high levels of national debt, and grossly
underfunded pension systems that are threatening to bankrupt state
budgets in the not too distant future. But since 1991, much has begun
to change.

The Euro

The year 1991 will be remembered as a watershed in European economic history. In Maastricht, a provincial Dutch town wedged between
Germany and Belgium, the European Union finally committed itself to
what Richard F. Hokenson, European analyst at Donaldson, Lufkin &
Jenrette, regards as "one of the most significant global changes since
the end of World War II—European economic and monetary union."

From the Roman Empire through the Third Reich, a history of Europe could be written based on the search for unification, or more aptly
put, for domination. It has been a passion that at one time or another
has intrigued leaders of nearly all European nations. What Caesar and
Napoleon couldn't do, what Hitler and Stalin wrecked a continent failing to accomplish, is peacefully, democratically being effected by EMU.
And if it succeeds, greater political union will follow.

EMU forged dramatic macroeconomic improvements by having
member states meet the following requirements:

➤ Reduction of national debt to no more than 60 percent of GDP,
➤ Government deficits of no more than 3 percent of GDP,
➤ Domestic inflation and interest rates within 1.5 percentage points of the average of the three best-performing economies within the euro-zone, and
➤ Stable foreign exchange rates.

Common currency's most significant impact has been as a policy sur-rogate. As PaineWebber's chief international economist Alison Cottrell explains, "Maastricht has achieved what local legislators could never do on their own—government fiscal discipline."

For instance, in the early 1990s, with Italian debt running above 125 percent of GDP and unemployment pushing toward 13 percent, to imagine Rome qualifying for monetary union was absurd. But it did. And today, the country's inflation has been averaging around 2 percent a year, and interest rates have been cut by two-thirds. Italian macro-economic indicators converged with those of the rest of Europe prior to the euro's introduction in January 1999, and Italian equities thrived. Between 1996 and 1998, the local market ran up nearly 30.7 percent a year in dollar terms.[11]

Common currency has done more than force governments to get their economic houses in order. Supported by a wide range of Europe-an Union directives seeking to open up markets and competition, eco-nomic and monetary union has helped unleash a more effective form of capitalism rippling across the entire continent. Here's how.

Privatization and Deregulation
To cut public deficits and to help pay down their debt burden to meet EMU's fiscal requirements, governments have sped up the sell-off of corporate assets to help raise cash. Because these privatized firms were often monopolies, market deregulation was essential to promote com-petition and more efficient operations. This more open business envi-ronment is requiring companies to restructure to effectively compete in larger and freer markets. And this in turn is encouraging the merg-er of complementary business interests and the spinning off of noncore operations to firms who can better exploit these assets.

In Austria, for instance, more than 20 percent of the country's indus-trial output, which had been in state hands at the beginning of the

European Privatization in $U.S. Millions*

COUNTRY	1994	1995	1996	1997	1998	1999†
Austria‡	700	1,035	1,300	2,654	2,426	138
Belgium	549	2,748	1,222	1,817	2,277	
Czech Rep.	1,077	1,205	994	442	469	781
Denmark	229	10	366	45	4,502	19
Finland	1,166	363	911	835	2,068	3,645
France	4,136	5,099	8,189	12,951	9,509	
Germany§		13,228	1,125	364	6,734	
Greece	73	44	558	1,395	3,892	4,880
Hungary	1,017	3,813	1,157	1,966	353	88
Ireland		157	293			4,846
Italy#	6,493	7,434	6,265	27,719	13,619	25,611
Netherlands	3,766	3,993	1,239	831	335	1,481
Norway	118	521	660	35		454
Poland	725	1,101	1,442	2,043	2,079	3,422
Portugal	1,132	2,425	3,002	4,930	4,260	1,624
Spain	1,458	2,941	2,679	12,522	11,618	964
Sweden	2,313	852	785	1,055	172	2,071
Switzerland					4,426	
United Kingdom**	1,341	6,691	7,610	4,544		
EU 15	24,939	32,829	44,557	67,661	58,484	61,522
Global total	**66,274**	**67,599**	**92,107**	**157,455**	**131,039**	**144,765**

Source: "Recent Privatization Trends," Ladan Mahboobi, *Financial Market Trends* 76, OECD June 2000 46.

* The amounts shown are gross proceeds from direct privatizations. These do not necessarily correspond to the net amount available to the government. The figures are on a calendar-year basis and they may not add up to published budget figures.
† Provisional
‡ Statistics refer only to privatizations by the central government.
§ Up to 1997, information on trade sales is not available.
# Including convertible bond issues (INA) of U.S. $2,055 million in 1996 and indirect privatizations raising U.S. $2,658 million in 1996 and U.S. $2,620 million in 1997
** Debt sales for years 1994–97 (fiscal years) amounting to £5,453 million, £6,429 million, £2,439 million, and £4,500 million, respectively

1990s, is now privately managed.[12] Besides using sales receipts to improve government finances, privatization has helped expand European productivity by 5.1 percent a year over the past decade. This has cut per-unit labor costs. And with real wages increasing, these trends have helped propel GDP growth.[13]

Danish competition has been enhanced through the privatization of nearly $6 billion of state-run operations in the 1990s and market deregulation, especially in transportation, telecommunications, financial services, and energy exploration.

Though not participating in the initial round of monetary union, Britain was one of the first European nations to realize the benefits of privatization—from elimination of perennial industrial subsidies to increased tax collection. Once a financial black hole for the government, British Steel has now become one of the lowest-cost steel producers in the world. Previously known more for its ineptness than service, British Airways is one of the largest and most efficient international carriers around.[14]

In Italy, as in most other European countries, the issuance of new telecom licenses eliminated the monopoly enjoyed by the former state phone operator, Telecom Italia. "This pushed TI to become a more efficient operation," observed Paolo Bianco, equity analyst at JPP Euro Securities in Milan, "to develop more innovative service and international agreements to attract market share and enhance shareholder value."

But deregulation of the Italian phone system also paved the way for one of the largest hostile buyouts Europe has ever seen. Olivetti, one of the new players in the industry and itself a major restructuring story, was only one-fifth the size of Telecom Italia when it initiated its takeover proxy. Ignoring traditional Italian business mores—guided by U.S. investment bankers in selling off assets, securing bank loans, and tapping into Europe's nascent corporate debt market to finance the buyout—Olivetti pulled off Europe's most remarkable corporate coup, highlighting the biggest change in the European corporate landscape: the explosion of mergers and acquisitions.

Mergers, Acquisitions, and Restructuring

Six major M&A stories broke on one day alone in October 1997. Although several of the deals fell through, the activity that took place during that autumn day revealed the pace of change and the fact that the rules of corporate governance are being rewritten.

Grand Metropolitan and Guinness, two huge British food and beverage operations both with strong brand-name recognition, cleared a major hurdle toward their $40 billion merger that was to become Diageo. Scandinavia's largest bank was created through a $10.6 billion merger of Finnish Merita and Swedish Nordbanken forming MeritaNordbanken. The Zurich Group purchased BAT's financial

services operations, creating a $35.7 billion powerhouse renamed
Zurich Financial Services. French building materials firm Lafarge
(one of the world's biggest) made a $2.8 billion hostile bid for British
Redland, which was subsequently bumped up to $3.02 billion and
accepted by Redland.

Though its offer was subsequently topped by Germany's Allianz,
Italian insurance giant Generali shocked French businessmen and
government officials with a $9.3 billion hostile bid for Groupe des
Assurances Générales de France (AGF).[15] U.K. scientific publisher
Reed Elsevier and Netherlands publisher Wolters Kluwer were on the
verge of consummating a $20 billion deal to create the world's largest
professional publisher, only to watch it fall through several months later.

By the end of 1997, European mergers and acquisitions exceeded
$400 billion, plowing past the previous record set in 1996 of $253 billion.[16] But all this activity seemed only prelude to 1998, when M&A
activity reached $800 billion. British Petroleum bought out Amoco for
$56.3 billion. Daimler-Benz and Chrysler created a $43.1 billion venture. The pharmaceutical industry witnessed two huge mergers: the
$33.4 billion deal bringing together the U.K.'s Zeneca and Sweden's
Astra, and the partial merger of Hoechst of Germany with Rhône-
Poulenc of France that created Aventis. Financial services giant Fortis,
itself a Belgian-Dutch merger, bought out Belgium's Générale de
Banque in the Continent's largest bank takeover for $14.2 billion. And
then late in 1998, French energy giant Total announced it was buying
Belgium's leading oil company, Petrofina, for more than $13 billion. No
sector seemed immune from the M&A craze.

The pace nearly doubled in 1999 with $1.5 billion in announced
deals, led by the world's largest takeover—U.K. telecom leader Vodafone's buyout of German industrial/telecom giant Mannesmann for
$183 billion. Veba and Viag merged into a $38 billion German utility
giant called E.ON, while the new French-Belgian oil giant Total-Fina
added Elf Aquitaine to its group at a cost of $53.2 billion.[17]

Several key developments triggered this frenetic pace of mergers
and acquisitions. Common currency offers transparent price comparison throughout the eurozone, leveling the marketplace and encouraging corporate expansion beyond state borders. The euro is also making
financing easier, promoting the use of common stock and euro-denominated debt.

Cross-border dealings have begun to erode the importance of corporate nationalism, enabling companies (and some governments with protectionist tendencies) to think more in terms of market share and shareholder value than traditional state concerns such as domestic employment, tax revenues, and corporate national affiliation.

Perhaps the most important force behind the urge to merge and acquire is the search for enhanced profitability. Toward that end, *The Wall Street Journal* observed, "many of Europe's old-style behemoths are reinventing themselves as new-style high-growth companies by redeploying capital in higher-margin business to boost lackluster earnings."[18] Specifically, companies are refocusing attention on core oper-

Largest European Mergers and Acquisitions through June 2000

TARGET	ACQUIRER	ANNOUNCED PRICE	COMPLETED	SECTOR
Mannesmann (Germany)	Vodafone AirTouch (U.K.)	$183.0 B	2/3/00*	Telecom
AirTouch (U.S.)	Vodafone (U.K.)	57.5	6/30/99	Telecom
Amoco Corp. (U.S.)	British Petroleum	56.3	1/4/99	Oil
Elf Aquitaine (France)	Total Fina (France)	50.7	2/9/00	Oil
Orange (U.K.)	France Telecom	46.0	5/31/00*	Telecom
Chrysler (U.S.)	Daimler (Germany)	43.1	11/13/98	Auto
Grand Met. (U.K.)	Diageo (U.K.)	39.0	12/17/97	Food
Nat'l Westminster Bank (U.K.)	Royal Bank of Scotland (U.K.)	37.8	4/10/00	Banking
Orange (U.K.)	Mannesmann (Ger.)	35.4	2/10/00	Telecom
Astra (Sweden)	Zeneca (U.K.)	33.4	4/26/99	Pharm.
Telecom Italia	Olivetti (Italy)	33.3	5/21/99	Telecom
Atlantic Richfield (U.S.)	BP Amoco (U.K.)	31.8	4/18/00	Oil
DATING (Italy)	Honeywell (U.S.)	24.0	4/29/97	Telecom
TSB (U.K.)	Lloyds Bank (U.K.)	21.4	12/28/95	Banking
Swiss Bank Corp.	UBS (Switzerland)	19.7	6/29/98	Banking
Promodès (France)	Carrefour (France)	17.0	4/3/00	Retail
Viag (Germany)	Veba (Germany)	13.7	6/19/00	Utilities

Source: Bloomberg

* Date of agreement

ations—sometimes redefining core activities—stripping away ancillary, often unrelated services, and acquiring operations that complement primary strategies, offering access to new markets and economies of scale.

Take, for example, the French conglomerate Compagnie de Suez, whose operations included the Banque Indo Suez (investment banking), Générale de Belgique (energy, mining, and insurance), and Compagnie Victoire (insurance). By the beginning of 1997, the company sold off its entire investment banking operations to Crédit Agricole Indosuez. Then, later in the year, it merged with Lyonnaise des Eaux, a global water distribution and construction firm. The strategy: combine Suez's energy component with Lyonnaise's operations to form a $10 billion worldwide utility. All unrelated functions of Générale de Belgique along with Compagnie Victoire were sold off. The result of all this corporate surgery was the creation of Suez Lyonnaise des Eaux, a "well focused player in a fast growing industry that will expand as utility deregulation spreads around the world," according to Eric Bleines, Indocam Asset Management European Equity portfolio manager.[19] (For more information on Suez Lyonnaise, see Chapter 9.)

Acquiring and demerging assets can help a company focus on its core competencies and unleash value. As European economic observer Antony Currie explains, "shareholders generally benefit from a more transparent corporate structure; analysts feel at ease with a company that is more focused; and investment banks can make more money on a spin-off IPO than they can on a trade sale."[20]

Whether the bulk of European mergers and acquisitions will realize the full economies of scale executives anticipate is far from certain. Corporations in many countries are still running up against strong labor unions more concerned with preserving jobs than boosting the company's bottom line. A study by BNP Paribas found that between 1996 and 1998 virtually all mergers and acquisitions in France involved few mass layoffs or sell-offs of underperforming assets.[21]

Shareholder Value

Privatization of more than $265 billion of European state assets between 1995 and 1999 has expanded the number of tradable securities and has exploded the market capitalization of bourses across the Continent.[22] Coupled with the exponential rise in mergers and acquisitions, fueled by privatization and an increasing percentage of sophisticated, active foreign shareholders—including the likes of Fidelity Investments and California Public Employees Retirement System—Europe is developing an equity culture focused on shareholder value.

DaimlerChrysler, Siemens, Preussag and Hoechst of Germany, TOTAL FINA ELF and Danone of France, British Petroleum of the U.K., the Swiss-Swedish ABB, Finland's Nokia, and Italy's ENI and Olivetti are among Europe's leading restructuring stories that are paying close attention to investor interests.[23] In contrast with state-controlled companies formerly concerned with the preservation of jobs and taxes, these companies are far more focused on the search for market share and profitability.

As *The Economist* explains, "behind this trend is a new generation of managers who understand that firms belong to shareholders, not to bosses or 'society.'"[24] Companies now set minimum returns on capital employed in response to demand for greater earnings. For instance, Daimler's target is 12 percent, and before it was taken over, Mannesmann's was 15 percent. This has significantly cut into the traditional conglomerate practice of cross-subsidization between profitable and loss-making units, resulting in a greater focus on a company's core competencies.[25]

It wasn't so long ago that stock price and earnings per share weren't driving concerns. A startling number of European CEOs wouldn't even have been able to tell you what their firms' cost of capital was.[26] According to Fidelity's Europe fund manager, Sally E. Walden, "market share and labor peace were the dominant corporate considerations. But what we're seeing now," Walden observes, "is a lot more senior managers being compensated based on financial and stock performance. Germany and Finland, for instance, just legalized stock options in 1998. And we're also finding new securities legislation aimed at making corporate stock buybacks feasible."

Another key shareholder-driven change involves capital reserves. Big European companies, especially in the United Kingdom, traditionally hoarded cash, paid large dividends, and maintained a high rate of interest cover. These characteristics were signs of fiscal strength. But as U.S. high-techs have demonstrated, plowing money back into research and development and buying back shares are far more effective means of driving up stock prices.

Improved financials are also being motivated by increasingly global competition for investors. "With common currency enabling European fund managers to make investment decisions irrespective of national boundaries," observes Michael Tory, a managing director at Morgan Stanley Dean Witter in London, "companies will be driven to change."[27] And at the same time, management is discovering a rising share price is the cheapest way to effect an acquisition or to ward off unwanted advances of a corporate raider.

Cost Harmonization

Adoption of the euro is furthering the dissolution of national borders by increasing price transparency and reducing the opportunities of exchange-rate-induced inflation. Industrial equipment manufacturers are now able to discern the cost difference between Belgian and German steel or Irish and French computer components, promoting more efficient use of capital and leading to cheaper finished products for both local and foreign markets. In addition, to help reduce competitive disadvantages in production costs across the Continent, government, businesses, and unions are working together to harmonize two critical costs: labor and taxes.

Labor costs vary dramatically from country to country. Differences in actual wages paid is one part of the story, but the biggest variance is often the nonwage component involving social security. In Germany this amounts to nearly 50 percent of total worker compensation and helps explain why labor costs in Portugal and Hungary are as little as one-sixth those of Germany.

However, things are changing. Two significant developments are slowing down total wage growth in Europe and helping to support economic expansion. First, there has been an explosion in flexible, short-term contracts, allowing companies to quickly respond to demand without assuming the long-term financial liabilities of permanent workers. "Before the early 1990s," explains Scott Clemons, comanager of the 59 Wall Street European Equity Fund, "temporary employment in most European states was illegal."[28] However, by the middle of the decade, rules had begun to change. Between 1995 and 1998, such contracts accounted for 70 percent of job growth in the eurozone. (Looking at the success of Swiss-based Adecco, featured in Chapter 9, provides a glimpse into the substantial role temporary work is now playing in Europe.)

The second major change in the European labor front is increasing union flexibility. Unions are now making concessions that would have been unheard of just a few years ago, when they were able to secure identical contracts for all workers, regardless of industry or regional cost-of-living differences.

In Germany, labor contracts are increasingly being negotiated on a per-company basis to promote efficiency and job flexibility. Volkswagen has been able to set up a two-tier pay scale to bring in temporary help 10 percent below the rate being earned by permanent employees; and before the merger with Chrysler, workers at Daimler-Benz agreed to a longer workweek. At the big chemical company Bayer, workers have accepted a reduction in bonuses and elimination of employee share-purchase programs in exchange for flexible work hours.[29]

Nationwide, "around 10 percent of the western German workforce has wriggled out of old-style collective bargaining arrangements," reports *The Economist*, "and in the poorer east, the figure is over 50 percent. These concessions have allowed many companies to adjust to their own market conditions."[30]

German union authority, especially in the country's largest firms, is being compromised by a decline in *Mitbestimmung*, or co-determination—the traditional arrangement that gave unions half the seats on companies' supervisory boards.[31] Diminishing influence has contributed to more modest pay hikes. In the spring of 1999 IG Metall, Germany's and Europe's largest union, accepted a 3.5 percent wage increase above inflation for the union's 3 million members.[32] And in March 2000, the German chemical union IG BCE established an even lower benchmark for the year, agreeing to a real wage increase of 2.9 percent, which the *Financial Times* called "reasonably in line with productivity growth in the economy."[33]

Outside of Germany, in the rural heartland of France, Pechiney SA, Europe's leading producer of primary aluminum, adopted a series of employee incentives shortly after the firm was privatized in 1995 that are enhancing productivity. Early retirement packages and increasing use of temporary workers are also making the firm more competitive and profitable.[34] And in Austria, while work rules are still quite rigid, companies are now permitted to operate seven-day shifts, and the number of hours in a workday has been expanded and includes Sunday.

However, not everything that's happening on the labor front is nec-

Annual Wage Increases

COUNTRY	1997	1998	1999	1994–99 AVERAGE
Germany	1.4	1.4	1.8	3.8
France	2.1	2.5	1.8	2.2
Italy	4.3	-1.7	1.9	3.1
Netherlands	2.1	2.4	3.5	2.3
Spain	3.5	2.3	2.2	3.5
Austria	0.9	2.9	2.5	2.3
Belgium	1.9	2.6	2.4	2.2
Finland	1.5	5.1	3.5	3.5
Ireland	4.1	2.0	6.5	3.5
Portugal	4.9	4.9	5.0	5.4
Eurozone (w/o Greece)	1.8	1.6	2.2	2.5

Source: ABN AMRO, as reported in Tony Barber, "Problem: How to Get the New Europe to Work?" *Financial Times*, 6 April 2000, p. 2.

essarily improving the prospect for jobs and the economy. To counter persistent unemployment, a number of European governments are turning to a shorter workweek. France has cut it from thirty-nine to thirty-five hours for white- and blue-collar positions. But because the new law prohibits any corresponding reduction in wages, the result may fuel inflation, make businesses less efficient, and encourage management to consider overtime schemes rather than the addition of more time-restricted positions.

Despite its poor industrial performance during the latter half of the 1990s, Italy maintains national collective bargaining. This means uniform wage levels are still negotiated across each industry, regardless of location, product, or efficiency.[35]

In Belgium, unemployment is still exacerbated by restraints on agency hiring and use of temporary labor, high social security payments, and the creation of common labor contracts to serve disparate sectors. Belgium's high wage taxes help pay for jobless benefits that are perpetual.

Back in Germany, the government's post-unification decision to equalize wages across the country forfeited access to the east's formerly less expensive (and less productive) labor market. Maintaining wage disparity would have helped the country retain jobs that are escaping to cheaper foreign markets. Distinct pay scales would also have helped Germany sustain its overall competitiveness, which has since suffered.

Varying national tax rates create an uneven playing field across Europe. They hurt both corporations unable to relocate to lower-taxed jurisdictions and governments that cannot afford to offer businesses better breaks.

A recent Dutch Finance Ministry study found statutory corporate rates ranging from Ireland's low of 21.94 percent to Italy's high of 50.48 percent.[36] Until taxes achieve a greater degree of harmony throughout Europe, capital will continue to flow to the least restrictive regimes.

In Sweden, one of the Continent's lowest corporate tax rates belies an extraordinarily high income tax schedule that the country relies upon to finance its extensive social security system. With personal rates topping out at nearly 60 percent, Sweden discourages highly skilled workers and executives from staying in the country. Many corporate boards have shifted headquarters outside of Sweden after merging with a cross-border rival.

➤ Astra, Sweden's leading drug company, teamed up with the United Kingdom's Zeneca, establishing headquarters in London.

➤ Stora linked up with Finland's Enso in creating Europe's largest forestry concern, with headquarters in Helsinki.

➤ Nordic Baltic Holding, the merger of Swedish and Finnish operations, designated Helsinki as its home base.

With formerly one of Europe's highest corporate tax rates of 45 percent, Germany has seen a more subtle response. According to Bärbel Lenz, comanager of the Dresdner RCM European Fund, "German taxes in the past encouraged companies to export operations to other countries to reduce their tax exposure." This stunted Germany's overall growth by limiting the trickle-down effect of economic activity that otherwise would feed down to domestic suppliers and services.

Tax considerations also kept some German firms from spinning off profitable subsidiaries or divesting themselves of unprofitable operations. Earnings-per-share numbers have been diluted by tax policy that encourages firms to issue new stock in lieu of cash dividends.

High corporate taxes also encouraged German companies to hide reserves and understate earnings by distributing assets across a less-than-clear network of ownership. Sheltering profits not only cuts into dividend distribution but also makes it difficult for analysts to discern a corporation's true worth, inhibiting development of an equity culture.

(For an in-depth discussion of key differences between U.S. and European accounting, see Chapter 11.)

But things are changing. The German Parliament passed a major tax reform bill in July 2000. The top personal income tax rate will drop in stages from 53 percent to 42 percent by 2005, while the standard corporate tax rate will be cut from 45 percent to 25 percent. Goldman Sachs estimates that between 2000 and 2005 corporate tax savings will likely amount to $28.68 billion.[37]

However, the most radical provision is the complete elimination of capital gains tax on cross-corporate shareholdings. This move promises to unlock up to €250 billion of corporate assets, which had been too expensive to unwind because of a capital gains tax rate of 50 to 60 percent.[38] Reallocating these assets will be a windfall, stimulating immense investment into core corporate operations.

The potential impact of this move will not stop at the German border. Typical of the manner in which change is spreading across Europe, the competitive advantage tax reform will give German companies is likely to encourage other nations to adopt similar tax changes. France is now planning to slash taxes by $18 billion by 2003. Italy's central bank has already hired a German law firm to study the potential impact Germany's tax cuts may have on Italian business and the country's economy.[39]

Although it may be difficult to discern on the surface, there are signs that taxes have already begun to harmonize across Europe. The aforementioned Dutch Finance Ministry tax study found effective rates corporations were actually paying were on average 9.6 percent less than those that were on the books. In Sweden, for instance, the effective rate of 27.47 percent was about 1 percentage point below the statutory rate. But in Belgium, where the statutory rate is 40.28 percent, the effective rate was just about half.[40]

Another important development: adoption of U.S. Generally Accepted Accounting Principles and International Accounting Standards is beginning to harmonize financial statements. This is helping to spotlight the differences between countries' real tax rates. Over time, the manager of the Germany Fund, Hanspeter Ackerman, believes tax reform will improve "disclosure of profits and hidden reserves, providing greater transparency and an improved investor environment." This, Ackerman speculates, will further encourage com-

National Income Tax Rates as of April 2000

Source: Ernst & Young, as reported in Kevin Brown, "European Connection Lifts Trade," *Financial Times* Survey of Inward Investment into the U.K., 14 October 1999. p. I.

COUNTRY	AVERAGE CORPORATE INCOME TAX RATES	PERSONAL INCOME TAX RANGE
Germany*	45	29-53
France	40	10.5-59
Belgium	40	25-55
Greece	37.5	5-45
Italy	37	19-46
Netherlands	35	7-60
Spain	35	20-56
Austria	34	10-50
Portugal	34	15-40
Denmark	34	40-58
Ireland	32	24-46
U.K.	30	20-40
Finland	28	5.5-56
Sweden	28	31-56

* Does not reflect descending rates resulting from Germany's new tax reform package adopted in July 2000

panies to replace their traditional reliance on expensive debt financing with public offerings, which ultimately will propel equity markets across Europe.

Pension Reform

European stock markets, both within the eurozone and without, are beginning to receive a substantial boost from pension reform. There have been two basic changes.

➢ Governments are now encouraging an increasing percentage of retirement funds to be redirected away from state coffers and directly into private pension funds.

➢ Regulatory changes are permitting these funds to reallocate an increasing percentage of their portfolios away from bonds—the traditional European retirement investment—and into stocks. As workers begin to see the profitability of their pensions invested in equities, they are likely to be more inclined to shift a greater portion of their own personal savings into stocks, further lifting markets.

What's triggering reform? A pending pension crisis across the Continent. Demographics and high unemployment are playing havoc with many countries' unfunded pay-as-you-go retirement systems, which rely on current payroll taxes to take care of today's retirees. With an increasing percentage of citizens getting ready to retire and a receding percent entering into the job markets, the money for pensioners just isn't there. According to a study published by Merrill Lynch, where there are now 4.8 workers financing each retiree, by 2030, the ratio drops to a budget-busting 2.6.[41]

This problem has been made worse by persistently high unemployment and falling wages that are reducing governments' take. With the move toward common currency placing new limits on national borrowing, pensions will likely have to be cut. Currently, France and Germany pay out 70 percent of a worker's annual net salary; reform in the Netherlands and the United Kingdom has cut pensions to only 30 percent of salaries.

Whether governments will raise the retirement age to help maintain high benefits or get out of the pension business altogether, what seems certain is that 401(k)-type plans are the only viable way to go from here. The financial industry thinks this decision is a fait accompli. Investment houses like Fidelity Investments, State Street Bank, Bankers Trust, J.P. Morgan & Co., and Goldman Sachs are trying to sell governments the "win-win" scenario that individual retirement plans offer.[42]

➤ They can relieve government of a huge expense that will otherwise require higher taxes, which ultimately discourages investment and growth.

➤ Pooling retirement money into mutual funds is likely to generate a far greater return for pensioners than governments could ever pay out.

➤ Best of all, local equity markets will explode with new-found liquidity—as they have done in the States.

European insurance companies have benefited greatly from the creation of private pensions, as witnessed by a substantial shift in assets from traditional bank accounts into unit-linked accounts or variable annuities. These life insurance products have proven to be so profitable for insurers that the industry is seeing a seismic shift by insurers away from property and casualty and into life sales. The industry paradigm has been the small Swedish insurer Skandia, whose five-year annualized

Demographic and Pension Characteristics

Source: William M. Mercer, "European Pension Fund Managers Guide 2000," as reported in Debbie Harrison, "Brussels Set to Publish Reform Plan," *Financial Times* Survey of Pension Fund Investment, 12 May 2000, p. V.

COUNTRY	POPULATION (M)	DEPENDENCY RATIO*	PENSION ASSETS ($B)	ASSETS/ RETIREE ($)†
Netherlands	15.8	18.8	607.0	204,350
Switzerland	7.1	22.4	306.2	192,530
Denmark	5.3	22.4	187.0	157,513
Sweden	8.9	26.6	270.5	114,260
U.K.	59.4	24.6	1,444.5	98,854
Ireland	3.7	16.7	45.9	74,284
Finland	5.2	22.7	60.0	50,830
Norway	4.5	25.0	49.9	44,355
Italy	57.7	25.0	250.0	17,331
Germany	82.0	23.5	294.1	15,257
Austria	8.1	22.1	26.7	14,915
Belgium	10.2	24.2	32.6	13,207
Portugal	10.0	22.1	11.8	5,339
France	59.1	24.6	64.1	4,409
Spain	39.4	23.2	29.1	3,184

* Population 65 and over as a percentage of domestic working population
† Pension Assets / (Population x Dependency Ratio / 100)

returns through 1999 in local currency terms have exceeded 61 percent. (For more details on this trend, see the analysis of the Insurance Sector in Chapter 8 and Dutch insurer AEGON in Chapter 9.)

While Europe's largest economies are still debating how to finance their underfunded pension systems, Europe's more independent and developing countries are actively pursuing reform. In Sweden, 12 percent of all pension kronor are channeled into securities. In Norway, 35 percent of all pension assets are now in stocks, while Switzerland directs 25 percent of all retirement francs into the country's blue-chip stocks. In central Europe, young Polish workers are required to direct 20 percent of their retirement zlotys into private pension funds. In Hungary, the figure is closer to 75 percent.[43]

This means pension fund assets are soaring. According to the *Financial Times,* "the value of pension funds in Ireland and the Netherlands exceeds the capitalization of their respective stock markets. In Denmark, Sweden, Switzerland, and the United Kingdom, these assets represent more than 100 percent of domestic GDP."[44] Moreover, what's got fund managers really drooling is the rising percent of pension fund assets going into domestic and international equities induced by the gradual lifting of restrictions on fund investment. According to the brokerage firm Dresdner Kleinwort Benson, pension reform could generate an additional flow of $4 trillion into Europe's capital markets by the year 2010.[45]

"European investors have been traditionally focused on fixed-income securities," explains PaineWebber's Alison Cottrell. "But with the Continent's low interest rates, retirement funds will be shifting an ever increasing portion of pounds and francs and lire into stocks, and this could turbocharge European equity markets as much as any other reform."

Productivity, the Euro, and the New Economy

Europe has made a stunning turnaround from the not so distant past, when it was common to see governments push businesses to effect social policy (jobs created, taxes paid, and pensions funded), and for large corporations to be more focused on serving this agenda rather than return on investments. Increasing adoption of the Anglo-Saxon business model is making Europe's corporations and governments more fit and efficient. Both are in much better shape to confront the demands of a global economy.

A gauge of this transformation: eurozone productivity is now close to parity with the States. This is a measurement of the increase in economic output over the input of labor and capital. In 1998, the region was found to be 94 percent as productive as the United States. In 1971, the comparison was a dismal 71 percent.[46]

Future European prosperity is hinged on continued productivity gains. These will be spurred on by further improvements in government finance and corporate operations. But they will also depend on the degree to which Europe embraces the New Economy. Keeping up with the United States will be quite a challenge.

There's evidence suggesting that the euro's weak start was linked to accelerated U.S. productivity that picked up from an average annual rate of 1.4 percent to 2.9 percent between 1995 and 1999. This change generated a stronger U.S. economy that has significantly increased the net flow of capital from Europe and into the States, which reached nearly $200 billion in 1999.[47] Stronger demand for U.S. assets—stocks, bonds, and businesses—has meant weaker demand for European assets and, hence, for euros with which to buy them.

U.S. productivity gains have been triggered by the creation of higher-quality IT products at cheaper prices. Increased application of these products, especially involving the Internet, is creating more productive links across the economy.

Although European IT spending has been steadily rising, it's still only half the U.S. rate. According to the Organisation for Economic Co-operation and Development and Morgan Stanley Dean Witter, Europe's accumulated IT investment as of 1998 (18.5 percent of GDP) has only caught up with U.S. 1990 levels.[48] E-commerce and Internet access has also been slower to develop in Europe than in the States.

In equity terms, computer hardware, software, and communications businesses account for 25 percent of Europe's total market capitalization. In the U.S., these stocks represent more than one-third of domestic market capitalization.

Several structural problems are behind this technology gap. The most significant barrier is that the European way of doing business still doesn't encourage young entrepreneurs to step out. That's why many of the region's technology leaders have been the well-financed and connected former state monopolies and the enterprises they have spun off, such as Spain's Telefónica and its Internet offshoot, Terra Networks (which was originally a small start-up the giant telecom bought out).

According to Dirk Hudig, secretary-general of UNICE, Europe's employers' federation, there are still dozens of restraints on start-ups. Leading the list:

➤ Very costly and time-consuming regulatory approval process,
➤ Discouraging balance between risk and reward, especially when considering the tax hit on stock options,
➤ Labor markets that are still too restricted and inflexible, and
➤ An unfortunate disconnect between research institutes and the private sector that, compared to the States, fails to join academic initiatives and business.

How important is this last point? Think where the Internet came from—two American professors trying to figure out a way to link their computers.

Proliferation of the Internet is also hamstrung by a host of systemic problems, which investors need keep in mind if they are thinking Europe's more-embryonic Web offers an opportunity to catch the ride that the States has already experienced.

➤ Size and wealth of the Continent suggests a solid market base on which to build. But credit card usage is much lower.

➤ PC penetration also significantly trails the States, reflecting a potential lag in accepting the Web as a means of doing business, especially on the retail level.

➤ Line-access costs are still high.

➤ Then there is the issue of language. With four dominant languages and a half-dozen secondary tongues, designing and integrating sites for the European market is no easy challenge.

Yet, despite all these impediments, technology initiatives are taking off across Europe. "Flying to Europe these days," observes a recent *Fortune* magazine article, "is like landing in Silicon Valley circa 1998. Office parks outside capitals from Stockholm to Rome are filling up with media companies and tech start-ups. Cafés are packed with jeans-clad twentysomething entrepreneurs yapping on cell phones to their venture capital backers. The number of public offerings—most of them tech—on the German stock exchange has doubled every year since 1997. And all across the region, Internet usage is taking off."[50]

Initially financed by venture capital, many of these companies are receiving a second-stage boost from public offerings on a slew of so-called new markets that have been popping up, performing like hyper cousins of the Nasdaq. In 1999, Germany's Neuer Markt rose 53 percent in local currency terms, and France's Nouveau Marché soared 127 percent. The Pan-European Easdaq gained 84 percent. And in its first year of trading, through June 2000, Milan's Nuovo Mercato catapulted 644 percent.

As in the United States, information technology stocks have been some of Europe's leading tech stories, especially those with a telecom connection. This area is where Europe is developing a distinct advantage over the States.

The Continent excels in wireless technology and application, led by industry-leaders Nokia and Ericsson. Whereas the U.S. mobile network is compromised by four competing operating systems, Europe enjoys a superior seamless network based on one common platform—

GSM. Product and infrastructure advantages have also propelled European mobile phone penetration well beyond levels in the States.

Many analysts believe this network advantage should result in substantial productivity gains for Europe, especially when wireless Internet communication is in place. And a new generation of companies is preparing to exploit this new means of doing business.

Vodafone is the first mobile operator to offer a fully integrated European network linked with the United States (see Chapter 9 for more information).

MobilCom, an independent German phone network and Internet service provider (ISP) started up in 1991, has seen sales propelled by a series of acquisitions. Since its October 1997 IPO, the stock was up more than eightfold through 1999.

Intershop Communications, another German start-up, is a leading provider of Internet commerce software. It has become a market favorite, also having soared eightfold since its IPO in July 1998 through the end of 1999 on triple-digit annual sales growth.

Tiscali, an Italian telecommunications provider, was one of the first ISPs to offer free Internet access along with e-commerce services. Acquisitions are helping to position the company across Europe, which has helped send shares rocketing by more than 900 percent over its first four months of trading, through February 2000.[51]

While European tech stocks have proven to be as volatile as their U.S. counterparts, they do reveal a comparable thirst by European investors for exposure to the New Economy—providing entrepreneurs support they would never have found from traditional sources even five years ago. This bodes well for long-term productivity gains, economic growth, and equity investors.

The New Europe

Norwegian Sea

SWEDEN

NORWAY

FINLAND
€

Baltic
Sea

ESTONIA

RUSSIA

North
Sea

DENMARK

LATVIA

LITHUANIA

IRELAND
€

UNITED
KINGDOM

NETHERLANDS
€

BELGIUM
€

—LUX. €

GERMANY
€

POLAND

BELARUS

CZECH REP.

UKRAINE

FRANCE
€

SWITZERLAND

AUSTRIA
€

HUNGARY

MOLDOVA

SLOV.
CROATIA

BOSNIA
HERZEG.

YUGO-
SLAVIA

ROMANIA

ITALY
€

BULGARIA

Bl

SPAIN
€

MAC

ALBANIA

TURKEY

PORTUGAL
€

Mediterranean Sea

GREECE
€

C h a p t e r Two

Understanding Europe: Investment Geography

T HE MOST RECOGNIZABLE investment region in Europe is the eurozone—the eleven countries initially participating in EMU. These include Austria, Belgium, Finland, France, Germany, Ireland, Italy, Luxembourg, the Netherlands, Portugal, and Spain. And in January 2001, Greece was the first addition to the eurozone.

These nations compose a broken landmass ranging from Finland in the northeast, Ireland in the northwest, Portugal in the southwest, and Greece in the southeast. The eurozone's population is roughly the same as that of the United States, with a gross domestic product that's nearly 80 percent of the States. But a more refined look at Europe reveals the existence of five distinct investment regions that extend beyond the borders of the eurozone, providing investors a better understanding of European finance and the various environments in which to invest.

The Core

EUROPE'S OLDER, DEVELOPED core includes Germany, France, Italy, Switzerland, and the United Kingdom. The first three nations comprise nearly two-thirds of the eurozone's wealth; the latter two are not currently part of EMU. During the phase-in of common currency, these economies had the least to gain, since the primary goal of economic and monetary union is to bring the rest of Europe up to their financial standards.

Save for Italy, the currencies of the other four core countries had been Europe's most stable. Ironically, since its introduction in January 1999, the euro has so far been shown to be much more volatile than the German mark and the French franc, having lost nearly 25 percent of its value during its first sixteen months of trading.

Still, the public finances of these core nations, again save for Italy, are the region's soundest; and their strong private sectors, including Italy, are home to some of the world's best-run companies.

As monetary union enhances economic integration, companies based in these large core countries should enjoy increased market share across Europe, especially through mergers and acquisitions. Common currency and the prospect of expansion of the eurozone will also enable them to reach into less developed areas, like Portugal, Greece, and Hungary, with less risk. The magnitude of these economies assures a reasonable degree of stability. However, it also means that they will not be the source of the region's most aggressive growth.

The Tigers

EUROPE'S TIGER ECONOMIES lie on the periphery of the Continent. The growth rates of Ireland, Spain, Portugal, and the Netherlands have been running close to twice the rate of Europe's core economies (in Ireland's case, three times the core average), and they can credit their good fortunes in large part to the move toward common currency.

The prospect of economic and monetary convergence with Europe's stronger core economies and the sense of legitimacy that has come with it have encouraged these smaller, less developed economies to clean up their fiscal acts. Cutting debt and reducing spending and deficits have helped bring down interest rates and inflation. In addition, their governments' commitment to tackle structural reform, including more flexible labor laws, wage restraint, and privatization of prized national assets, has triggered rapid expansion of foreign direct investment within their borders. This has led to perennial GDP growth of 4, 5, and 6-plus percent.

The Independents

THE NORDIC REGION—comprised of Denmark, Sweden, Norway, and Finland—is one of the most prosperous economic zones in the world, enjoying an average annual GDP growth of 3.3 percent between 1995 and 1999. Reflecting the region's independent character, only Finland decided to join the EMU. The other countries, remaining suspicious of Brussels and EU policy, have decided for the time being to maintain their own fiscal and monetary sovereignty.

Denmark hedges its economic independence with a monetary policy that shadows the euro, which pulled the krone down nearly 18 percent in 1999 against the dollar. In contrast, the Swedish krona and Norwegian krone held up fairly well in 1999, depreciating only 6 to 7 percent against the dollar. While strong market ties between Scandinavian and eurozone economies will ultimately dictate equity performance, the region's independent stance offers investors a non-euro alternative to European growth. However, pending public referendums on joining EMU could change the region's policy toward eurozone membership over the next several years.

Latent Reformers

BECAUSE OF THEIR SLOWER pace of structural reform, Belgium and Austria have been underperforming the rest of the eurozone. Their core businesses have not kept up with the rapid growth of some of their neighbors, and they will find it difficult to initially benefit from common currency.

Significant unemployment, high taxes, and government spending, plus a debt-to-GDP ratio that's the highest in western Europe has stifled competitiveness in Belgium. Not surprisingly, many of its blue chips have become acquisition targets, especially by French firms that are in a better position to unlock their intrinsic value.

The Austrian market is far more commodities-oriented than the rest of Europe, lacking telecoms and technologies that have been driving growth and efficiency in other European markets. Development of a pro-business and equity culture has been handicapped by a nepotistic political system. And early in 2000, inclusion of Jörg Haider's ultra-right Freedom Party in the ruling coalition government soured markets and resulted in European Union sanctions against Austria.

Nevertheless, Austria's geographical position on the edge of central Europe's emerging markets provides it with a real competitive advantage that's attracting thousands of multinationals. And this should benefit Austria significantly as the European Union expands eastward.

Greater liberalization will also come to both economies as restrictive domestic policy eventually gives way to EU-driven reform. While these changes will be initially disruptive, especially to the less competitive industries, more efficient firms will thrive and grab increasing market share.

Emerging Markets

DEFINED BY THEIR LOW LEVELS of income per capita, Europe's three core emerging markets lie just east of Germany and Austria. Poland, Hungary, and the Czech Republic are all enjoying a high degree of inward foreign direct investment from foreign corporations in search of cheaper labor and low production costs with proximity and free-trade access to western Europe's central markets.

Greece is also part of Europe's emerging market. Like its counterparts to the north, Greece has enjoyed solid economic growth and substantial macroeconomic improvements. And it will benefit further from common-currency membership.

While all four economies offer investors potential exposure to rapid growth, the big risk is that these countries are still learning the realities of capitalism. Their political, legal, and economic infrastructures are still evolving. Corruption remains a significant concern. In addition, their markets, from both a business and an investment point of view, are still not efficient.

Exchange rate stability is also a major issue. Although Greece will turn in its drachmas for euros, the currencies of the other three eastern European economies are far less stable than those of the rest of Europe. This instability is due to higher inflation and interest rates, proximity to Russia, and the need for additional structural reform.

WHEREAS THE ABOVE CLASSIFICATIONS are configured around historic, economic, and cultural similarities, some analysts see Europe's investment potential in simpler terms: Who are the "new capitalists," embracing change and technology, and who are not?

Jean-Yannick Liatis, head of French equity research at BNP Paribas, points to the United Kingdom, the Netherlands, Ireland, and Finland as leaders in deregulating and privatizing markets, with corporate cultures that have been quick to embrace shareholder best practices. While slower out of the gate, France and Germany are now moving in this direction as well.

Eric Bleines, Indocam Asset Management European Equity portfolio manager, observes that Belgium, Austria, Portugal, Greece, and Italy fall along the other end of the curve. These nations have been slow to open up domestic markets, which makes it difficult for them to compete in the global marketplace. A general failure of domestic corporate strategy to focus on bottom-line efficiency and European integration results in less attractive investment opportunities.

Part Two

Individual
Countries

Chapter 3 Three

Core Countries

France—A Quiet Revolution

I N PROVENCE, Gemplus SCA, the world's largest manufacturer of smart cards, has made English its spoken language. The company is waging battle against the French unions, planning new production facilities in countries where labor is cheap, and working out details for an initial public offering in the States.[1]

In France's rural heartland, Pechiney SA, Europe's leading producer of primary aluminum, adopted a major restructuring program shortly after the firm was privatized in 1995. Employee incentives are enhancing productivity while the combination of early retirement packages and increasing use of temporary workers is making the firm more competitive and profitable.[2]

Compagnie d'Assurances Mutuelles contre l'Incendie, an insurance firm founded in 1817 in northern France, adopted a moniker in the 1980s that could be pronounced similarly in nearly every western European language. In linguistically minded France, nothing is closer to anathema. A decade later, after buying controlling stakes in Equitable Life; Donaldson, Lufkin & Jenrette; and Alliance Capital Management, and with $789 billion in assets under management as of the end of 1999, Paris-based AXA has become the world's second-largest asset manager, right behind Fidelity.[3]

Despite the political rhetoric and the election of a new Socialist gov-

The Core

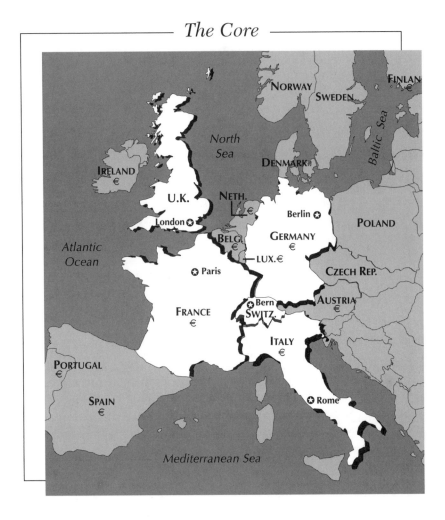

ernment in 1997 as the country was preparing to meet the stiff fiscal requirements of monetary union, France is in the midst of an economic revolution. Change may be slow, and the French may argue that they aren't trading in their socialist affections for capitalism. But continued privatization of major state operations and the desire to increasingly promote free enterprise to ensure that these new public offerings succeed in the global marketplace speak most clearly about where France is heading. *BusinessWeek* illustrated the point in a lead story that identified "a small but growing army of citizens wanting to shrink the state's role (where government outlays are 54 percent of GDP, the highest of all G-7 nations), reverse a pervasive hostility toward entrepreneurs, and erase the handout mentality that is ingrained in French society."[4] And for this to be happening in a country with the second-largest economy in Europe that's experienced only a single year of recession since the end of the Second World War bodes well for investors.

Strong Performance

French stocks have been among the best-performing European shares over the second half of the 1990s, having appreciated 24.07 percent a year in dollar terms between 1995 and 1999.[5] In 1998, the year leading up to EMU, French shares soared nearly 40 percent. In 1999, they tacked on another 28 percent—nearly 50 percent in euro terms.

The rally has been broad with all sectors reporting substantial gains in 1999, led by telecommunications, retail, industrial, and information technology shares. The year's biggest winners in local currency terms included France Telecom, up 94 percent; shares of luxury goods manufacturer LVMH rose 190 percent; the big French construction company Bouygues soared 264 percent; and semiconductor giant ST Microelectronics more than quadrupled, up 356 percent.[6]

Two dominant factors have fueled the growth in French equities. The first was broad European and global strength throughout much of the 1990s that made France the third-largest recipient of foreign direct investment in the world and the largest within the eurozone. The second force was expanding domestic consumer confidence spurred on by real wage growth, optimism about monetary union, and the country's solid economic performance, illustrated by the following statistics.[7]

➤ Corporate investment has been increasing at an annual rate of more than 7 percent.
➤ Gross national savings have crept up from 18.6 percent of GDP in 1995 to 20.5 percent in 1999.
➤ Domestic demand has grown by an average of 2 percent a year.
➤ Inflation declined to a Continent-low 0.5 percent in 1999.
➤ Between 1995 and 1999 the French GDP grew by an average of 2.2 percent a year.
➤ Strong exports have helped create a trade surplus that's been averaging 1.36 percent of GDP per year.
➤ A positive trade balance and net foreign investment income flow has pushed up France's current account balance from 0.7 percent of GDP in 1995 to 2.5 percent in 1999.

➤ Declining government bond yields, from 7.6 percent in 1995 to 5.5 percent in 1999, have helped reduce the country's budget deficit from 5.5 percent of GDP to 1.8 percent.[8]

Weaknesses

However, there are two sour spots: debt and jobs.

While having barely satisfied the terms of monetary union, France's high debt-to-GDP ratio has in fact been trending the wrong way as the government seeks to cushion some of the hardship brought on by the demands of Maastricht. Corporate subsidies, dubious job programs, extensive unemployment, and healthy social security benefits have pushed the ratio up from 48.5 percent in 1994 to 59 percent by the end of 1999 while other eurozone nations' debt positions have been improving.

Given the increase in public outlays, this leaves Marie Owens Thomsen, economist at Merrill Lynch in Paris, to question the degree of fundamental change that has been achieved. She believes that current positive trends are more the result of "greater economic activity, not reform of old and stale ways, leaving France critically exposed to the business cycle next time it turns."[9]

Looking at France's troubled employment picture suggests that Thomsen may have a point. The government's most significant jobs policy—shortening the workweek from thirty-nine to thirty-five hours—is supposed to force businesses to increase the number of employees. However, because the law prohibits any corresponding reduction in wages (although it does give employers greater scheduling flexibility), the result may fuel inflation, make businesses less efficient, and encourage management to consider overtime schemes or temporary labor rather than the addition of new thirty-five-hour-a-week workers.

The Jospin government has resorted to the shorter workweek strategy because, paradoxically, steady economic growth has failed to substantially cut into the country's high jobless rate. While having finally broken below 10 percent in 2000, unemployment had been fluctuating between 10.6 and 12.5 percent during the latter half of the 1990s. This suggests that increasing corporate profitability has been based more on enhanced efficiencies rather than domestic expansion. And it may indicate corporate hesitancy to take on the liability of permanent workers.

Certainly the case can be made that the country's changing business culture is departing from the traditional focus on job creation and market share, focusing instead on shareholder value. And clearly, the increasing role of foreign institutional investors in French equity markets (who now own more than 40 percent of CAC 40 shares) has been a driving force behind this change.

Shareholder Value

After reviewing the operations of the country's largest firms making up the SBF 120 index, BNP Paribas, France's largest investment bank, made the following discoveries.

- ➢ 28 percent have drawn up economic-value-added–based management programs.
- ➢ 38 percent have announced or are pursuing share buybacks.
- ➢ 43 percent have set return-on-equity objectives by division.
- ➢ 49 percent have instituted stock option programs.
- ➢ 58 percent have eliminated share or cash dividends to end this traditional dilution of earnings per share.[10]

The result: annual earnings per share growth increased from an average of 2.9 percent in the early 1990s to 16 percent in 1998.[11]

While BNP Paribas observed that "French companies still contain a significant untapped reservoir of shareholder value, especially when compared to other European countries (Switzerland, the Netherlands, Sweden, the United Kingdom, Germany, and Spain)....The impact of these trends has helped boost stock prices, bringing better visibility of strategy and higher valuations."[12]

The link between government and business that for so long had kept management focus on jobs is also being severed with the phasing out of a practice known as *noyau dur.* Management and board members of France's largest privatized firms often came from the bureaucratic ranks of government, lacking expertise in their assigned businesses. Further, officials would often hold voting positions at several different firms at once, establishing a significant cross-shareholder network among the country's largest companies. The goal was to sustain government involvement in corporate decision-making and to prevent hostile takeovers, particularly by foreign concerns.

However, this layer of bureaucracy that stretched across much of the country's privatized landscape has retarded corporate restructuring, and in certain instances has led to some big losses, including those at UAP (now AXA), Elf Aquitaine (now TOTAL FINA ELF), and Credit Lyonnaise during the mid-1990s.[13] The BNP Paribas study found that between 1996 and 1998, "virtually all mergers and acquisitions in France involved almost no mass layoffs," while at the same time, underperforming assets were rarely sold off.

But all that is beginning to change as the concept of corporate governance enters into the Gallic vocabulary. Diminishing state regulation is enhancing French companies' ability to operate more efficiently and profitably. And in the more competitive climate of common currency, even the socialists are realizing that proceeding in this direction holds the best hope for the French economy and the welfare of her citizens.

Germany—The Potential for Change

DEVELOPMENT OF THE European Union and creation of a common currency show just how far the nations of Europe have come since being torn apart by the Second World War. None has journeyed further than Germany. And the metamorphosis of the German state offers the best evidence that substantial change is possible, brightly coloring the prospects and opportunities for Europe in the twenty-first century.

From the ashes of Dresden and Berlin, Germany has rebuilt itself into the world's third-largest economy and the biggest in Europe, generating 30 percent of the Continent's total gross domestic product. Of Europe's top 500 companies ranked by market capitalization, 60 are German.[1] And unlike any other country on the Continent, corporate Germany includes world-class players in every major sector: Deutsche Telekom (telecommunications), Deutsche Bank (finance), Allianz (insurance), DaimlerChysler (industry), Bayer (pharmaceuticals), Metro (retail), BASF (chemicals), Siemens (engineering), SAP (software), and Lufthansa (transportation).

Yet, despite the range of corporate behemoths, the Germany economy during the second half of the 1990s has been lethargic. GDP expanded by an average of only 1.5 percent a year between 1995 and 1999. That's among the weakest performances anywhere in western Europe. How is that possible?

The 1990s were characterized by inconsistency in German corporate restructuring and market reform. This has led many market-friendly politicians to complain that the country is a *blockierte Gesellschaft,* or blocked society, with stunted growth the result.[2]

At the same time, the government transferred massive sums of capital to eastern Germany after reunification. Subsidizing development, rather than promoting more efficient and productive markets, continues to weigh on the country's overall economic performance.

Strong Equities

Nevertheless, the country's stock market has been among Europe's top-performing bourses over recent years. Between 1995 and 1999 the German bourse appreciated by nearly 25 percent a year in euro terms (19.26 percent in dollar terms). Three-year annualized gains were even better, up by more than 33 percent. And in 1999, German equities soared 39 percent, paced by banks, industrials, and telecoms. Among the best-performing issues were Deutsche Bank, which gained nearly 71 percent, Siemens, whose shares shot up 131 percent on the heels of restructuring, and Deutsche Telekom, which rose an amazing 153 percent.[3]

What's to explain the paradox of a weak economy and a strong market?

As the list of top gainers indicates, a key explanation goes back to the matter of corporate size. Market-cap weighted indices are driven by Germany's largest firms, and these fellows have proceeded ahead of the rest of the country in three key ways: mergers and acquisitions, restructuring, and a new focus on shareholder value.

Corporate Reform

Large German businesses reinvented themselves in the late 1990s, fueling strong profit growth. There was perhaps no greater metamorphosis than that of Daimler-Benz. After several years of record losses in the mid-1990s, the venerable industrial began selling off noncore businesses, relocating certain activities to cheaper foreign locations, cutting back staff, and raising productivity. It adopted U.S. accounting standards to make its finances more transparent and to gain listing on the New York Stock Exchange, which subsequently prepared the company for executing the largest merger in auto industry history. According to the *Financial Times,* the creation of DaimlerChrysler highlighted "the transformation that has been ripping through German industry over the past five years."[4]

Expansion of corporate Germany has also been primed by Deutsche Bank's $10.1 billion buyout of Bankers Trust, Hoechst's $25 billion merger with French pharmaceutical concern Rhône-Poulenc in forming Aventis, and Allianz's $10.3 billion acquisition of Assurances Générales de France.

Yet, German business strategy has also been shifting its focus away from sheer corporate size and top-line revenue to a new emphasis on return on investment and shareholder value. After years marked by wild diversification and underperformance, corporate giants including Viag, Veba, and Siemens began shedding billions of dollars' worth of businesses to help them refocus efforts on their core, more profitable activities. Siemens was the country's top turnaround story in 1999, and in its rejuvenation spun off two of the hottest IPOs: semiconductor-maker Infineon and electronics manufacturer Epcos. Meanwhile Viag and Veba merged, creating the giant German utility E.ON.

In addition to downsizing and spin-offs, German firms are now experimenting with share buybacks to enhance shareholder value. Within a year after the state legalized buybacks in 1998, more than sixty German firms announced their intentions to reacquire shares, including multinational chemicals giant BASF, drugmaker Schering, and engineering group Linde.[5]

Shareholders are also benefiting from increasing adoption of U.S. and Internationally Accepted Accounting Standards. This is improving corporate transparency, valuation estimates, and access to U.S. stock exchanges. NYSE listing is improving the visibility of Daimler-Benz, Deutsche Telekom, and SAP in the world's largest market, raising additional equity for expansion, while providing the necessary currency (U.S.-based stock shares) for subsequent merger and acquisition.

Equity value is also being created through privatization and deregulation of once heavily state-controlled markets, including telecommunications and energy, which is helping to bring down customer costs while promoting broader economic growth. Germany's main telephone service provider, Deutsche Telekom, was initially privatized in November 1996. In January 1998, competition was opened up, and now there are more than 120 new telephone service operators, with a comparable number awaiting licensing. The result is that long-distance prices have fallen by more than 70 percent while industry employment has increased by 150,000 jobs.[6]

German electricity costs traditionally ran 25 percent higher than the European average. But with the partial privatization of German utilities and pending access to foreign suppliers, prices are expected to fall by 10 to 15 percent over the next several years.[7]

Labor Reform

Improving labor contracts are also helping the bottom line. Traditionally, unions have negotiated industrywide contracts applicable to workers across the nation, despite differences in regional living costs and unemployment levels. But five basic elements have been eroding union strength.

> ➤ German wages are the highest in the world.
> ➤ Total annual number of hours worked is only eighth-highest among major industrial powers, behind Britain, Sweden, Italy, France, and the Netherlands.[8]
> ➤ Until recently, German corporate competitiveness ranked poorly.
> ➤ Unemployment hit a postwar high of 11.3 percent in 1998.
> ➤ The traditional arrangement that gave unions half the seats on companies' supervisory boards, *Mitbestimmung*, is being compromised.

A recent Morgan Stanley survey found 30 percent of employers are now paying wages below rates stipulated by industry contracts.[9] Volkswagen set up a two-tier pay scale to bring in temporary help at wages 10 percent below those earned by permanent employees. Workers at DaimlerChrysler have agreed to a longer workweek. And the big chemical company Bayer has gotten its workers to accept a reduction in bonuses and elimination of an employee share-purchase program in exchange for more flexible work hours.[10] IG Metall, the country's biggest industrial labor union, agreed to autoworker salaries based on performance and prevailing market trends in exchange for a shortened workweek, from forty to thirty-five hours.[11]

Economic Improvement

All of the above changes are generating broad improvement in the country's macroeconomics, which is beginning to show up in the numbers.

➤ New manufacturing orders, which contracted in the first quarter of 1999 by 5.2 percent, steadily increased throughout the year, soaring by more than 10 percent in the fourth quarter.

➤ Exports, which likewise contracted in the first quarter of 1999, ended the fourth quarter pushing ahead by 9.1 percent.

➤ Gross fixed investment, which rose an anemic 0.9 percent in 1998, increased by 2.1 percent in 1999.[12]

➤ Despite a year-over-year (1998 to 1999) falloff in annual industrial production growth from 4.2 to 1.1 percent, fourth quarter 1999 and first quarter 2000 numbers were rebounding.

➤ Unemployment managed to nudge down throughout 1999, from 11.1 percent in March to 10.3 percent in December.

➤ The budget deficit shrank from 3.4 percent of GDP in 1995 to 1.1 percent in 1999.

➤ Inflation in 1999 was running at the barely perceptible rate of 0.6 percent.[13]

Perhaps most important, 1999 witnessed a steady climb in business confidence, which spilled over into the first quarter of 2000, boosted by two key events. The first was tax legislation that will help unravel close to €250 billion in cross-shareholdings among the country's largest firms and encourage more efficient redistribution of capital. The second was the government's decision to steer clear of Vodafone's takeover of core German industrial Mannesmann. This wasn't necessarily expected so soon after the administration propped up the failing giant construction concern Holzmann. Permitting shareholders to decide the fate of Mannesmann suggests the administration's commitment to a more laissez-faire business policy, sending the message that accelerated corporate reform, not government intervention, is what companies need count on to fend off hostile bids.

Structural Problems

Still, Germany struggles with several major structural problems that will continue to impede growth. With wages more than 25 percent higher than the eurozone average—more than 40 percent higher than in the United States—German industry has been exporting operations abroad.[14] Audi manufactures nearly all its engines in Hungary, where labor costs are one-sixth of those in Germany, and the company intends to begin assembling cars there as well.

Such wage disparity further weakens German job and economic growth by undermining the country's ability to attract foreign direct investment. *The Economist* reports that there is limited external investment in Germany "chiefly because foreign business prefers to go to countries like Britain and Ireland where costs are lower and regulations less cumbersome." In fact, a 1999 U.N. Conference on Trade and Development found Germany to be a weaker destination for investment than Peru, India, Iceland, and Gibraltar.[15]

German reunification seemed to have offered a real chance to remedy corporate flight through access to eastern Germany's cheaper labor market. However, the government's decision to rapidly equalize living standards throughout the country raised eastern German wages to 90 percent of the national rate. And even after the transfer of more than DM 1 trillion (the equivalent to more than 4 percent of the country's GDP on an annual basis) to rebuild the east's shattered economic infrastructure, productivity in the region is still 30 percent less than in the west.[16]

Costs of reunification have significantly contributed to the country's financial woes. In 1994, debt as a percent of GDP was a manageable 50.2. By 1996, it had soared to 60.4 percent, fractionally above Maastricht's guidelines, and has remained around that level since.

At the same time, officials are only now beginning to grapple with the issue of high taxation, which continues to drag heavily on the economy. Recent reform will lower the standard corporate tax rate from 45 to 25 percent while dropping the top personal income tax rate from 53 to 45 percent. Officials are also talking about cutting the basic income tax rate from 22.9 percent to 15 percent by 2005.[17]

As of the second quarter of 2000, social security payments by both employee and employer amounted to a whopping 42 percent. While pending legislation may change this later, *The Economist* observes that when "taking into account all taxes and social security charges, including employers' contributions and consumer taxes, the nonwage costs of labor are still higher in Germany—50 percent of total wages—than in all other industrialized countries."[18]

As for the pension system, a look at the country's demographic trends clearly shows Germany's pay-as-you-go approach heading for bankruptcy. The Bundesbank calculated that while today's sixty-year-olds may receive up to three times what they've paid into the system, twenty-year-olds will likely see only half of their pension contributions, without any appreciation, by the time they retire.[19]

However, privatizing at least a portion of the pension system not only will help safeguard retirement but also will dramatically fuel development of Germany's evolving equity market. And this will bode well for investors.

Italy—Beyond the Idiosyncratic

WHAT TO MAKE OF a country that has had fifty-eight governments since the end of World War II? What to make of a government that had been so rife with corruption that before it was dissolved in 1994, one-third of Parliament was under investigation? What to make of a nation's representatives who threw out the prime minister, a leader who had agilely courted the nation through a most unlikely and remarkable path to the brink of European monetary union, just two months before common currency commenced?

Italy indeed seems to founder in perpetual chaos.

And yet for those investors who saw past Italian idiosyncratic behavior to the changes that are slowly, fragilely enveloping Europe's third-largest economy, the returns over the years leading up to European Monetary Union were more than compensatory. They were some of the best the Continent has had to offer.

Euro-Induced Reform

Despite a flat performance in dollar terms in 1999, Italian stocks rose by more than 21 percent a year between 1995 and 1999. The annualized rate of return from 1997 through 1999 topped 31 percent.[1]

In the year leading up to monetary union, 1998, Italian equities soared more than 54 percent, driven by nearly every major sector.[2] However, in 1999 only telecoms and basic industries scored significant advances: Telecom Italia soared 92 percent in local terms, and Italcementi's stock rose 27 percent.[3]

The key behind the country's strong equity performance during the last half of the 1990s was the prospect of membership in common currency. Qualifying for the euro has brought about a fiscal discipline previously unseen in Italy, and this impressed the markets. By the end of

1998, a Merrill Lynch poll found fund managers consistently over-weighting Italian equities because of extensive benefits Italy is expected to derive from EMU.[4]

Many of these improvements were quite dramatic. For example, a 10 percent government deficit in 1993 was reduced to 1.7 percent by 1999. Driving this improvement was a cut in the country's huge debt service as interest rates plummeted from double digits in 1995 to the European Central Bank's 3 percent rate set at the end of 1998 in preparation for monetary union.

Paralleling the drop in interest rates has been a steady decline in inflation, which fell from 5.4 percent in 1995 to 1.6 percent in 1999. Low inflation has promoted business and consumer confidence and had a positive influence on the lira—historically western Europe's most volatile currency. Since its readmission to the European Union Exchange Rate Mechanism in 1996 (required before admission into monetary union), the Italian lira had held steady, aided by strong trade and current account balances and broad improvement in the country's overall finances.

Public finances were further assisted by Italy's privatization program, the Continent's largest, which has so far raised $77 billion between 1992 and 1998.[5] The extensive shift of public enterprises to the private sector, especially in banking, insurance, and utilities, has spurred a wide range of mergers, acquisitions, and restructurings that are slowly altering Italy's cumbersome and inefficient corporate culture, increasing focus on return on equity, and enhancing shareholder value.

Economic Risks

Two large macroeconomic concerns remain: government debt and a persistently high jobless rate. With indebtedness having ended 1999 at 115 percent of GDP, nearly twice the limit set by EMU, Italy had the second-worst debt position in the eurozone. However, just four years earlier, in 1995, the Debt/GDP ratio was 125 percent. Such improvement got Italy past the requirements of Maastricht. By 2001, the Economist Intelligence Unit expects it to be down to 107 percent.

Unemployment surged to a six-year high of 12.6 percent in October 1998 (23 percent in the country's impoverished south) at a time when the job picture in the rest of Europe had been improving. According to

Riccardo Barbieri, senior economist at Morgan Stanley Dean Witter, this trend suggested that many of the country's gains in public finance and equities were more dependent on one-time events (such as a euro-surcharge on income taxes to close the budget deficit) than on structural changes required to effectively turn around the economy.[6] And GDP performance between 1994 and 1999 does give pause, displaying a far more erratic pattern of growth than in the rest of Europe, reflecting the paradox that seems to define Italian economics. Over the 1990s, total economic growth in Italy ran 7 points lower than the average expansion of the other ten charter eurozone economies.[7]

In 1998 the Asian crisis began washing up onto Italian shores, cutting into this export-driven economy, slowing expansion to only 1.5 percent, well below the eurozone average of 2.9 percent.[8]

With economic growth having shown no improvement in 1999 (GDP up a paltry 1.4 percent), unemployment nudged down only modestly, ending the year at 11.4 percent. Eurozone joblessness was nearly 2 full percentage points lower.

One key reason for stagnant job and economic growth is the country's arcane labor laws. Management often chooses not to add workers because wages are set nationally without regard to productivity or regional differences in the cost of living. Approximately 44 percent of basic wages goes to "nonwage" costs.[9] In addition, laying off workers is still virtually impossible. However, work laws are slowly changing.

➤ Greater labor flexibility is being achieved in exchange for a reduction in corporate profit taking.
➤ Businesses are able now to rely increasingly on temporary and part-time positions, assisted by the legalization of private employment agencies.
➤ Performance-related pay is becoming a reality.
➤ New jobs are now costing employers less in social security payments.[10]

Still, Italian labor remains uncompetitive, a reality that's most clearly illustrated by the low flow of direct foreign investment into the country, despite incentives that are as lucrative as those in Ireland and Wales.[11]

According to Sergio de Nardis, economist with Confindustria, the national federation of Italian industrials, "excessive labor costs, inadequate infrastructure, high taxation, and a byzantine bureaucracy are enormous deterrents to foreign investment. Italy is just not competitive." In 1997, whereas England attracted $36.9 billion in direct foreign investment and France $18.2 billion, Italy attracted only $3.5 billion.[12]

Further compounding the problem of erratic economic growth and the poor rate of job development is Italy's need to ultimately increase taxes to pay down her staggering debt and pension liability, the latter of which is currently running at 15 percent of GDP.[13] Such revenue needs hamstring the state from extending significant tax breaks to encourage greater investment and employment. The *Financial Times* aptly observes that while "Italy has made considerable [fiscal] progress in the last few years, behind this facade lies a series of unresolved structural economic and political problems that need to be addressed quickly."[14]

Political Vacuum

But of all her difficulties inhibiting revival, Italy suffers worst from the lack of strong political leadership. The problem dates back to Mussolini's abolishing the country's short-lived parliamentary system in 1924 and aligning the country with fascism and Hitler. Reaction to his dictatorship subsequently distanced the country from embracing strong central government. The postwar constitution of 1948 significantly cut into executive authority and established parliamentary rule that continues to dominate government to this day. The result is that the average length of an administration since the end of the Second World War has been less than one year. The lack of consistent leadership has kept the country from effectively addressing its most pressing problems: jobs, pensions, taxation, transportation, and political reform.

EMU has begun to alter all that. While governments still come and go in Italy, administrations have shared the common policy of keeping the state a part of the most significant economic and political alliance Europe has ever known. And that has been good news for business and investors. During the next few years, competing in the New Europe may spur structural economic change, which could generate more consistent political leadership. But don't hold your breath.

Switzerland—Curious Independence

ALTHOUGH INVESTORS IN SWISS equities have been treated to very good returns over recent years, the country's economy paints a rather confusing image about what exactly is driving up share prices. Swiss economic growth has been among the slowest in western Europe, barely averaging 1 percent a year throughout the 1990s. Yet, domestic stocks returned more than 25 percent a year in local currency terms between 1995 and 1999, helping to make the country among the wealthiest in the industrialized world, with GDP per capita the second highest in Europe.[1]

Switzerland has not been benefiting from European integration. In fact, it remains the most unaligned nation in Europe and is highly skeptical of European union. Yet, no other country speaks more foreign languages. Private banking laws make it the repository of one-third of the world's offshore accounts.[2] Construction of two major rail tunnels through the Alpines—the largest construction project in the country's history—will integrate Switzerland into Europe's high-speed rail network, vastly improving international passenger and commercial travel across the heart of western Europe.[3] And the active pace of Swiss mergers and acquisitions has created some of the world's leading multinationals.

Swiss Giants

Though it has only 7 million inhabitants and its economy ranks twenty-third in size globally, Switzerland has twenty-three companies in the *Financial Times* European Top 500 Index, with a composite market cap of $580 billion.[4] Swiss equities are collectively worth more than the Italian, Dutch, and Swedish bourses combined.[5] Some of the country's most prestigious names:

➤ Pharmaceutical giants Novartis and Roche are two of Europe's top ten largest companies.

➤ Nestlé is the world's largest food company.

➤ Merger of Union Bank of Switzerland and Swiss Bank created the largest bank on the Continent, United Bank of Switzerland (UBS), with a $62 billion market cap. UBS followed the domestic merger with the acquisition of two major foreign brokerage houses, Warburg Dillon Read and PaineWebber.

➤ Credit Suisse Group, the country's other global-scale financial services operation, acquired the country's biggest life insurer, Winterthur; the U.S. mutual fund group Warburg Pincus Asset Management; and the U.S. financial services firms First Boston and DLJ.

➤ Swiss Reinsurance and Zurich Financial Services are two of the world's largest insurance companies.

➤ Holderbank is the world's largest cement company.

➤ Schindler is the number-one manufacturer of escalators and the second biggest manufacturer of elevators.

➤ ABB Alstom Power (the combination of a Swiss-Swedish firm and a French-British firm) is the world's third-largest manufacturer of power generating equipment.[6]

➤ The linkup of Swiss Stratec and U.S. Synthes has created one of Europe's largest medical technology companies.[7]

In 1998, Europe's biggest IPO was Swisscom, the country's primary telecom provider. The $5.6 billion offering is the largest in the country's history and the first privatization of a state asset. But most telling about the offering was that it took place in the middle of the fall 1998 market correction and yet it was three times oversubscribed, reflecting both the broad appeal of Swiss equities and the restructuring that much of corporate Switzerland has been going through.[8]

Well before it went public, Swisscom installed new management that consolidated the company's seventeen units into four. Annual capital expenditures were cut by 40 to 50 percent, and the workforce was slimmed down from 22,000 to 15,000.[9] The company sold off its noncore fiber-optic network[10] and its mobile telephone interests in India and Malaysia.[11] And with 14 percent of its traffic generated from northern Italy, Swisscom decided to set up its own landline service in the region at prices that are 40 to 50 percent below prevailing rates.[12]

Corporate and Economic Disconnect

With corporate Switzerland developing a dominant global presence, how then was it possible for Swiss GDP to have averaged only 1.26 percent annual growth between 1995 and 1999?[13]

The most likely answer: the nation has simply thrived beyond the limits of its geography, forcing Swiss corporations to shift much of their resources beyond the border. Between 1995 and 1999, domestic firms channeled close to SFr 100 billion in foreign direct investment out of Switzerland. That's roughly four times more foreign investment than that which came into the country.[14] This shift in capital has meant that much of the economic benefits and trickle-down effects of Swiss corporate expansion are being captured by the foreign economies where these firms are operating.

Look at Swiss research and development. The country commits the third-highest percent of GDP (2.7 percent in 1996) to R&D in the OECD.[15] However, half of this work is carried out on foreign soil, suggesting Switzerland's manufacturing base is not fully realizing the benefits of advanced technologies.[16]

What does this all mean for domestic economic growth? "With Switzerland's large companies producing the bulk of their output abroad," observes the London-based Economist Intelligence Unit, "this leaves the vast majority of domestic manufacturing executed by smaller (slower-growing) companies employing 10 to 100 people."[17]

While globalization diversifies the Swiss economy, taking some of the edge off its cyclical swings, it also enhances currency risks and points to another paradox. The Swiss franc has traditionally been thought of as a safe haven. This means when export growth suffers due to the collapse of emerging market economies, Swiss companies are subsequently socked a second time by increasing demand for the franc. Greater demand for the currency pushes up its value, making Swiss exports more expensive, especially to nations whose currencies are moving in the opposite direction. This occurred most recently in 1998, when Swiss exports of machinery, electronics, and metal industry fell by 14 percent as a direct result of the protracted Asian economic crisis that spread to Latin America.[18]

However, monetary policy has helped ease matters. To reduce upward pressure on the currency and to stimulate growth, the Swiss central bank continued to cut interest rates. Yields on three-month money market accounts, which were as high as 4.8 percent in 1993, fell to 1.4 percent in 1998. Coupled with a significant decline in unemployment, from 5.2 percent in 1997 to 3.9 percent in 1998, this boosted consumer confidence and overall domestic demand. At the same time, inflation was barely perceptible. All this helped the economy make its strongest showing of the decade, expanding by 2.2 percent. This was followed by 1.7 percent growth in 1999.

Early in 2000 the central bank—fearful of accelerating growth, a tightening labor market, and the import of inflation due to the Swiss franc having weakened 20 percent against the dollar in 1999—quickly pumped up interest rates by 1 full percentage point. Was this an overly defensive move? Looking at the country's equity markets for guidance on the matter, it would seem that at least over the past several years, the central bank's Goldilocks-like monetary policy seems to be "just right."

Equity and Currency Performance

Between 1994 and 1998, Swiss stocks' one-, three-, and five-year stock returns (in dollar terms) have been Europe's most consistent, appreciating 23 percent a year on average, with the Swiss franc having been the great equalizer. Between 1996 and 1998, returns in local currency terms actually averaged nearly 30 percent a year. But depreciation of the franc from SFr 1.24/$ to SFr 1.44/$, driven by the substantial cut in long-term interest rates from 4.2 percent to 2.4 percent, reduced the market's dollar-based return. In 1998, the franc's rebound, stimulated by the rush to quality during the emerging market meltdown in the fall, transformed a relatively modest 15.91 percent return (based in francs) into a 23.09 percent dollar-denominated gain.[19]

The market, however, stumbled in 1999, turning in the weakest performance of any major European bourse, rising only 7.44 percent in local currency terms. Dollar-based investors were down nearly 8 percent due to the sharp decline of the franc.[20] Besides the Swiss franc depreciating in sync with the euro against the dollar, investors were hurt because the Swiss market is dominated by an above-average number of Old Economy stocks. Approximately two-thirds of the country's market cap is comprised of pharmaceuticals, chemicals, and financial services shares.[21] The more tech- and telecom-seasoned eurozone markets, in contrast, rose 37.47 in local terms, and 17.35 percent in dollar terms in 1999.[22]

Still, several Swiss sectors had a strong year. The cyclical services group, led by the doubling in share price of global temporary staffing agency Adecco, was up 67 percent in local currency terms. Swiss industrials soared by nearly 85 percent in 1999, led by the turnaround of the engineering and electrical conglomerate ABB, whose stock more than doubled. While the banking sector as a whole had an off year, Credit Suisse rose 47 percent.

Two recent developments further buoy the prospects of Switzerland's leading stocks.

➤ Reform of the retirement system will funnel up to 25 percent of the state's $17.4 billion pension fund into Swiss blue chips.[23]

➤ A new alliance between the Paris Bourse and the Swiss Exchange should not only trigger greater demand for domestic equities but also will better position both exchanges as stock markets consolidate across western Europe.[24]

Switzerland and Europe

Perhaps the biggest concern facing Swiss macroeconomics and equity growth is the nagging question of European integration. Once held up as a model of growth, the Swiss economy's weak performance during most of the 1990s has been blamed in large part on Switzerland's isolation from Europe.[25] The *Financial Times* pointed out in its survey of the country's banks and insurance companies, "if Swiss financial institutions are to continue to grow, they have to expand internationally, and this means that increasingly they must fall into line with the rules and regulations of other countries."[26] With more than 60 percent of Switzerland's exports heading into the EU and nearly 80 percent of Swiss imports coming from the EU, greater European integration would appear to be unavoidable.

Toward that end, Swiss leaders signed the Vienna Accords at the end of 1998. This agreement spelled out greater integration of EU and Swiss policy regarding roads and air transport, free movement of labor, public procurement, research, agriculture, and establishment of trade standards.[27]

However, enactment of the accords is hardly assured. First, they must be approved by Switzerland's various representative layers, including a majority of her twenty-six cantons. These are the country's historic regions, many of which passionately hold onto anachronistic visions of inviolable independence. The entire voting process could take years to complete.

Even more contentious is the sheer cost of further European integration. Compliance with the accords could cost Switzerland up to SFr 950 million a year.[28] Of course, Swiss companies would realize certain savings. SwissAir projects it could slash SFr 200 million in expenses. Overall, the agreement is expected to boost Swiss GDP by 0.5 percent, a rather substantial amount given the economy's perpetually anemic growth. And that potential may be enough of a carrot to get the accords approved.

However, sentiment against the treaty asserts that passage could be an irrevocable and costly step toward Swiss membership in the European Union.

➤ Because of the country's substantial wealth, joining would likely mean outward transfers of nearly SFr 3 billion into EU coffers.

➤ Subsequent interest rate convergence could cost the Swiss an additional SFr 20 billion.

➤ Indirect taxes could potentially double (the country's low VAT is currently less than half the EU's average).

➤ EU membership would also threaten the country's prized private banking laws, the source of huge inflow of assets into Swiss-based accounts, and this could destabilize the Swiss franc.[29]

All of this is likely too high a price to pay, especially since the prize of EU membership—adoption of the euro—is clearly not of prime concern to the Swiss at this time given its strong corporate performance.

United Kingdom—Continental Divide

AN INDEPENDENT ANGLO-SAXON character has placed Great Britain in the fore of European change. Government reform and corporate restructuring, which only began catching on in Europe in the early 1990s, started a decade earlier in the United Kingdom, closely paralleling the U.S. experience. Whereas European nations needed the carrot of common currency to begin getting their economies in order, a revitalized Britain has been content holding onto its sterling.

Overall, the U.K. financial picture is compelling. Having jump-started privatization, mergers and acquisitions, restructuring, market deregulation, and labor and pension reform well before the rest of Europe, Britain has created an economy that looks more like that of the United States than any on the Continent. This helped British stocks to average gains of nearly 17 percent a year in dollar terms from 1995 through 1999.[1] This economic distinction from the mainland also explains why Britain's business cycle has been out of phase with most other European markets—a reason the country's financial leaders seek to keep the United Kingdom out of common currency.

British officials fear that complying with a monetary policy designed for the twelve-country eurozone could endanger Europe's third-largest economy. A look at Britain's initial attempt at Continental monetary linkage points to the basis of this concern.

Britain and Europe

Only several years after belatedly joining the European Union Exchange Rate Mechanism (the precursor to monetary union) in the late 1980s, Britain was forced out, unable to stabilize sterling's exchange rate with the deutsche mark. The reason: huge spending accompanying reunification overheated the German economy and led the Bundesbank to push up interest rates while the British economy was mired in a protracted recession. Higher rates made the mark stronger. Because Britain couldn't sustain similar measures, the required trading bandwidth between sterling and the mark was broken, forcing Britain out of ERM.

However, economic disparity between the United Kingdom and Continental Europe went beyond the issue of currency. Between 1991 and 1994, as the British economy was pulling out of recession, the eurozone was lapsing into one. Since 1995 the two economies have shown closer correlation, more frequently trending in the same direction. Still, diametric monetary conditions continued. Then, in 1998, as eurozone interest rates converged down toward 3 percent, U.K. rates shot up to 7.5 percent, sending the pound soaring. Sterling ended the year trading at €1.42.

By the middle of May 2000, the pound had appreciated by an additional 16 percent against the euro and held fairly steady with the dollar, while three-month U.K. interest rates of 6.25 percent were nearly 50 percent above those in the eurozone. Not only does such monetary disparity expose British trade to substantial risk—with half the country's exports going to the eurozone—but also it suggests difficulty maintaining convergent growth. This and the sterling's currently high exchange rate impede U.K. membership in EMU.

A New Fiscal Code

At the heart of this cyclical problem has been the volatility of the British economy. A 1998 OECD economic survey observed that "booms and busts have been characteristic of the United Kingdom over the last several decades." Analysts at the Economist Intelligence Unit blame this phenomenon in part on myopic U.K. policy makers responding to short-term electoral considerations. They see "unsustainably strong growth countered by excessively corrective policy that slows the economy far too sharply, giving the country periods of high inflation, currency volatility, and sharp macroeconomic policy reversals."[2]

Soon after taking office in 1997, Prime Minister Tony Blair set out to replace this volatility "with the prospect of real stability."[3] His strategy was based on enactment of a new Code for Fiscal Responsibility, based on the following policy initiatives:

➤ Consolidating monetary authority with the Bank of England (taking control of interest rates away from the Chancellor of the Exchequer),

➤ Promoting tax and social security reform,

➤ Maintaining strict debt and inflation levels,

➤ Requiring government spending to be financed through current revenues instead of long-term borrowing, and

➤ Eliminating the deficit.

So far, his policies seem to be working. Government budget deficit, which was nearly 6 percent of GDP in 1995, turned into a small surplus in 1998 and 1999. Public debt also declined from 45.5 percent of GDP in 1996 to less than 39 percent in 1999. Inflation held steady below 3 percent across the last half of the 1990s, enabling long-term interest rates to decline from 8.2 to 5.2 percent.

At the same time, unemployment steadily declined from 8.7 percent in 1995 to under 6 percent in 1999. This helped accelerate domestic demand from 1.8 percent to 3.4 percent, while capital investment expanded at an annual rate of 6 percent.

GDP grew at an average of 2.6 percent a year during the last half of the 1990s, peaking at 3.5 percent in 1997. Despite several emerging market crises and the continuous rise of the pound during 1998 and 1999, both of which cut into U.K. exports, the economy still managed to average more than 2 percent annual growth during those years.[4]

If Britain can smooth out its business cycle, extending periods of expansion, then it will go a long way toward addressing one of the country's most significant deficiencies: productivity.

According to the international consulting firm McKinsey, U.S. productivity is 37 percent greater than Britain's; German and French rates are 25 percent greater.[5] A primary cause of this gap has been inhibited investment. An unpredictable business cycle makes it difficult for managers to make timely capital commitments to increase production and increase efficiency. Moreover, instead of driving growth by making products more affordable, companies seem to hinge expansion on explicit evidence of demand.

The ability to charge substantially higher retail prices in Britain, often 20 to 50 percent above those in Europe and the United States, also contributes to corporate complacency that neglects productivity improvements. According to a survey by *The Economist,* the country's relatively inexpensive labor has encouraged "British companies to employ more people and less capital (for productivity improvements) than their counterparts in France and Germany."[6] However, several external and internal forces are beginning to exert pricing pressures that will likely lead to enhanced efficiencies.

Efficiency Improvements and Foreign Direct Investment

Privatization, deregulation, and increased focus on shareholder value continue to drive competition and price cutting. Having regularly required substantial subsidy, British Steel is now one of the lowest-cost steel producers in the world. British Airways, while mired in a protracted industry slump, is still among the largest and most efficient international carriers around. Privatization of British Telecom and subsequent deregulation of the telecom industry has helped cut phone bills by more than half.[7]

Booming foreign direct investment, opened up by the Thatcher government in the early 1980s, is also driving efficiency. According to the *Financial Times,* "one-third of recent productivity growth in British manufacturing is attributable to production and management techniques introduced by foreign investors."[8] For example, Nissan's operations in Sunderland have become the most efficient manufacturing plant in the industry, helping to make the United Kingdom the fourth-largest carmaker in the EU.[9] Meanwhile, investments by Siemens, Samsung, Fujitsu, Motorola, and NEC have helped transform Britain into the world's second-largest semiconductor manufacturer.[10]

Besides improving productivity, foreign direct investment (FDI) is driving the British economy. Foreign companies poured more than

$36.4 billion into the United Kingdom in FY 1998, representing 10 percent of the world's total foreign investment and 25 percent of all foreign investment that flowed into the EU.[11] Britain captured 20 percent of all U.S. foreign-directed capital and 40 percent of all Asian exported capital. Two significant foreign acquisitions of British properties were Merrill Lynch's $5.2 billion purchase of the venerable money management firm Mercury Asset Management and French insurance giant AXA's purchase of Guardian Royal Exchange for $5.6 billion.

During FY 1999, the *Financial Times* reported "a record 652 new inward investments—worth nearly $72 billion—created or safeguarded 118,000 jobs."[12] Several of the largest deals:

➤ U.S. conglomerate TRW's purchase of the British auto parts concern Lucas Varity for $6.6 billion;

➤ AES Corporation, the largest U.S. power-plant developer, acquired National Power energy station for $3 billion;

➤ Huntsman, the private U.S. chemical concern, purchased four units from Imperial Chemical for $2.7 billion.[13]

In FY 2000, FDI climbed by another 23 percent, or $76 billion, pushing the total stock of foreign inward investment to $384 billion.[14]

The reasons for Britain's appeal: a transparent open market; free trade with all EU countries; access to the world's largest and most sophisticated capital markets; a flexible, relatively inexpensive, well-trained labor force that speaks English; a corporate tax rate that's among the lowest in Europe; and a government committed to stable macroeconomic policy. According to a World Economic Forum survey, these benefits have helped the United Kingdom become the fourth most competitive country in the world.[15]

However, capital is also flowing out of Britain. Reflecting an increasingly aggressive corporate culture seeking to expand the bounds of the country's limited marketplace, British investment abroad totaled more than $111.6 billion in FY 1998, far exceeding capital inflow.[16] Almost one-third of exported capital flowed into the United States, with 80 percent of foreign mergers and acquisitions involving U.S. firms.

Several of the largest deals:

➤ Vodafone's transatlantic acquisition of AirTouch Communications for $55 billion (subsequently topped several years later by its audacious takeover of Mannesmann for $183 billion),

➤ British Petroleum's purchase of Amoco for $53 billion and Atlantic Richfield for $27 billion,
➤ The $34.6 billion pharmaceutical merger of Britain's Zeneca and Sweden's Astra, and
➤ British Telecom and AT&T's $3 billion joint venture.[17]

Equity Performance

In 1999, while shares of AstraZeneca managed only to break even, the other three deal makers generated strong gains. BP was up nearly 30 percent in local currency terms, Vodafone gained more than 58 percent, and British Telecom soared by more than 67 percent.[18]

Overall, British stocks performed very well in 1999. Consumer cyclicals rose by a third, basic industries were up 36 percent, industrials and resources both gained 46 percent, telecommunications appreciated by 65 percent, and information technology stocks more than doubled.[19]

Sterling's strong performance in 1999, down by less than 5 percent against the dollar, helped U.S. investors retain most of these gains. But it also suggests that Britain may still be more economically correlated with the United States than with the Continent. And in currency terms, this gap not only places greater strain on U.K. exports to its prime eurozone trading partners but also renders thoughts of U.K. membership in monetary union moot—at least until the euro rebounds or the pound weakens substantially.

Chapter Four

Tigers

Ireland—Testing the Limits of Common Currency

I RELAND IS ONE OF THE hottest economies in the world, expanding at a rate that would've been the envy of any of the Asian tiger economies before they were defanged.

GDP growth averaged 8.4 percent per annum between 1995 and 1999. Unemployment significantly declined, from 12.2 percent in 1995 to 5.7 percent by the end of 1999, while labor productivity increased at three times the EU average.[1] Private consumption was up by nearly one-third to 30 billion Irish punts, and gross fixed investment nearly doubled to I£ 14 billion, while inflation was kept under control through the end of the decade.[2]

Meanwhile, Ireland's phenomenal growth has been a boon for government finances, leading to tax cuts and a drastic reduction of debt as a percent of GDP from 88 percent in 1995 down to an estimated 46 percent in 1999.[3] This, in turn, has diminished the government's drain on capital markets, freeing up more investment dollars for the private sector.

Growth and Inflation

Expansion has come as a result of pro-business government policy that's lured in big multinationals via tax breaks, a well-educated labor

The Tigers

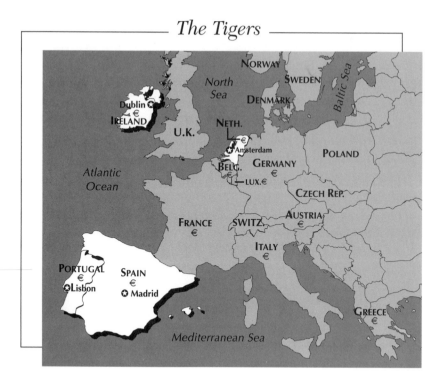

pool, and being the only EMU-member country with English as its first language. All this has generated business confidence in Ireland that has consistently exceeded the EU average since 1990.[4]

Growth has also been the product of supportive demographics. Where Continental Europe faces pending pension crises due to an aging workforce and too few younger workers capable of supporting retirement demands, Ireland is blessed with just the opposite. The number of so-called active individuals, between the ages of fifteen and sixty-five, has been increasing by 1 percent a year, while the remaining dependent age groups have been declining. A reduction in birth rates and the increasing return of expatriates of working age help explain these trends, which, according to David Poutney, a bank analyst at London-based securities firm Panmure Gordon, are expected to continue for the next ten years. And this is generating higher incomes, greater tax revenues, and a reduction in government assistance.[5]

Ireland is in the extraordinary position of possessing all the energy and growth of an emerging market economy with the political, legal, and social stability and transparency of a mature industrialized state.

However, even with all its strengths, Ireland is in a very vulnerable position, testing the most basic premise of common currency.

Growing three times as fast as the average eurozone economy during the latter half of the 1990s, Ireland maintained high interest rates to restrain inflation. But with rates having converged with the rest of the eurozone (yields on 3-month Treasury bills were cut in half, falling from 6.2 percent in 1994 to less than 3 percent by the end of 1999) and with private credit expanding by 25 to 30 percent a year[6] (nearly three times the pace of the eurozone), higher prices seem a foregone conclusion.[7]

Housing and fuel prices have shot up dramatically. But as of early 2000, strong growth and low interest rates still had not yet triggered broad inflation. David Poutney believes that "because Ireland's boom was superimposed onto an open, small economy operating well below capacity, marked by high unemployment, inflation has been subdued."[8] But this calculus was predicated on Ireland's control of its monetary policy. Because the Irish economy represents only 1 percent of the GDP of the European Union, the country's macroeconomics will have little influence on broad European Central Bank decisions—especially in determining where interest rates are set.

This leaves local fiscal policy (taxing and spending) as the primary means government has to keep inflation at bay. But a good bit of this discretion has already been spoken for in the country's labor policy— Partnership 2000—wherein government has negotiated 3 percent per annum wage increases in exchange for income tax cuts that will effectively increase wages by 4 to 5 percent. At the same time, the government has pledged to gradually reduce corporate taxes to 12.5 percent by 2006 and hold them at that level for the next twenty years.[9]

If Ireland is unable to restrain inflation, then the country will challenge a core component of monetary union: that a single interest rate can prevail effectively across countries whose individual economies are in various stages of growth and contraction. With Spain, Portugal, Finland, and the Netherlands all potentially facing the same scenario, Ireland has become a keen focus of the European Central Bank.

As in most industrialized economies, Ireland's growth has been driven by the service sectors, which generate more than half the country's GDP. Most business is still state owned. Private financial and consulting services now represent more than 11 percent of GDP and should continue to expand. With privatization just beginning to creep into various facets of the economy, Ireland could well be on the brink of enhanced economic competitiveness and expansion.

In July 1999, the government sold off its remaining 50.1 percent stake in Eircom, the country's primary telecom service provider, for $5.5 billion. It was one of Ireland's largest public offerings, having added 2.5 percent to the market capitalization of the Dublin Stock Exchange. Just as important is a novel share ownership arrangement that will pass 14.5 percent of the company to Eircom's workers. Highlighting the government's partnership with its people (as well as with business), Ireland's minister for public enterprise, Mary O'Rourke, explains, "the workers have contributed to the value of the company, and you have to have them with you." And Eircom's CEO, Alfie Kane, sees the arrangement as "a groundbreaking deal in industrial relations that will free up the culture of the company and accelerate restructuring in cost cuts and improvements in work practice."[10]

In addition to an expanding service sector, the Irish economy also is drawing strength from a unique feature of a developed market: an expanding industrial base. Manufacturing activity has tripled since 1985, and currently, the industrial sector generates more than 40 percent of GDP.

A key industrial driver has been the addition of high-tech multinationals onto Irish soil. More than 470 U.S. companies have invested in Ireland,[11] and their names read like a list of Who's Who in U.S. Technology: IBM, Intel, Oracle, Microsoft, Novell, and Compaq. Gateway 2000 set up its 1,600-person European headquarters just outside of Dublin. Digital (Compaq) set up its European Software Center in Galway, employing 500 workers. And Dell added 3,000 jobs to its 1,400-worker operations, making the company the biggest private sector employer in the country.[12]

Remarkably, 30 percent of all U.S. information technology investment into Europe is going into Ireland. This has helped the country become the largest software exporter in the world. If company sales executives are wondering how to penetrate the European technology market, all they need do is look at Ireland—the source of one-third of Europe's computers, 40 percent of its software, and 60 percent of its business applications.[13]

How does all this bode for Irish stocks? Pretty darn well.

Equity Performance

Three- and five-year annualized returns (in local currency) through 1999 both exceeded 19 percent. However, these returns were substantially depressed by the market's lackluster performance in 1999 as the market barely broke even in local currency terms.

Whereas participation in common currency enhanced equity expectations, the reality is that EMU cut into stocks during the first year of the euro in two basic ways. First, there was a flight of institutional capital out of Ireland as portfolios rebalanced their holdings to reflect their new eurozone benchmarks. Some local stocks were oversold. And unfortunately, there was no corresponding inflow of foreign capital to make up for the loss in demand for domestic shares. By the second quarter of 2000, however, there was some evidence of this happening.

The second hit to Irish equities was the plunge in the euro's value. Although the MSCI Ireland Index rose 0.72 percent in euro terms in 1999, the index fell by 14 percent in dollar terms.

Financials took the brunt of the hit in 1999. Allied Irish Banks and Bank of Ireland fell 25.9 and 16.8 percent, respectively, in euro terms, despite profits remaining strong. Because of its asset size, financials depressed Dublin's overall performance in 1999.

However, there were a number of strong nonfinancial performers. CRH Public Limited Co., a multibillion-dollar construction company, climbed 45.3 percent. The upstart discount airline Ryanair continued to soar, rising nearly 74 percent, while shares in the country's leading paper and packaging group, Jefferson Smurfit, nearly doubled.[14]

Exchange Rate Issues

How will EMU subsequently affect Irish equities? Despite an initial rough start, and assuming inflation doesn't run rampant, common currency should be as welcome as a pint of Guinness. In eliminating the exchange risk, buying and selling stocks with the euro will open up local shares to new investors from the eleven other countries participating in EMU. And with Irish exports leading the country's economic surge, common currency—offering pricing transparency from country to country while limiting currency risk—will likely trigger even greater Irish expansion.

One outstanding concern in joining common currency is that Ireland's major trading partner, Great Britain, has not. Nearly one-quarter of Irish exports head for the United Kingdom, while 39 percent of Irish imports come from the United Kingdom.[15] In fact, unlike the average euro country that does 88 percent of its trade inside the eurozone, two-thirds of Irish trade is conducted with countries outside the eurozone, thus making exchange rates no incidental matter.[16]

So far, the steady decline in the euro against sterling and the dollar has made Irish products and services even more competitive. But it has also introduced the threat of imported inflation as the currency-translated price of non-eurozone goods has risen. Coupled with the threat of continued housing price and wage increases, this could make the Irish economy overheat and begin to extinguish its competitive advantage.

However, that would not necessarily be bad news in the larger scheme of things. Rather, it would reflect the increasing convergence of Irish living standards with the rest of the EU, while permitting market forces to nudge Irish growth down in line with the rest of western Europe. And this will ultimately enable Ireland to thrive under a single monetary policy.

The Netherlands—Dutch Miracle

PERHAPS IT'S A MATTER of topography, the ingenuity that comes with the threat of living below sea level, that has made the Dutch a resourceful people. Creating an intricate network of dikes and water locks has earned the Dutch a reputation as world-class engineers. The country's latest land venture captures the imagination: creating a series of man-made islands along its North Sea coast to accommodate expansion of Europe's busiest port and the Continent's third most active airport.

It's little wonder then that during the past twenty years the Dutch have engineered one of the great turnaround stories in recent European economic history.

Back in the early 1980s, the country was stalled in a deep recession. Inflation was pushing toward 7 percent, and lending rates topped 14 percent. Soaring labor costs and borrowing rates so crippled productivity that the country's current account plunged from a surplus of $3.5 billion to nearly a billion-dollar deficit.[1] Job loss ensued, shooting up unemployment from 5.6 percent in 1980 to 17 percent in 1983.[2]

Further, the government deficit had nearly doubled in just two years, to nearly 8 percent of GDP, while the national debt soared to over 50 percent of GDP. The most remarkable statistic: public expenditures represented 61 percent of everything the country produced.[3]

Economic Restoration

However, toward the end of the 1990s, the *Financial Times* reported that "the Netherlands boasts the Continent's most competitive economy,"[4] while the OECD cited the Dutch as "the leader in structural and regulatory reform in Europe."[5] The numbers are indeed impressive.

➤ Since the first quarter of 1993, the last time GDP declined, the economy has been averaging over 3 percent real growth per year. Between 1997 and 1999, annual economic expansion ran at a remarkable 3.7 percent.[6]

➤ Inflation and interest rates have fallen dramatically, converging with Maastricht's guidelines.

➤ Unemployment ended 1999 at 3 percent, one-third the eurozone's average.

➤ Government deficit has been virtually eliminated.

➤ Current account balance closed the decade running at a positive 6 percent of GDP, spurred on by strong export growth.[7]

Two major forces were behind the Dutch renaissance. First, to settle volatile exchange rates and ease trade imbalances, the government pegged the guilder to the German mark, in essence linking its monetary policy with the Continent's most influential economy and its largest trading partner. This brought stability and discipline to the Dutch economy and was a boon to exports when the dollar soared in the 1990s.

The second development was to rein in labor costs. Reflective of the society's consensus-building approach to problem solving, workers, business, and government agreed to a broad policy that exchanged sharp wage growth for jobs.

➤ Automatic wage indexing was eliminated, and growth in social security benefits was slowed.

➤ Labor rules were liberalized, encouraging the creation of more temporary and part-time jobs.

➤ Minimum wages were frozen, taxes were cut for low-income workers, and tax brackets were raised, which gave back more money to workers.

The result: between 1983 and 1995, labor costs declined significantly relative to the country's industrialized rivals, giving Dutch industry as much as a 15 percent cost advantage over its chief German competitors.[8]

According to its 2000 survey of world competitiveness, the Lausanne-based Institute for Management Development found the Netherlands to be the fourth most competitive country in the world and among the most attractive places for foreign business.[9] "And with a low public deficit, a current account surplus, strong economic growth, and unemployment below 4 percent," the Economist Intelligence Unit regards "Dutch economic policy a model for the euro area."[10]

Industry Leaders

The depth of the country's economic recovery is no better illustrated than in its disproportionately large number of world-class multinationals: oil giant Royal Dutch/Shell, insurance leader AEGON, global electronics manufacturer Philips, world-beloved brewer Heineken, semiconductor equipment manufacturer ASM Lithography, consumer goods producer Unilever, entertainment leader Polygram, multinational food retailer Ahold, and publishing giant Elsevier.

Dutch companies were early to realize the competitive advantages of restructuring and mergers. Since the 1980s, for example, the country's extensive network of financial services and insurance operations has largely been consolidated, leaving three firms controlling three-quarters of the market. Stronger players and soaring equity values have fueled mergers and acquisitions, enabling Dutch companies to refine and expand operations well beyond the country's borders.

Evolution of financial services giant ING Barings offers the clearest look into the contemporary dynamics of the Dutch marketplace. In 1989, Nederlandse Middenstandsbank merged with the state-owned bank Postbank. Two years later, the bank merged with the Nationale Nederlanden insurance group, forming ING. The group picked up the British investment bank Barings after it collapsed in scandal in 1995, creating ING Barings. Then in 1997, in the largest Dutch banking takeover ever, ING Barings bought out the big Belgium bank Banque Bruxelles Lambert for $4.7 billion.

Dutch firms have been on a buying binge ever since. Between 1998 and the middle of May 2000, they cut twenty-five deals of $1 billion or more, worth a total of $84 billion. The top three takeovers:

➤ Dutch/Belgian financial group Fortis purchased Belgium's Générale de Banque for $14 billion.

➤ AEGON, the country's largest insurer, paid $10.9 billion for San Francisco–based Transamerica.

➤ The Netherlands' former telecom monopoly, KPN, teamed up with Bell South in buying E-Plus Mobilfunk, a leading German mobile service operator, for $9.1 billion.[11]

Globalization coupled with monetary union is drastically altering the way Dutch business leaders are thinking, driving cross-border acquisitions. As Gerben Kuyper, senior executive vice president of ABN AMRO, observes, "Dutch companies are managing their businesses as portfolios, which means they are much more relaxed about buying and selling parts of their businesses. In the process, they are redefining the boundaries of what they call a market."[12]

Top Stocks
What has this meant for Dutch stocks? Consistently strong returns. The Amsterdam Stock Exchange rose nearly 25 percent annually in local terms between 1995 and 1999. Dollar-based returns averaged more than 19 percent over that time.[13]

Most sectors continued humming in 1999, with the broad market gaining 23.3 percent in euro terms. But the euro's weak performance during the year brought down dollar-based returns to only 5.25 percent.[14]

Among the country's top stocks for the year were the international investment bank ABN AMRO which gained 38.4 percent in euro terms. Royal Dutch/Shell rose 43.4 percent, KPN soared 127 percent, and a restructured Philips did even better, roaring ahead by nearly 129 percent.[15]

With business investment and consumer spending expected to remain strong, and with many Dutch firms positioning themselves to benefit from common currency and greater competition, the Netherlands is in very good shape.

Two Concerns
However, there are two concerns. Even after years of strong growth and slowing government spending, national debt in 1999 was still high at 60 percent of GDP. Though it has descended from 75 percent in only

five years, some worry that if the government doesn't maintain its fiscal vigilance, the country's debt will be a drag on growth, especially when the economy slows.

Equally troubling is the debate over real unemployment in light of a wide-reaching national disabilities program that removed 850,000 from the workforce in 1997. If all able-bodied workers were counted, some officials estimate that unemployment might actually be in the high teens.[16] Continuation of generous benefits or the need to fund additional work programs, especially when tax revenues are not as strong as they are currently, would further strain government finances.

Toward that end, in February 2000 the government passed sweeping tax reform. According to the EIU, "it's the most radical shake-up of the Dutch tax system since the Second World War."[17] The changes hope to promote job growth by offering earned income tax credits and reducing the fixed employer costs of hiring additional workers. At the same time, the changes are simplifying the system, reducing tax rates for many by expanding the tax base and cutting public spending.

Portugal—From Emerging to Developed Status

RESTORATION OF PORTUGAL'S STATUS as a vibrant European state reflects the economic transformation sweeping across the Continent and the power of the European Union to effect change. In 1998, Morgan Stanley Capital Index reclassified the country from emerging- to developed-market status largely due to the impact of two major EU initiatives: the transfer of tens of billions of dollars to promote development and Portugal's inclusion in monetary union.

By the end of the 1990s, these two stimuli, assisted by broad European economic expansion, had helped propel GDP per capita from 56 percent of the EU average to over 70 percent in just ten years. They helped cut double-digit inflation down to 2 percent and sliced unemployment by more than half, down to 4.1 percent. Real economic expansion steadily rose, having averaged 3.2 percent between 1996 and 1999.[1]

EU funds are financing vast infrastructure improvements that will enhance access throughout the country and better link Portugal with the rest of Europe, helping to exploit her ocean access for world trade. In 1998 alone, $2.4 billion was spent on highway and rail projects, and $558 million went into modernizing the country's ports. These improvements have boosted exports, which rose by more than 70 percent between 1993 and 1999.[2] All told, "EU transfers," explains Jose Salgado, executive director of Banco Finantia, "will trigger extensive economic activity for many years to come."[3]

Qualifying for European Monetary Union imposed a fiscal discipline on the country's public finances that had been lacking. This has made Portugal a much more attractive place for doing business. In the mid-1980s, as the country was struggling with its fledgling democracy and requirements of European Union membership, the government deficit stood at more than 12 percent of GDP. By 1999, the deficit was down to 2 percent of GDP. Since 1995, government debt has declined from 65.9 percent of GDP to less than 57 percent in 1999. In addition, interest rates on 10-year government bonds have plummeted from over 20 percent in 1985 to under 6 percent in 1999.[4]

Fundamental Gains

Structural improvements have transformed Portugal from an economic backwater into a legitimate site of international investment and expansion.

➤ In 1985, one-fourth of the workforce was employed in agriculture; only 10 percent is now, and that figure continues to fall.

➤ Manufacturing jobs make up one-third of the economy, indicative of the country's modernization. Machinery, transportation, and related equipment have displaced textiles and garments as the country's leading exports.[5]

➤ A vast array of state-run financial, transportation, and building operations have been privatized, with total proceeds in the 1990s having exceeded $22.5 billion.[6]

➤ Between 1985 and 1995, productivity increased by 20 percent.

Institutional Investor reports that "Portugal's sound economic fundamentals, political stability, EU membership, vastly improved infrastructure, and government grants and tax breaks have combined to attract an increasing number of foreign investors."[7] Many of these players are big multinationals, setting up highly efficient production centers to serve growing demand. And these new operations are proving to be exceedingly profitable, given the country's inexpensive labor costs and an overall tax burden that's among the lowest in the European Union.[8]

Some recent examples:

➤ Ford and Volkswagen created AutoEuropa, a $2.54 billion joint venture that's manufacturing minivans for the entire European market;

➤ Mitsubishi established its European truck production center;

➤ German engineering giant Siemens built a new $360 million memory-chip plant;

➤ Texas Instruments and Samsung set up a $137 million semiconductor joint venture; and

➤ Philip Morris paid $213 million for a controlling share in Tabaqueira—the state tobacco company—transforming it into PM's production center for all of southern Europe.

Privatization is a key component of the government's economic strategy. "In selling off state enterprises," explains Fernando Teixeira dos Santos, secretary of state for Treasury and Finance, "we are seeking to reduce the government's role in the economy, stimulate capital markets, attract foreign investors, and reduce the public debt."[9]

Privatization proceeds topped out in 1997 with the sell-off of $4.93 billion in state assets. The year's largest deal was a 30 percent offering of Electricidade de Portugal, the country's main utility. Orders for 6 billion shares chased after the 180-million-share offering, eventually raising $2.1 billion for the state. In 1998, a second comparably sized tranche exploited the company's rising share price and raised an additional $4.49 billion.

Portugal also sold off 65 percent of Cimpor, its blue-chip cement and concrete company, whose business has boomed with government's huge commitment to infrastructure improvements not only in Portugal but also in Spain, Mozambique, Morocco, and Brazil. In addition, Portugal Telecom, which has been 75 percent privatized, is playing a key role in the country's economic networking and expansion, forging worldwide links with MCI WorldCom, British Telecom, Spain's Telefónica, and Telebras in Brazil.

Equity Performance

All this news has bode very well for Portuguese stocks, which were on a long-term rise until side effects of common currency temporarily derailed equities. Through 1998, Portuguese stocks had one of Europe's best track records. Five-year annualized returns in dollar terms exceeded 20 percent; three-year returns topped 33.5 percent.

But the first year of the euro witnessed substantial portfolio redistribution. Domestic funds that had been largely restricted to Portuguese stocks were now able to branch off into the rest of the eurozone. The net outflow of funds, coupled with a double-digit decline in the euro, left the *borsa* down by nearly 11 percent in dollar terms in 1999.

Bank and telecom shares, however, did manage to keep pace with the broader European markets in local currency terms. These sectors were led by Banco Português do Atlantico, one of the nation's leading commercial banks, whose shares rose 16.6 percent, and by Portugal Telecom, the country's principal telephone service provider, which gained nearly 40 percent in 1999.[10]

Concerns

The recent downturn in the market has highlighted several key weaknesses in the Portuguese economy. The combination of an expanding economy and low interest rates could fuel greater consumption and inflation. Three-month interbank rates fell from 7.4 percent in 1996 to 3.4 percent in December 1999, while over the same period, real GDP growth ran above 3 percent. Although private consumption grew by 5 percent and government spending by 10 percent in 1999, consumer prices still held steady, below 3 percent.[11] But the question is how much longer can inflation be held at bay?

Another concern is one born of the country's success. As the country becomes wealthier, the flow of funds from the European Union to finance major improvements will slow. Moreover, completion of two of the biggest EU-assisted projects, Expo 98 in Lisbon and construction of the ten-mile Ponte Vasco da Gama (Europe's longest bridge), will leave an economic void. In the future, funds for which Portugal is eligible will be increasingly redirected across the former east-bloc countries as they are absorbed into the EU over the next several years. The cheaper land and labor markets of Poland, Hungary, and the Czech Republic will be competing intensely with Portugal for public and private investments, offering the added benefit of closer proximity to Europe's largest markets.

A final issue: domestic spending and reduced capital inflows catapulted Portugal's current account deficit from 4.8 percent in 1998 to nearly 7 percent in 1999. While common currency reduces the monetary implications of this imbalance, Miguel Namorado Rosa, a senior economist at the Banco Commercial Portuguèse, believes a rising trade deficit and declining public and private capital inflows could threaten the country's economic stability and competitiveness.[12]

Spain—Emerging Corporate Aggressiveness

THE EXPLOSIVE RESURGENCE of the Spanish economy in the 1990s leading up to charter membership in the Economic Monetary Union was to a large degree a response to decades of living beneath the constraints of a closed society.

It's easy to forget that Spain carried the dictatorial legacy of World War II further into the century than any other European country. This profoundly retarded growth for nearly fifty years. Corporate culture was unable to modernize and evolve as rapidly as the rest of Europe, privatization was an unknown concept, and Spain's participation in the international marketplace was severely restricted.

But now, "Madrid is becoming a capital of corporate aggressiveness and clout," reports *Business Week,* fueled by "government trimming its role in the economy, privatizing state companies, and embracing free markets.... Liberalization has unleashed Spanish executives' pent-up competitive spirit, supported by eurozone membership, which now enables corporate chiefs to tap the bourses of an entire continent to finance their big foreign acquisitions."[1]

Franco's rigid control over the Spanish economy didn't cease until his death in 1975. Democracy was only formally adopted in 1977, and it took another decade before the establishment of fundamental political and economic order demonstrated to its neighbors that Spain belonged in the European Union.

The impact of gaining EU membership in 1986 was dramatic. Modest rises in GDP during the early 1980s were replaced with three consecutive years of 5-plus percent growth between 1987 and 1989.[2] Aggressive government spending, a cheap, plentiful labor force, and the country's newly gained trade access to the rest of western Europe is enticing new foreign investment.

However, the boom of the late '80s was accompanied by rising inflation that approached 7 percent by the end of the 1990s. Attempting to slow the economy, the central bank's escalation of interest rates to further attract more foreign capital led to overvaluation of the Spanish peseta. This, coupled with the Continent's recession in the early 1990s, strangled export growth and led to a huge current account deficit, bottoming out in 1992 at nearly $22 billion.

Three devaluations within nine months, between fall 1992 and spring 1993, began to correct some of the imbalances within the Spanish economy. But more important, they highlighted the need for Spain to join common currency.

Economic Rejuvenation

Spain's qualification was considered a pipe dream by many who saw her badly outclassed by Europe's more evolved and sophisticated economies. However, setting out to meet the requirements of Maastricht imposed a fiscal discipline upon the government that led to widespread privatization and restructuring of corporate Spain. It also helped the nation become the largest recipient of transfer funds from the EU to promote badly needed infrastructure improvements and job development. Today, these efforts have brought Spain into the EMU and have transformed her economy into what Ken Wattret, senior economist at BNP Paribas in London, described as "the shining light of the European Union."[3]

The numbers explain his assessment.

➤ Between 1995 and 1999, real GDP growth has been steadily rising, averaging 3.3 percent a year.

➤ Private consumption has also been expanding steadily, up 4.4 percent in 1999.

➤ Fixed investments have been soaring on the back of rising business confidence, up 9.2 percent in 1998 and 8.3 percent in 1999.

➤ Short- and long-term interest rates have sharply declined, from double-digit levels in 1993 to 3.4 and 5.4 percent, respectively, by the end of 1999.

➤ Inflation has been cut by more than half since 1993, registering a modest 2.3 percent in 1999.

➤ Government deficit, which ran as high as 7 percent of GDP in 1993, was down to 1.1 percent in 1999.[4]

➤ A sharp rise in productivity more than doubled exports between 1993 and 1999.

➤ This helped to cut 1994's $6.9 billion current account deficit down to $1.6 billion in 1998. However, a substantial increase in Spanish investment abroad and strong consumer spending exploded the current account deficit in 1999, which shot up to a record $12.5 billion.[5]

Besides a soaring current account deficit, Spain must contend with two major structural problems: unemployment and government debt. Nearly one-quarter of the workforce was out of work during the 1992–1993 recession. However, Spain has been generating new jobs faster than any other country in Europe. Toward the end of the 1990s, the nation's job growth accounted for half of all the jobs created in the eurozone and reduced unemployment to under 16 percent by the end of 1999.[6]

As recently as 1996, debt exceeded 72 percent of GDP. The figure came down to 67.1 percent by the end of 1999. However, with the European Central Bank requiring nations to keep the ratio below 60 percent, Spain's indebtedness leaves the government little flexibility to counter any future economic slowdown.

Reform Strategy

Privatization has been the key government strategy to help remedy its employment and debt problems while addressing needed structural reforms to the Spanish economy. In just the first two and a half years in power, the center-right government of Prime Minister José Mariá Aznar sold off $28 billion in state-run operations. This included the sell-off of several gems of the Spanish economy:

➤ Telefónica, the country's leading telecom group and first multinational;

➤ Argentaria, a collective of state-owned banking groups that subsequently merged with Banco Bilbao Vizcaya to form Spain's second-largest bank; and

➤ Repsol, Spain's $27 billion energy concern.[7]

By 2001, the government expects to have privatized every public enterprise, except for mining operations.[8]

In addition to using the proceeds to pay down the country's huge debt, privatization is restructuring much of the private sector. According to the local brokerage firm BBV Interactivos, "privatization is playing an essential role in the liberalization of Spanish business. It has boosted efficiency and has made corporate behavior more competitive, eliminating dependency on the state budget."[9] The result has effected wide-ranging structural reforms.

➤ The telecommunications industry now includes several new fixed and mobile operators.
➤ Production of electricity and fuel distribution has been deregulated.
➤ Minimum prices have been eliminated from a variety of professional trades.
➤ More land is now available for development.
➤ New motorways and railroads will be developed and run by privatized operators.
➤ The cost of terminating permanent workers is being cut and the long-term financial risks of hiring are being reduced to encourage more efficient reallocation of labor and greater employment.

On a global level, privatization and reform have enabled Spanish firms to aggressively expand into international markets. Before the 1990s, *multinational* was an imported concept, a reference solely to foreign groups who would come into the country and revitalize and expand underperforming assets. For example, Spain is the third-largest producer of cars in Europe, but not one of the local manufacturers is Spanish.

Today, Spanish multinationals offer the most aggressive investment opportunities in Latin America. BSCH is the region's largest bank. Endesa will have invested $2.6 billion into Latin American operations by 2002.[10] And Telefónica is Latin America's leading telephone operator, having plowed $5.7 billion into the region,[11] with plans to invest an additional $3.8 billion in Brazil.[12]

Telefónica's Internet portal, Terra Networks—itself a remarkable story of Spain's blossoming New Economy—has acquired Internet service providers in Chile, Peru, Guatemala, Brazil, and Mexico. And with its $12.5 billion acquisition of the major U.S. search engine Lycos and massive content support from German media giant Bertelsmann, Terra has strengthened its hold over Latin America while grabbing significant market share in the United States and Europe.

Shareholder Culture and Value

Evolution of a shareholder culture has given Spanish economic expansion a huge push. It has not only offered companies a more efficient means of financing but also brought wealth to a wide range of families, further fueling consumer spending and corporate growth. Today, more than 25 percent of all households own stocks. Small investors bought two-thirds of the $4.3 billion 1997 offering of Telefónica. In February 1998, they purchased nearly the same portion of Argentaria's $2.3 billion tranche. And several months later, in April, more than 70 percent of the $2.2 billion issue of the state tobacco concern Tabacalera went to individual investors. As of the end of the 1990s, small investors owned 500 million shares, worth $9.6 billion.[14] And these investors have been generally well served.

The Spanish equity market has been booming. Outside of the telecom-driven bourses of Finland and Sweden, Spanish stocks outperformed the rest of Europe over the last half of the 1990s, rising by more than 29 percent a year in dollar terms between 1995 and 1999. In local currency terms, the gains were even more impressive, in excess of 35 percent a year.[15]

Following a remarkable year in 1998, when Spanish stocks outperformed nearly all developed markets, up 48 percent in dollar terms, Spanish equities rose a meek 5 percent in 1999. The problem: a collapsing euro. In local currency terms, the Spanish market was up a healthy 23 percent, led by the country's large caps.[16]

Spain's largest bank, BSCH, gained 32.6 percent, energy-giant Repsol added more than 50 percent, and shares in Telefónica more than doubled, becoming the country's largest company, with a market cap exceeding €80 billion by the end of 1999.[17]

C h a p t e r **5** *F i v e*

Independents

Denmark—A Link to the Future

A NEW $3 BILLION TEN-MILE tunnel and bridge now spans the Oresund strait linking Sweden with Denmark. It is the centerpiece of a new transport network that will finally make possible direct road and rail access from Scandinavia into the heart of western Europe. It is expected to increase Denmark's already remarkable growth, fixing her place as a strategic hub of the Nordic region and a link to the Baltic states beyond.

The Nordic countries are one of the fastest-growing regions around. But their historic diffidence to political and economic integration with the rest of Europe is an impediment to both the region's and the Continent's expansion. Norway remains outside of the European Union. Finland doesn't belong to NATO. Denmark initially rejected the entire concept of the euro. Although they all qualified for admission into the EMU, Finland was the only country in the region to participate in the first round of common currency.

But this new physical link between Scandinavia and the western portion of the Continent is symbolic of coming change, manifest in the mergers and alliances forged among companies, stock exchanges, and currencies of northern European nations. And given that Denmark shares the only Nordic border contiguous with western Europe via Germany, it's of little surprise to find the Danes at the forefront of

The Independents

economic liberalization and deregulation in Scandinavia.

The OECD credits Denmark's current success to fiscal consolidation, monetary policy credibility, and structural reform. Specifically, it cites improvements in the tax system, the labor market, and education. Competition has been enhanced through the recent privatization of $5.6 billion of state-run operations[1] and market deregulation, especially in transportation, telecommunications, financial services, and energy exploration.[2]

Two examples:

➤ Just twenty-four months after deregulation, the Danish telecom market now includes France Telecom, Sweden's Telia, and a U.S./ Dutch alliance known as Sonofon, along with the dominant local provider, Tele Danmark. The result: expanded services and reduced prices.

➤ Partial privatization helped fund a 50 percent expansion of the Copenhagen Airport, which will support further regional expansion.

These structural improvements are raising expectations about the economy. And recent macroeconomic figures support that optimism.

➤ Between 1995 and 1999, Denmark's GDP expanded by an average of 2.8 percent a year.

➤ Unemployment has plunged from more than 12 percent in 1994 to 5.7 percent in 1999.

➤ GDP per capita exceeds $32,000, the second highest in the EU.[3]

➤ Private consumption has been increasing by an average of 2.8 percent a year.

➤ Household savings have been rising annually by 6 percent.

➤ Long-term interest rates declined from double digits in the early 1990s to below 6 percent in 1999.

➤ Foreign direct investment soared to DKr 37 billion in 1998, three times the annual average FDI for the decade.

➤ Corporate taxes have been falling from a high of 50 percent in 1988 to a competitive 34 percent in 1999, with plans to cut rates even further to 26 percent by 2002.

➤ A 1994 government deficit of 2.7 percent of GDP was transformed into a 2.6 percent surplus in 1999.

➤ Government debt has shrunk from 74 percent of GDP to less than 52 percent.

Underperforming Equities

Despite these positive macroeconomic trends, Danish stocks were able to register only modest gains from 1995 through 1999. During those years the FTSE index for Danish stocks averaged an annual return of 16.37 percent in dollar terms, 4 points below the European average. In local currency terms, returns were quite decent, averaging 23 percent a year.[4]

One reason Danish equities have underperformed the Continent's could be in part that Europe's current market boom has been powered by large-cap stocks. The Danish economy is comprised primarily of small- to midcap issues, which have generally lagged the market everywhere.

Little surprise then that in 1999 the country's top-performing shares included several of Copenhagen's largest stocks: FLS Industries, an engineering and aerospace group, rose 43 percent (in local currency terms); Dampskibsselskabet af 1912, the country's largest shipping concern, saw its shares soar by 95 percent; and Tele Danmark, the country's principal telecom provider, whose market cap represents nearly one-quarter of the local index, managed an industry-modest 29 percent gain.[5]

Merrill Lynch believes the Danish market has been punished for remaining on the fence regarding monetary union.[6] A linked exchange rate is nothing new for the Danish currency. Since the early 1980s, the krone has maintained trading parity with the deutsche mark. And the government is continuing this monetary connection by entering into the second phase of the European exchange rate mechanism that requires the krone to trade closely in line with the euro.

While shadowing the euro eliminates currency risk for eurozone investors buying Danish shares, this policy exposes the economy to problems that euro membership would otherwise avoid.

For example, when the emerging market crisis reheated in the summer of 1998 as Russia devalued its currency and defaulted on its debt, many of Russia's closest trading partners as well as nearly all commodity-driven currencies got hit. Although Denmark doesn't fall into either category, the Nordic region as a whole does, and the Danes got caught in the draft. The value of the krone dropped, forcing the central bank to push up interest rates, thus slowing growth. Previous monetary conditions were reestablished within two quarters; however, the incident reveals the risk Denmark runs in staying outside monetary union.

Danish stocks also have been hurt by declining competitiveness. Despite Denmark's being the third most productive country in the OECD in terms of units produced per worker, a rapid rise in wages—up more than 4 percent in 1998 and in 1999—is increasing the costs of domestic goods and services.[7] And while the country was ranked the eighth most competitive economy globally in 1999, ahead of powerhouses like Ireland, Sweden, and the United Kingdom, that represents a decline of three notches from her 1996 ranking.[8]

While Danes are proud of their extensive welfare system, some observers argue that it has contributed to the country's declining competitiveness. Total government outlays have been among the highest in the OECD—54.5 percent of the GDP in 1999.[9] Not surprisingly, then, Denmark's personal income tax also ranks among the highest in the world, topping out at 58 percent. And this hardly encourages corporate residency, despite a competitive corporate tax rate of 34 percent.

But changes in the system are occurring. Unemployment compensation is now being handed out in concert with job training and proof of active job searches, and the duration of benefits has been cut back. Extension of the official retirement age and a tax policy that's encouraging the adoption of private pension plans are helping to mitigate a pending pension crisis.

But the state's extensive safety net will always be an integral part of the Danish system. It's characteristic of the way the country cares for its people and the manner in which government works. Employers and workers generally enjoy a far more cooperative relationship than is seen in most other European countries. Even more impressive is a recent global survey that found Denmark the least corrupt place in the world for doing business.[10] And that speaks volumes about the fundamental integrity of investing in Denmark.

Finland—Riding Nokia

IT MAY BE ONE OF THE coldest industrialized corners on the globe, a place that most investors would be hard-pressed to find on a map. But the Finnish stock market has been the hottest on earth.

Revealing the depth of the current boom, five-year annualized returns through 1999 in dollar terms were up 54 percent. Three-year annualized gains were even better, averaging 85 percent a year. But even these profits pale in comparison to the market's 1999 performance, when stocks shot up an incredible 151 percent.[1]

Financials and basic industries helped power returns in 1999. Pohjola, the country's largest insurer, gained 60.8 percent in euro terms. Metal manufacturer Outokumpu jumped 78.5 percent, while StoraEnso—one of the world's largest forestry concerns—soared 132.5 percent.[2]

However, these days the Finnish equity market is charged by telecommunications, reflecting the country's increasing push into technology and global markets. Scandinavia's leading mobile service provider, Sonera, more than quadrupled during its first year of trading in 1999.

But make no mistake, the mobile phone and network maker Nokia, with its $200 billion market cap—far and away the country's largest—is the gorilla driving the market, representing more than half the Helsinki stock index. Company sales have been growing on average by 50 percent a year, which has boosted yearly revenues beyond $20 billion. And with net profits also soaring at an annual clip of 50 percent, the market has driven Nokia's shares up a remarkable twentyfold between 1994 and 1999.

How did such a remote, sparsely populated country turn into a Continental powerhouse?

Geography and Economics

The answer is rooted in the geopolitical reconfiguration of post–Cold War Europe, which turned attention away from Moscow and focused on Brussels—the capital of the European Union. Finland's 1,300-mile border with the former Soviet Union and history of ten wars between the two nations had kept Helsinki especially mindful of Soviet policy, so much so that Finland never joined NATO. With up to 25 percent of its trade having been with the big neighbor to the east, exports were geared to Russia's often unique product needs—which often had limited demand elsewhere.[3] But when the Soviet Union ceased to exist in 1991, at a time when recession racked economies throughout the world, Finland slid into her worst recession of the century. In the early 1990s, output fell 15 percent, unemployment was close to 20 percent, and external debt topped out at a record 60 percent of GDP. Bursting of the 1980s-inspired asset price bubble and loss of competitiveness led to the devaluation of the Finnish markka and forced the government and business to make some fundamental changes.

Finland observed that to regain her economic footing, she was going to have to develop a more global vision. Privatization, mergers, restructuring, and low corporate taxes were going to be necessary to revitalize the private sector, while commitment to meeting the stiff macroeconomic requirements of monetary union would do the same for government finances. The results have been no less than miraculous.

Starting the 1990s with four straight years in the shadow of the Soviet Union's collapse, the Finnish economy has since been on a tear.

➤ Between 1994 and 1999, average annual GDP growth has exceeded 4.4 percent—among Europe's top performers.

➤ Gross fixed investment between 1995 and 1999 has been exceedingly strong, increasing by nearly 9.2 percent a year.

➤ Exports of goods and services have been expanding at an annual rate of 8.5 percent.

➤This has helped Finland to sustain a large current account surplus, which has been averaging 6.16 percent of GDP per year.[4]

➤ Since 1994 unemployment has been declining, ending 1999 at 9.3 percent, less than half the jobless rate of the early 1990s. While still a major problem in the country's more remote agrarian regions, elsewhere unemployment is increasingly a matter of deficient skills rather than the lack of opportunity.

➤ Since 3-month yields peaked at 13.3 percent in 1992, Finnish interest rates have fallen dramatically. The country's decision to join common currency, coupled with an inflation rate of around 1 percent and vastly improved macroeconomic conditions, has resulted in short-term interest rates of 3.43 percent as of the end of 1999.

➤ Recession in the early 1990s pushed gross public debt to 59.6 percent of GDP. However, since 1994, GPD has been on a slow decline, ending 1999 at 45.8 percent of GDP, well below the eurozone's average.[5]

➤ Government deficit followed a similar trend, peaking at a record 8 percent of GDP in 1993, transformed into a 3 percent surplus in 1999 due to solid economic growth and tight control of spending.[6]

However, with large pension obligations looming down a not too distant road and with high unemployment still putting a strain on finances, Helsinki may face difficulties when economic growth does finally slow. No longer in control of interest rates, fearful that raising taxes could exacerbate an already high unemployment picture, and with a longstanding commitment to preserve the country's extensive social safety net, officials will not have many options at their disposal to effectively counter recession.

Privatization

The one trump card it does have: a stable of highly regarded, well-run public assets, many of which will eventually be sold off. Finland's privatization program raised $2.1 billion in 1998 and $3.6 billion in 1999. The highlight was the auction of the first tranche of Telecom Finland, now known as Sonera. The IPO was a huge hit. The 22.2 percent stake in the company was oversubscribed by more than twenty times. Shares shot up by more than 37 percent on their first day of trading and raised more than $1.39 billion. Then in October 1999, the state sold an additional 18 percent stake, raising $3.3 billion that went to cutting the national debt.[7]

In 1998, the government offered shares in the new energy giant formed by the merger of Neste and Imatran Voima, known as Fortum, and raised more than $1 billion.

However, the biggest deal to date was the $1.5 billion IPO of one of the world's largest paper manufacturers, StoraEnso.

The Economist Intelligence Unit reports that Finland's privatization effort is "not only generating additional revenue used to reduce the public debt, but it is also helping to intensify competition between firms, thereby reducing inefficiencies in the Finnish economy."[8] Just as important, taking a company public gives it the necessary freedom and currency (tradable shares of stock) to deal in the global marketplace.

With a booming economy, strong domestic spending, and interest rates geared to the slower-growing core economies of the eurozone, Finnish prices have remained remarkably stable, defying basic macroeconomic principles. With the weak euro boosting import prices, commodity prices returning to health, and domestic wage pressure building, one wonders just how long Finland can keep inflation at bay.

Ultimately, investors need to watch the two key markets that drive the economy and stocks: commodities (especially pulp and paper-related products, which account for 30 percent of all exports) and the mobile phone industry. With Nokia responsible for 20 percent of exports, one-third of all corporate research and development, and 60 percent of Helsinki's entire market cap,[9] when telecoms begin to sniffle, Finnish investors will become aware just how far north they are.

Norway—Europe's Sheikdom

THE NORWEGIAN ECONOMY is Europe's most distinct. It is driven by oil. Norway is the world's sixth-largest producer of crude and its second-largest exporter.

This wealth has generated one of Europe's fastest-growing economies, averaging 3.2 percent annual GDP growth between 1995 and 1999. Unemployment has consistently been among the lowest in the Continent, ending 1999 at 3.2 percent, while inflation averaged a modest 2.16 percent from 1995 through 1999. In the late 1990s, gross national savings were peaking at more than 30 percent of GDP, while domestic investment was reaching 25 percent of GDP.[1]

Norway's oil wealth has enabled the country to run a perennial budget surplus that's serving the country in two big ways. First, it has helped keep a lid on borrowing, despite the country's extensive commitment to social welfare, which has pushed government spending up to 45 percent of GDP.[2] In 1995, the Debt/GDP ratio was one of Europe's lowest, at 41.1 percent. By the end of 1999, it had diminished to 34.1 percent.[3]

Oil's second boon: it has enabled the government to set up a huge Petroleum Fund—equivalent to 19 percent of Norway's 1999 GDP—

that will help finance its retirement obligations for generations. And by investing up to half of the fund's $28.5 billion in international securities, the fund is effectively diversifying Norwegian assets to ensure consistent long-term growth.[4]

It's not surprising that given such strong macroeconomics, Norwegian GDP per capita is among the highest in the OECD. "By any standards," observes *The Economist,* "Norway is exceptionally rich."[5] And this wealth has helped the country maintain its economic and political independence.

Though it's a member of the European Economic Area, which qualifies it for participation in the free-trade zone, Norway decided to stay out of common currency. In fact, it's the only western European nation besides Switzerland that's not a member of the European Union, because of policy differences involving farming, small businesses, environmental protection, and assistance to the poor, both within Norway's borders and throughout the third world.[6]

Fundamental Risks

Whereas oil prices soared in 1999, helping to send Norwegian stocks broadly higher, the collapse of oil prices in 1998 displayed the fundamental risks of an economy driven by natural resources with linked exchange rates. As the 1997 Southeast Asian crisis has shown, commodity-driven economies are exposed to currency problems when prices sink and current accounts descend deep into the red. Although the Norwegian economy is fundamentally far more sound than any of the Asian Tigers', the Norwegian krone weakened as the nation's oil surplus revenues plummeted in 1998 from a projected Nkr 92 billion to an actual Nkr 27 billion,[7] and the current account turned negative for the first time in ten years.[8] Unlike any other European market, the link between Norwegian crude and currency is so tight that Merrill Lynch analyst Richard H. Woodworth likens trading the krone to "a proxy for the oil market."[9]

How is that possible? The currency is itself a commodity. Half of all Norwegian exports are energy related. So when demand for the krone falls, because less of it is needed to pay for declining Norwegian oil prices, so then does its value. The krone has also been under pressure from inflationary fears fueled by double-digit domestic demand growth, 5 to 6 percent wage growth, and the minority government's inability to tighten fiscal policy.[10]

With the central bank committed to maintaining a stable exchange rate with the country's European trading partners (who purchase 75 percent of Norway's exports and sell 68 percent of its imports), short-term interest rates were pushed up seven times in 1998 in attempts to defend the krone. By August 1998, interest rates, which had started the year at 3.5 percent, were above 8 percent, virtually stifling the economy. Ian Amstad, an international economist at Bankers Trust in London, aptly commented that Norway's currency crisis "once again demonstrates the folly of operating a fixed-exchange-rate system in an economy whose fortunes are tied to a volatile commodity."[11]

At that point, the government abandoned further currency intervention and decided to permit the krone to float. Even though that pulled the plug on speculator pressures, the damage had been done. The combination of falling oil prices, inflationary fears, and sharp increases in interest rates sent Norwegian stocks reeling in 1998 by more than 27 percent in local currency terms, nearly 30 percent in dollar terms, making Oslo the worst-performing stock exchange in Europe.[12]

Equity Performance

But what a difference a year makes. In 1999, oil prices tripled, the krone recovered, and Norwegian stocks soared by nearly 49 percent in local currency terms—more than 41 percent in dollar terms.

Except for utilities, every sector excelled in 1999, from natural resources and industrials to telecom and banking. The large-cap winners included oil producer Petroleum Geo-Services, up 47.4 percent, and Norway's largest full-service bank, Christiania, whose stock rose nearly 50 percent. Shares in global forestry group Norske Skogindustrier climbed 88 percent, while the price of mobile telecom provider Netcom more than doubled.[13]

However, despite the country's strong turnaround in 1999, Norwegian stocks were among the Continent's weakest performers during the last half of the 1990s. Between 1995 and 1999, Norwegian shares gained on average only 13.45 percent a year in local currency terms. Dollar-based investors saw annualized gains of less than 10 percent. That's well below half the MSCI index performance for Europe, which realized annual gains of 22.55 percent over the same period.

What's depressing the country's equity growth?

Norway is precariously behind the rest of western Europe in priva-

tizing state assets, restructuring inefficient and overly diversified operations, and encouraging mergers and acquisitions in pursuit of greater
market share. The government still controls energy, telecom, and commercial banking, limiting inward foreign investment and preventing
consolidation and market expansion of three of the most dynamic
European sectors.

However slow the pace of corporate change, the status quo shows
signs of finally giving way.

Restructuring, Mergers, and Acquisitions

In 1999, after reporting its worst full-year results in a decade, govern-
ment-run Statoil, the country's largest company, cut nearly 10 percent of
its staff, reduced investments by up to 30 percent, and trimmed explo-
ration costs by 30 percent.[14] At the same time, management made the un-
precedented call for at least partial privatization to enable the company to
participate in regional and global consolidation and realize associated cost
savings.[15] Norsk Hydro is also cutting jobs and investments while looking
to sell off some of its noncore assets.[16] And Aker RGI, a major oil and gas
conglomerate and Norway's largest industrial holding company, is selling
off assets to redefine itself as an investment company.[17]

There were several big moves in the shipping industry.

➢ The Norwegian firm Wilhelm Wilhelmsen and Swedish company
Wallenius merged to create the world's largest shipping line special-
izing in car transport.[18]

➢ Bahamian-based Teekay Shipping, operator of the world's largest
fleet of medium-sized oil tankers, bought Norway's Bona Ship-
holding for $450 million.[19]

➢ And Kraerner, the troubled Anglo-Norwegian engineering and ship-
building company, is undergoing substantial restructuring involving
cost cutting and the sale of nonessential assets after reporting a pretax loss of $171 million in 1998.[20]

A series of financial mergers and acquisitions in 1999 marked greater government acceptance of domestic and cross-border consolidation
of Norwegian assets.

➢ Norway's largest financial group, DNB Holding, acquired state-
owned Postbanken, boosting assets to more than $41 billion and the
bank's domestic market share to 21 percent.[21]

➤ Den Danske Bank, Denmark's largest bank, acquired Norway's fourth-largest lender, Fokus Bank.[22]

➤ Scandinavia's largest bank, Sweden's Svenska Handelsbanken, bought Bergensbanken, a regional Norwegian bank.

➤ Seeking to energize the industry's low growth rate, Norway's largest insurance company, Storebrand, merged its nonlife operations with Sweden's Skandia in an effort to create a Pan-Nordic operation with 20-plus percent market share.[23]

➤ The Norwegian government launched an auction in June 2000 for its remaining 35 percent stake in Christiania Bank after having sold a 17 percent tranche in the country's second-largest bank in 1999.[24]

Now that government and business appear committed to consolidating and restructuring corporate operations, and with oil prices rebounding, the prospects for Norwegian equities have significantly improved.

Stocks will receive an added boost from two recent developments. Pension reform is now permitting funds to invest 35 percent of assets in stocks, up from a previous limit of 20 percent.[25] And greater foreign investor activity is expected from Oslo's decision to finally adopt screen-based trading and to ally itself with the new NOREX exchange, joining Denmark and Sweden in Scandinavia's first regional market.[26]

Sweden—A Compromised Model

BECAUSE IT MODELS ITSELF as the "middle way" between capitalism and socialism, Scandinavia's largest economy may be the most difficult to truly understand. There are a host of attractive investment opportunities in various industries. Yet structural deficiencies set them at cyclical risk, while a huge tax burden has prompted corporate flight out of the country.

On the surface, the numbers are impressive. While having slowed recently, domestic stocks returned on average more than 33 percent a year in dollar terms between 1995 and 1999. That's 11 percent a year better than the broad European market.[1] During that time, GDP expanded 2.9 percent a year, exports grew by 9.4 percent a year, and long-term interest rates were nearly cut in half, ending 1999 at 5.2 percent, while inflation virtually disappeared. The country's overall economic strength has helped eliminate a double-digit deficit.

Swedish Paradox

Yet Sweden's effort to foster growth of some of the world's most successful operations is compromised by a debt-choking commitment to social welfare. In 1999 government expenditures amounted to 56 percent of GDP, among the highest in Europe, while the country's Debt/GDP ratio was 66 percent.[2] Diametric goals have produced policies that pull the economy in opposite directions, deterring corporate expansion within Sweden's borders.

With one of Europe's lowest corporate tax rates (28 percent), the country seems bent on drawing business from across the Continent. And yet it counters this attraction with extraordinarily high income taxes, topping out at 56 percent.

High income taxes, along with asset taxes, make it difficult for domestic firms to attract the most qualified talent. This problem is made worse by a wage scale that fails to significantly differentiate pay between skilled and unskilled workers.[3] Unionization of 90 percent of the workforce may help explain this condition. But what thoroughly muddles the matter is that Sweden is a society that embraces high tech, spending more than 3 percent of GDP on information technology (second in percent only to the United States), but then fails to compensate workers accordingly.[4] A recent study revealed that computer and information technology professionals earn one-third to two-thirds less than their counterparts in Silicon Valley.[5]

Another paradox is that Sweden is the home of a variety of world-class corporations: Ericsson (telecom), Electrolux (consumer goods), and ABB (engineering). Other industry leaders that have recently merged with foreign firms include Saab and Volvo (transportation), Stora (forestry products), and Astra (pharmaceuticals). Yet in a society that prides itself on fairness and shareholder rights, one investor—the Wallenburg Family—controls the fate of these and many other businesses. Its holding company, Investor, owns more than 40 percent of the market cap of the Stockholm Stock Exchange.[6]

Even more disconcerting is that in the past several years Sweden has lost claim to half these name-brand companies via foreign deals that have resettled corporate headquarters outside the reach of Stockholm's high taxes.

➤ Astra has merged with the British pharmaceutical company Zeneca, establishing a world-class drug company with headquarters in London.

➤ The main offices of Europe's largest forestry company, created by the merger of Stora and Finnish concern Enso, are in Helsinki.

➤ So is the headquarters of the merged banking operations of Merita-Nordbanken, a Swedish-Finnish enterprise that is now one of the region's largest banks.

➤ The country's largest private employer, Ericsson, maintains an ongoing threat to shift its corporate headquarters to London.[7]

The Swedish National Board for Industrial and Technical Development found that 20 percent of the country's largest 500 public companies anticipate shifting their headquarters abroad within the next five years because of exorbitant income and payroll taxes.[8]

Still another bit of wonder: Despite having more than half her trade with EU countries, Sweden was very late in joining the European Union, gaining membership in 1995. Like most Nordic nations, Sweden is skeptical about European political and economic integration. Although Sweden may relinquish the krona within the next few years, there is substantial opposition not only to giving up sovereign monetary policy but even to remaining in the EU. The essential concern: adherence to Pan-European policies will eventually force Sweden to compromise its long-standing commitment to social welfare.

However, maintaining a dual commitment to growth and to social spending has already shown strains on the economy by exaggerating Sweden's business cycle. When corporate expansion can support the country's high taxation and spending programs, the economy expands rapidly; when it can't, the economy contracts just as quickly.

The 1991–1993 recession was the worst since the 1930s, triggered by extensive credit and strong domestic demand. Inflation soared, weakening the currency, which led to further deterioration of this trade-driven economy.

Seeking to stabilize the krona and increase investor confidence, the government linked the krona with the ecu (a statistical predecessor to the euro). But sensing the currency's inherent weakness, speculators attacked. Overnight interest rates shot up as high as 500 percent in a vain effort to defend the currency.[9] Subsequent devaluation paved the way to an export-led recovery that continues to this day. But the experience has left Sweden wary of common currency.

Privatization and Deregulation

Since the recession, the government has pursued moderate reform through privatization and deregulation, which has helped improve the country's competitive position. Sweden was the first European nation to deregulate its telecom industry. Today, competition among its twelve service providers has led to the development of one of the world's best fiber-optic infrastructures and tariffs that are among the lowest in Europe. After failing to pull off the first cross-border merger of state telecom assets (with Norway's Telenor), Sweden sold off 30 percent of Telia, the state's major telecom operator, worth $8.8 billion. The company is expected to become one of Sweden's largest stocks by market cap, second only to Ericsson.

The Swedish steel company SSAB was initially privatized in 1991 and has since become one of Europe's most cost-effective steel producers.[10] In 1994, pharmaceutical company Pharmacia was privatized and subsequently merged with the U.S. drug company Upjohn, creating one of the industry's biggest players.

Mergers and acquisitions have been driving investment in Sweden. In 1998 alone, J.P. Morgan reported that Swedish M&A totaled $52 billion. That was $6 billion more than went on in Germany, whose economy is ten times the size of Sweden's.[11]

Equity Performance

After shaking off a sluggish 1998, when local equities rose only 9.2 percent in local currency terms, 1999 was a blowout year, led by telecom manufacturer Ericsson. Shares in Sweden's dominant company soared 170 percent. At the end of 1999, Ericsson was worth 44 percent of the entire Swedish market.

Industrials had a very good year, with construction, forestry, metals, and engineering industries rising an average of 50 percent. But the two other large-cap stocks that captured Europe's attention were fashion retailer Hennes & Mauritz—up 72 percent—and life insurer Skandia, whose shares more than doubled.[12] (For a detailed discussion of H&M, see Chapter 9.)

Swedish equities are receiving a boost from progressive pension reform, which *The Washington Post* described as "radical even by American standards and nearly unheard-of in Europe."[13] With Swedish retirement benefits nearly three times those in the United States and with only 3.6 adult workers per retiree (Germany's ratio is 4.5:1 and that of the United States is 5.2:1), the government has introduced private retirement accounts that are channeling more than 12 percent of all retirement kronor into securities.[14] The success of these investments is encouraging Swedes to allocate more of their nonretirement savings into the market as well.

Swedish shares may also receive support from the recent introduction of stock buyback rules. In March 2000, Stockholm was the last major European market to pass such legislation, which is expected to boost acquisitions and company incentive programs while improving capital ratios.[15]

Demand for Swedish securities is also expected to increase as a result of the recent merger of the Stockholm and Copenhagen exchanges. With a total market cap exceeding $500 billion, the NOREX alliance (as the new exchange is known) runs both markets on a common trading platform, offering Denmark unfettered access to Swedish stocks. It also sets the foundation for a Pan-Nordic exchange that would further fuel equity expansion in Sweden, the region's most developed market.[16]

Overall, prospects for continued economic growth are good. The International Monetary Fund concluded that "with fiscal consolidation coming to an end and with interest rates low and asset prices high, conditions for a strong and balanced recovery in the near term are in place."[17] And Sweden will be receiving an added boost from her strategic relations with the neighboring Baltic states, a region that is primed to take off with 70 percent of its headquarters in Stockholm.[18]

But there is a caveat. The nation remains hampered by several structural weaknesses, most notably in the labor market, where total costs are very high, downsizing is next to impossible, and real unemployment is running near 10 percent. And if the Swedes remain outside the collective economic security of the eurozone, where exchange risks are minimized and interest rates are likely to remain low, the question goes begging: will the economy bend or break the next time corporate and government agendas conflict?

Chapter 6 Six

Latent Reformers

Austria—The Undiscovered Country

FOR INVESTORS AUSTRIA HAS been an enigma. GDP averaged a decent 2.32 percent per annum from 1995 through 1999. Industrial production and exports, which shot up by 8 percent in 1998, continued their strong showing in 1999, up 5.4 and 4.7 percent respectively. This helped nudge unemployment down to 4.4 percent by the end of 1999—less than half the EU average. And inflation has been nearly nonexistent, ending 1999 at only 0.6 percent.[1]

Austria's annual deficit, which had been over 5 percent in 1995, ended 1999 below 2 percent. At the same time, government debt fell from nearly 70 percent of GDP in 1995 to an estimated 62.4 percent in 1999.[2]

Recent membership in the European Union has heightened Austria's regional importance as a gateway into the burgeoning economies of eastern Europe. A thousand multinationals have set up shop in the state primarily for just that reason. And membership in monetary union further enhances integration of the economy with the rest of western Europe.

So why then has the Viennese bourse been one of the worst-performing exchanges not only in the eurozone but in the entire industrialized world? Austria ... the former hub of the Hapsburg empire ... whose currency and monetary policy have been linked with Germany,

The Latent Reformers

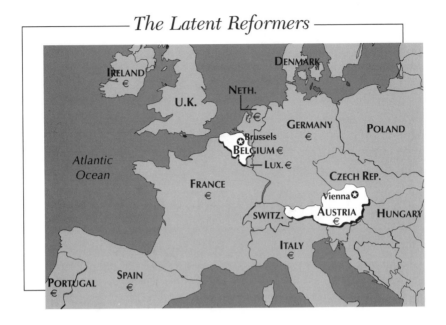

her major trading partner, for the past twenty years ... with one of Europe's most storied and urbane capitals? In the context of broad European expansion, the country's poor equity showing makes no sense.

Struggling Stocks

While European stocks as a region have averaged 19.84 percent annual gains in dollars between 1995 and 1999, Austrian shares have actually declined by nearly 3 percent a year over that time. Even in the year leading up to EMU, 1998, when recovering western European economies sent markets soaring by 27.54 percent as a group in anticipation of common currency, Austrian stocks lost 0.72 percent.[3]

Led by utilities, banks, and basic industrials, the market recovered a bit in 1999, up 4.88 percent in euro terms. Some of the top-performing shares: EVN, one of the country's largest power companies, rose by nearly 25 percent in local currency terms; Bank Austria, the country's largest company, climbed 29.2 percent; and VA Stahl, the partially privatized steel manufacturer, saw its shares soar by more than 75 percent.

Two prominent factors help explain the market's more recent stumblings: the failure of the Russian economy and the collapse of commodity prices in the late 1990s. Austrian financial institutions were hit badly in 1998 when Russia defaulted on its foreign loans, sending the ruble into a tailspin. At the same time, Austrian cyclicals, like those in much of the world, were dragged down by falling steel, coal, wood, and energy prices. With nearly half the Austrian market made up of these two sectors, the slump in equity prices hardly comes as a surprise, and points to systemic problems.

Mark Breedon, portfolio manager of the closed-end Austria Fund, sees two obvious differences between the Viennese bourse and most other European markets. First, telecoms and technologies, which have been driving most western markets, are underrepresented in Austria. The country suffers from a weak entrepreneurial spirit and a low rate of start-ups. Unfavorable tax laws, excessive regulation, and bankruptcy laws discourage risk taking, and there is a heavy reliance on partisan politics to get anything done.[4] This has led the OECD to conclude that "the economy lacks a large enough group of rapidly growing enterprises to underpin growth prospects over the longer term."[5]

The second major difference Breedon observes between Vienna and other western markets is that "expanding local demand for stocks and equity mutual funds in Europe is simply not a phenomenon in Austria." Less than 5 percent of the country's total market capitalization is owned by individual investors, and the majority of the country's small mutual fund industry is invested in cash and bonds. Domestic demand that's driving up stock prices in other European countries just isn't happening in Austria.

Moreover, development of a strong equity culture is being retarded by companies still relying upon bank debt instead of equity financing, although certain EU regulations may challenge this tradition. Also, Austrians tend to stash away their savings in anonymous numbered savings accounts that often go undertaxed. "Investors are still shy about setting up open transparent accounts, required for equity investing," Breedon explains, "especially since stocks haven't consistently proven their worth."

Not surprisingly, then, the Austrian market is driven by foreign institutional investors. This fact, coupled with the lack of a domestic ownership base, contributes to the general illiquidity and volatility of the Viennese exchange, keeping it a minor European player.

Vienna's decision to ally itself with the Frankfurt exchange may help visibility. But that's only a start. "We need to give the international investor more security that we are operating in an open market," observes Andreas Treichl, chairman of the First Austrian bank. He adds that "we need more publicly owned companies to attract investment from pension funds and insurance companies. Right now, you can count on one hand the number of companies in which you could buy a significant stake."[6]

Another Austrian anomaly: "The fact that the country's most successful business leaders are to be found outside Austria, heading companies such as Roche, Nestlé, and Volkswagen," observes the *Financial Times*, "says something about career prospects inside Austria."[7]

Some economists argue that the dominance of middle-size family-run companies—Austria's version of the German *Mittelstand*—has also held back the Austrian market. The *Financial Times* found that "even industry-leading firms like glass gem and optical instrument producer Swarovski and engine manufacturer AVL List receive little attention because they remain family controlled."[8]

Larger Austrian firms are also suffering from an inability to significantly restructure. Even when companies merge, significant cost savings are not being realized because laying off workers is expensive and generally avoided. They have also been reluctant to cut or spin off unprofitable activities, which has inhibited industries from more efficiently reconfiguring operations.

Stock prices are also depressed because companies tend to keep large amounts of cash on their balance sheets. This practice may make corporations appear financially stable, but it depresses return on equity. Breedon points out that the average ROE of Austrian companies is only two-thirds that of corporate Europe. Maintaining significant cash positions also inhibits business investment and expansion, keeping Austrian companies from generating competitive levels of return.

Finally, there has been the Haider effect. The entry of Jörg Haider's right-wing Freedom Party into Austria's coalition government in the beginning of 2000 has led to EU sanctions and raises questions about Austrian political stability—two elements that certainly don't enhance the appeal of an already troubled bourse.

The sum effect of these issues is corporate valuations 30 percent below the rest of Europe. Breedon believes that although these problems won't stand in the way of the country's continued expansion, they will undermine the competitiveness of Austrian stocks. And until these problems are corrected, he doesn't expect the valuation gap to significantly close.

Market Liberalization

Privatization of state assets, however, is slowly bringing fundamental change. The government began selling off nationalized operations in the early 1990s as part of the restructuring process to counter heavy losses sustained in the 1980s. Nearly 25 percent of the country's industrial output, which had been in state hands at the beginning of the 1990s, is now privately managed.[9] Besides helping Austria pare down its deficit and debt, privatization has helped expand productivity by 5.1 percent a year over the past decade. This has brought down per-unit labor costs, and with real wages increasing, these trends have helped propel GDP growth.[10]

Policy reform has also enhanced business performance. In 1994 corporate taxes were lowered from 55 percent to a flat rate of 34 percent, eliminating multiple tariffs and making Austria one of the lower-taxed nations in western Europe.[11] While still quite rigid, labor laws have loosened a bit. Companies can now operate on seven-day shifts. The number of work hours in a day has been expanded and now includes Sunday. The application process for new plant approvals has been sped up, with 80 percent of requests resolved within three months.

Government still retains controlling or substantial stakes in many of the country's leading businesses: 75 percent of Telekon Austria; 41 percent of Austria Tabak; 40 percent of Austrian Airlines; 50 percent of the Vienna stock exchange; and 39 percent of the country's leading steel producer, VA Stahl.[12] Maintenance of government shareholdings in the country's major corporations interferes with restructuring and the pace of mergers and acquisitions. It deters foreign investors and further impedes corporate Austria from effectively competing in Europe's increasingly more open markets.

Another concern is the possible loss of trade advantages the country has historically enjoyed with Poland, Hungary, and the Czech Republic if they join the European Union. EU membership will enhance access by the rest of western Europe to these emerging economies.

Despite all of the difficulties facing the country, Austrian stocks hold substantial potential over the long term. Liberalization sweeping across the Continent's markets will bring change from both within and without. Austria will realize significant gains from its exposure to the rapidly expanding economies in eastern Europe. And given the overall soundness of the economy, the relative cheapness of Austrian equities suggests significant upside.

Belgium—The Cost of Division

NO OTHER COUNTRY IN Europe is as economically and culturally fractured as Belgium. The differences are intensified by its being among the smallest and most densely populated states on the Continent. Although this has impeded development of a strong economic environment, investors were treated to surprisingly good equity returns over the last half of the 1990s.

Belgium is comprised of three regions. There is the prosperous Dutch-speaking northern district known as Flanders, the old industrial French-speaking area in the south, and the capital region around Brussels—the headquarters of numerous Pan-European organizations. The challenge of negotiating policy for three distinct constituencies has hindered the pace of broad economic reform. The most troublesome byproduct of this inertia has been continuous loss of Belgian corporate independence and domestic wealth due to a slew of cross-border acquisitions, executed primarily by the French. The goals of these takeovers are to unlock value that's been stifled by the lack of substantial market liberalization and corporate restructuring and to bulk up for the more competitive world of common currency.

French-Belgian Connection
The French energy group Total bought out Petrofina, the largest Belgian oil firm. Dutch-based ING bought Banque Bruxelles Lambert, Belgium's third-largest bank. The big French insurer AXA took full control of the country's second-biggest insurer, Royale Belge. Then, in one of the biggest Continental bank takeovers ever, financial services giant Fortis (itself a Belgian-Dutch merger) acquired Générale de Banque. But nothing was larger and more telling than when the French conglomerate Suez Lyonnaise des Eaux bought out Société Générale de Belgique, the country's biggest holding company, with stakes in 1,200

Belgian firms involving one-third of the country's entire economy.

While the creation of these bigger multinationals may prove beneficial to Belgian firms in the long run, loss of regulatory control over large operations reduces the influence of domestic policy, specifically on employment, taxes, and private investment. This is on top of the loss of monetary authority ceded to the European Central Bank.

How has the economy responded to this new economic order?

Toward the end of 1998, Standard & Poor's/DRI found the economy to be the strongest it had been since 1990, "fueled by a revival of private consumption and strong trade performance."[1]

➤ Inflation and interest rates, which had benefited greatly by the government's 1990 decision to link the Belgian franc to the German mark, have declined and converged with the eurozone's low rates.

➤ Government deficit, which was over 7 percent of GDP in 1993, fell dramatically to 0.9 percent in 1999.

➤ While the national debt was an atrocious 115 percent of GDP in 1999 (the highest within the eurozone), that was down substantially from 135.2 percent in 1993.[2]

➤ GDP growth, which had slowed to 1 percent in 1996, averaged 2.7 percent annual expansion between 1997 and 1999.

However, many observers, including the International Monetary Fund, have been troubled by the country's inability to reduce government spending.[3] Not surprisingly, then, the drop in debt hasn't given the economy the kind of boost one would have expected, especially as total tax revenue as a percent of GDP has been going up. According to Ernst & Young, Belgians are among the heaviest-taxed Europeans, with corporate and individual rates topping out at 40 and 55 percent, respectively.[4]

Manufacturing still drives a substantial portion of the economy, representing one-quarter of GDP. However, industrial production has been erratic: contracting in 1995 and 1996, up 4.9 percent in 1997 and 3.2 percent in 1998, then flat in 1999.[5]

Belgium is also suffering from naggingly high unemployment that has shown only modest improvement after several years of substantial growth. The IMF found that structural deficiencies have perpetuated joblessness among youths and the long-term unemployed. Hiring has been discouraged due to high social security payments, restraints on agency hiring and on temporary work, and labor contracts that are legally binding across entire sectors. White-collar layoffs require six-month severance pay. Moreover, the country's high level of wage taxation and unlimited jobless benefits don't particularly encourage the unemployed to get off relief.

Regional Disparities

The unemployment picture is also reflective of the country's regional economic disparities. According to Herman Daems, professor of strategy and international management at Catholic University in Leuven, "the Belgian economy is an average of several completely different economies."[6] The old industrial French-speaking region to the south, Wallonia, hosts only one-third of the workforce but has half the nation's unemployed. The capital region, around Brussels, which is also the capital of the EU and host to a wide range of Pan-European organizations, has only 9 percent of the workforce. But 13 percent of those are unemployed.[7] The old agrarian Dutch-speaking region to the north, Flanders, has become the most dynamic region in the country, growing at four times the rate of Wallonia.[8] It generates 60 percent of the country's GDP, attracts 60 percent of all foreign investment, and is responsible for 70 percent of all goods exported.[9]

Whereas the relatively recent division of the country into a federation of three regions was a means of ensuring sufficient independence to keep the country's different-speaking peoples together, the new order often seems bent on pulling the country apart. The more affluent north feels that it's being cheated in having to help support the south's higher rate of unemployment. There's aggressive competition among the regions to lure in foreign investment. Furthermore, with each region reliant upon separate tongues, language has become a political tool regulating the flow of information and power. In one instance, a conflict ended up adjudicated by the Council of Europe, which declared the denial of adequate translation a discriminatory act.

To the chagrin of most businesses, creation of the federation also added a new layer of government to an already bloated bureaucracy composed of local and provincial bodies, a federal parliament, and a national government. With confusion over responsibilities, compromise is a necessity, and hard decisions often don't get made. It is easier to spend more on everyone rather than decide where to make cuts.

As a result, government debt has exploded.

On the positive side, federation has inadvertently sped up the process of privatization and restructuring. Wallonia didn't have the resources to modernize the country's biggest steelmaker, Cockerill Sambre, which it inherited when Belgium divided. So it ended up selling off 54 percent of the company to the French group Usinor for BFr 26 billion, creating Europe's largest steelmaker.

Equity Performance

However, for all its problems, Belgian stocks have not performed badly. Three- and 5-year annualized returns in local currency terms through 1999 were 24.94 and 20.84 percent, respectively. In dollar terms, yields were substantially less, 15.46 and 15.30 percent.[10]

These numbers were substantially depressed by the market's flat showing in 1999, echoing the country's economic slowdown. No sector performed well that year, and overall, stocks were down 1.33 percent in local currency terms, off 15.77 percent in dollars.[11]

Still, several medium- to large-cap issues performed well. Groupe Bruxelles Lambert, an investment holding company with broad exposure to energy and financial activities, gained 15 percent in local currency terms. Solvay, a diversified multinational chemicals group, gained 28 percent. And Bekaert, a steel wire and cable manufacturer operating in twenty-eight countries, tacked on 30 percent.[12]

Near-term economic prospects are improving. According to the IMF, Belgium should benefit from expansionary fiscal and monetary policy, strengthening French and German economies, declining unemployment, and continued gains in household confidence and spending.[13] All this bodes well for Belgian stocks, despite the persistence of structural handicaps that cloud the country's long-term outlook.

Chapter Seven

Emerging Markets

Czech Republic—The Impression of Change

THE POTENTIAL OF the Czech Republic is no better illustrated than in the turnaround of its venerable carmaker Skoda. Forty years of state-run management eroded the company's reputation as a producer of well-engineered automobiles. By 1990, its 23,000 workers were turning out a modest 188,000 cars a year, most of which were sold domestically; only 10 percent were exported to western Europe.[1]

A year later, Volkswagen made the first foreign direct investment in the country, picking up a 30 percent share in the company, which subsequently grew into a 70 percent stake by 1995 and total ownership by 2000. Sinking $1.6 billion into the business, VW has created a new fully modernized production facility. It replaced most of management, designed new models that shared a common manufacturing platform with other VWs, and with almost 20 percent fewer workers has nearly doubled production.[2] Skoda now exports nearly two-thirds of its output, equivalent to 6 percent of the country's entire GDP.[3] And in a recent J.D. Power customer survey in the United Kingdom, Skoda automobiles came out on top.

However, transition of the Czech economy from one of the former Eastern Block's most rigidly controlled systems to a free marketplace has been one of great disappointment. The performance of the Prague Stock

The Emerging Markets

Exchange tells the story. Soon after its main index, the PX 50, was created, it lost nearly half its value, falling from 1,000 to 557.2 by the end of 1994. Although it has been quite volatile since, it ended the decade down an additional 12 percent, closing at 489.70. Why was so much expected of this emerging market economy, and what went wrong?

The Czech Republic earned a reputation as the vanguard of peaceful, democratic change: from the brief thaw in communist rule it showed the world in the Prague Spring of 1968, to its rapid claim to independence via the 1989 Velvet Revolution and the anointment of a dissident poet as president, to the country's orderly breakup into Czech and Slovak Republics in 1993. This disciplined, well-educated nation seemed to hold the promise of all eastern European economies, which had been mired for three generations under Nazi and communist rule. Although the Czech Republic is now arguably on the right track for establishing a sound economic system, the first ten years of self-rule have revealed the immense difficulties of creating free-market capitalism.

A key problem, lessened but still extant, is a misunderstanding of the importance of regulatory oversight in an efficient marketplace. Jan

Müller, former head of the Czech Securities Commission, says, "a key principle of the new republic was one of total freedom."[4]

Troubled Vouchers

No doubt a backlash against decades of blundering socialist rule contributed to the government's laissez-faire approach to privatization and the stock market. By 1995, the state had sold off most of its corporate assets through a voucher system, which disseminated ownership among its citizens as a means of equitably distributing the country's wealth while germinating the seeds of capitalism across the republic. The state also oversaw the concurrent development of a stock exchange that at best could be described as a freewheeling marketplace to trade privatized shares.

In practice, both policies turned out to be huge mistakes.

Instead of selling off controlling corporate interests to qualified foreign businesses (like Volkswagen) that would have imported much-needed hard currency, expertise, and access to foreign markets, the democratization of Czech corporate assets through vouchers fractured ownership, delayed restructuring, and ironically reverted shares to state control. Capital markets gained a notorious reputation for fraud due to the lack of adequate safeguards. Worst of all, the country forfeited the leadership role it had established in eastern Europe in the early 1990s as the champion of political and economic reform.

What exactly happened?

Czechs exchanged their corporate vouchers for shares in newly created investment privatization funds (IPFs). Laws prohibited a fund from holding more than 20 percent in any individual corporation, a stake that has since been lowered to 11 percent.[5] Because the system prevented consolidation of substantial blocks of shares, meaningful corporate governance—an unknown concept to the Czechs—was lacking. Further, many IPFs were being managed by major Czech banks, which were still largely state run. But signs that corporations were grappling poorly with their newfound freedom were evident even before the first vouchers were handed out.

In 1991, the government devalued the koruna by 50 percent. Instead of taking advantage of the windfall export profits to restructure, lay off, and make capital investments, most Czech businesses did nothing, satisfied that their newfound profitability justified the status quo.

Then came substantial wage growth and extra income derived from the sale of privatization vouchers. This may have helped convince citizens that the revolution was on the right track. Instead, rising consumer demand served only the illusion that effective reform was being made. There was no corresponding increase in industrial and service productivity. GDP growth peaked at 6.4 percent in 1995. However, the failure to restructure ate away at the Czech Republic's devaluation-induced export advantage as the rest of Europe was becoming leaner and more competitive.

By the end of 1996, as imports soared and exports leveled off, the trade gap hit nearly $6 billion. The country's current account deficit shot up toward 8 percent—among the highest anywhere—and currency speculators began to circle.[6]

At the same time, the country's banking system was headed for disaster. Government policies that discouraged layoffs, bankruptcy, and the breakup of failed enterprises led to a huge upsurge in nonperforming loans. Inefficient and corrupt financial markets virtually closed down the flow of equity capital, leaving banks the primary source of domestic financing.

Though nearly one-third of most bank loan portfolios were in trouble, state-run banks found themselves still forced to extend risky loans to failing companies they directly or indirectly managed through investment funds.[7] Even more bizarre, according to the OECD, "banks began subsidizing these loan losses by charging above-market interest rates to healthier firms in which they, or their IPFs, had controlling stakes."[8]

Devaluation and Recession

The facade of reform supported by several years of impressive economic growth broke apart by the spring of 1997 when the government was forced to relinquish the koruna's link with the deutsche mark and the U.S. dollar. Within a period of six months, the koruna lost more than one-third of its value, and the sound foundation that was thought to have underpinned the Czech renaissance was revealed to have been based on only the impression of change.

In the aftermath, the economy fell into recession, contracting on average by more than 1 percent a year between 1997 and 1999. During that time, Czech stocks lost 3.4 percent in local currency terms in 1997, then nearly 14 percent in 1998.

By the end of 1999, finance, banking, service, and utility shares rebounded, helping to push the PX 50 up by nearly 25 percent as the economy began once again to expand. This still left 3- and 5-year annualized returns in dismal shape. And this was especially so in dollar terms, where the Prague Exchange was down an annual average of -4.52 percent between 1995 and 1999 and -7.82 percent between 1997 and 1999. All this was indicative that on a corporate level the market was never sold on the Czech miracle.

Reality and recession finally forced Czech officials to begin, albeit timidly, to implement more substantial reform. The pace of privatization and market liberalization picked up as the level of state subsidies began to decline.

The immediate impact took the luster off the country's once impressive macroeconomic numbers. Unemployment, which traditionally hovered around 3 percent, shot up to 5.2 percent in 1997, hit 6.3 percent in 1998, and ended 1999 at 8.5 percent. Excessive domestic demand, which expanded by 8.5 percent in 1996, contracted by 1.1 percent in 1999. Real annual wage growth, which had averaged more than 8 percent between 1994 and 1996, dropped off sharply to 3.2 percent in 1997. Wages then actually declined in 1998 by 1.2 percent, helping to reestablish the economy's competitiveness, but then increased by more than 4 percent in 1999.

Government consumption, which grew by 4.3 percent in 1996, decreased by 1.8 percent in 1997 and 0.5 percent in 1998 before stabilizing in 1999.

Recovery and Reform

Broad economic slowdown reined in inflation, which had peaked at 10.7 percent in 1998, bringing it down to 2.1 percent in 1999. It also helped alleviate pressure on the country's bloated current account deficit, which ended the decade at a remarkable 2 percent of GDP.[9]

Most encouraging was the sharp turnaround in foreign direct investment, the primary engine that was driving corporate reform. Since it peaked in 1995 at $2.57 billion, FDI had collapsed to $1.29 billion in 1997. Yet a substantially weakened currency coupled with signs of economic reform revived FDI dramatically in 1998 and 1999, ending the decade at $4.9 billion.

The discount rate, which had peaked in mid-1998 at 13 percent in efforts to strengthen the koruna, fell to 5 percent by the end of 1999 as the central bank sought to prime the economy.[10] However, there has been a disconnect between monetary policy and growth, because corporate credit risk is still so significant that banks are reluctant to lend on top of unrestructured debt. The government's decision to tighten banking regulations and hasten the sale of the country's three largest publicly owned banks to established foreign financial interests will help clear up their balance sheets, recapitalize operations, and introduce a new loan discipline that will require troubled corporate borrowers to either restructure or liquidate assets.

Improved corporate governance is being prompted by the separation of commercial banking operations from investment fund management and by more active policing of stock exchange operations by the Czech Securities Commission, established in April 1998.[11] But the CSC's lack of independence makes it doubtful that it will be capable of quickly remedying the Czech financial markets' well-known "lack of transparency, poor protection of minority shareholder rights, and rampant insider trading."[12]

Though more than 1,000 companies have been delisted from the country's exchanges, leaving 194 active issues, liquidity remains thin.[13] Five companies account for more than half of the Prague Stock Exchange's total market capitalization and 80 percent of total trading.[14]

Two of these, Cesky Telecom and Ceske Radiokomunikace, are ranked by Credit Suisse First Boston as among the country's leading buys. CT, the republic's largest equity, is its primary telecom provider, with a $6.5 billion market cap. In 1999, its shares rose 26 percent in local currency terms, with earnings expected to grow at an annual rate of 20 percent. Ceske Radio is one of the country's primary TV and radio signal broadcasters, also providing mobile telecom and data business services. Its shares climbed 36 percent in 1999, raising its market cap to $1.5 billion. Earnings growth is projected to soar by nearly 50 percent between 2000 and 2001.[15]

Unfortunately, for most other publicly traded companies, the voucher system has left a systemically weak shareholder structure, ineffective corporate governance, and substantial debt, which will continue to drag down performance until foreign investors step in en masse.

A pipe dream? Not necessarily. The Czech Republic still has a lot going for it.

➤ It is the second-richest country in eastern Europe.

➤ The labor force is inexpensive and well educated.

➤ Czech membership in the European Union is likely within the not too distant future, further integrating the country with the rest of western Europe.

➤ Inward foreign direct investment is once again soaring, driven by the likes of Boeing, Siemens, Matsushita, and the General Electric Capital Corporation.[16]

➤ Depressed asset prices (made even cheaper by a weak currency that has been shadowing the euro) and the Czech Republic's pivotal location in the heart of central Europe make some of the country's strongest operations attractive takeover targets.

Maintaining this resurgence in FDI won't be easy, though, because of the recurring volatility of emerging markets, the proximity of Russian insolvency, and the increasing competitive advantages of neighboring Poland and Hungary.

Greece—Need for Continued Reform

THE GREEK ECONOMY surged toward the end of the 1990s, averaging 3 percent GDP growth between 1995 and 1999. The Athens Stock Exchange corroborated the good news, averaging annualized gains in dollar terms of over 39 percent during those five years, more than 66 percent during the three years, 1997 through 1999.[1] At the same time, Greek bonds generated tremendous returns as the country's double-digit interest rates converged with broad eurozone rates in preparation for the country's entrance into common currency in 2001.

This marks a remarkable turnaround from just several years earlier when Greece failed to qualify for charter membership in the euro club. In 1998, she exceeded each of the five key macroeconomic guidelines—inflation, long-term interest rates, government deficit and debt, and currency stability—by a wide margin.

Greece's economic problems were a product of the country's turbulent past. Like Spain, Greece carried the turmoil of World War II well into the 1970s while the rest of Europe was rebuilding and restructuring.

After decades of dictatorship and political struggles that shattered her economy, Greece became a democratic republic in 1974. Only after the country gained membership in the European Commonwealth (which became the European Union) in 1981 did Greek economic development and international trade begin to significantly evolve.

Even with strong global growth during the later 1980s and most of the 1990s, Greece still trailed other peripheral economies in making substantial reform. Spain managed massive restructuring of her economy to qualify for monetary union. So did relatively impoverished Ireland and ever-dysfunctional Italy. Even Portugal, the only EU member nation with a GDP per capita lower than that of Greece, managed to get its economic house in order in time to qualify for EMU.

Delayed Reform

Although the country as a whole generally supports the concept of currency union, people and institutions were slow to embrace the structural change necessary to get Greece to the mark. As in many socialist economies, in Greece, where approximately two-thirds of all business concerns are state owned, giving up guaranteed supports in return for the long-term benefits of the free market is an intimidating proposition. Take, for example, the 1998 initial public offering of the state-owned Ionian Bank—the largest privatization ever. This was supposed to be a showcase of Greece's commitment to change. But it failed, largely due to the show of union strength that coerced the government to stipulate that any new owner would have to keep all 3,500 employees who had been with the bank for more than three years.[2] Other instances of macro-inefficiencies: pensions are paid to retired workers who go back to work, and workers laid off after a corporate restructuring still receive their salaries.

This is not to say that the country hasn't made vast strides in recent years. According to the Bank of Greece, "growth in the economy is being underpinned by a surge in investment sustained by the healthy profit situation of domestic firms and a wide range of EU-supported public sector investments."[3] These projects—largely improvements to the country's poor transport infrastructure, including highways, shipping terminals, railroads, and airports—are expected to promote economic expansion that had been stifled by poor access. Despite the initial problems confronting Ionian's IPO, Greek privatization between

1998 and 1999 generated $8.77 billion. This included the sale of five major banks, along with a 49 percent stake in the country's dominant telecom operator, OTE, and the state's leading oil concern, Hellenic Petroleum.

Economic Recovery

Some highlights of Greece's recent economic performance:

➤ Real GDP growth rose from 2.1 percent to 3.5 percent between 1995 and 1999.

➤ Inflation declined from 8.9 to 2.4 percent over the same time.

➤ New labor agreements have reduced wage increases from 9.6 percent in 1996 to 3 percent in 1999.[4]

➤ Reductions have been made in government price controls of electricity, telephone, and public transport.[5]

➤ Investment and savings as a percent of GDP have been creeping up, from 18.6 percent and 16.5 percent in 1995, respectively, to 21.7 and 19.4 percent in 1998.

➤ Short- and long-term interest rates were both approaching 20 percent in 1994; by the end of 1999, money market rates were 10.2 percent, while 10-year government bond yields fell to 6.7 percent. (This inverted yield curve reflected near-term inflationary concerns as expansion collided with a substantial easing of monetary policy.)

➤ Government deficit declined from a whopping 9.2 percent of GDP in 1995 to a Maastricht-satisfying 1.5 percent by the end of 1999, assisted by declining interest rates and more efficient tax collection.

➤ Public debt remains quite high, falling slightly from a recent peak in 1996 of 111.3 percent of GDP to 104.2 percent in 1999, still well beyond the EMU ceiling of 60 percent; however, like Belgium and Italy, who maintain even greater debt-GDP ratios, Greece needs only demonstrate continued vigilance on this front to keep the European Central Bank happy.

Two large structural impediments remain: the slow pace of privatization, which has denied the government windfalls that other countries have relied upon to help pay down debt, and substantial cuts in the growth in government spending—a key to having qualified for monetary union.

Gaining access to common currency was important geopolitically.

Greece is the only member of the European Union that doesn't share an adjacent border within the alliance. It is isolated both in terms of trade and in shared priorities. Unrest across Albania, Bulgaria, Cyprus, Turkey, and the former Yugoslavia generates turbulence in Greek markets. According to Prime Minister Costas Simitis, joining EMU will more closely align Greece in the eyes of the global marketplace with the stability of western Europe, even though Greece still retains emerging-market status.[6]

Proof of his claim was seen during the summer of 1998 when emerging-market currencies and equities melted down as Russian and southeast Asian economies continued to unravel. The drachma held, and Greek equities moved increasingly in line with western markets.[7]

Strong Equities

With an eye focused on the pending benefits of euro membership, Greek stocks had a phenomenal year in 1999, rising 73.64 percent in local currency terms—47.58 percent in dollar terms. The rally pushed up stocks across every sector, from financials and information technology to transportation and industrials.

Some of the year's top performers:

➤ Greece's third-largest bank, Commercial Bank of Greece, was up 183 percent in local currency terms.
➤ Metal manufacturer Aluminum of Greece rose 186 percent.
➤ Transportation holding company Attica Enterprises more than tripled.
➤ Greece's leading software and hardware manufacturer, Intrasoft, soared 215 percent.[8]

Investors, however, need be mindful, as the Bank of Attica observed, that "despite important steps taken toward modernizing the economy, including the deregulation of Greek financial markets and the growth of modern products and institutions, it is clear that Greek reform still faces a long road."[9] To be truly competitive in the euro-zone, Greece needs to be more than statistically compliant with Maastricht; the government must maintain vigilance toward fundamental economic change, which is still far from second nature to the local corporate community.

Hungary—Embracing the West

IN NOVEMBER 1997, when global markets were in a highly unsettled state, Matáv, Hungary's primary telecom operator and the jewel of the Hungarian economy, became the first eastern European company to list on the New York Stock Exchange. Its IPO was priced at $18.65. The issue was 2.5 times oversubscribed and raised $1.2 billion.

A little over a year later, by the end of 1998, Matáv closed at $34.50, up nearly 85 percent.[1] And in early 2000, it was up another 20 percent, garnering widespread analyst support. More than just another hot telecom offering, Matáv's success reflected Hungary's effectiveness in modernizing and restructuring her economy over the past decade.

"Our starting point was that everything had to be privatized," observes Gyorgy Suranyi, president of the National Bank of Hungary, "and real privatization meant that we had to have responsible owners to increase efficiency and competitiveness and to help the economy become more flexible." That meant bringing in established foreign partners and their expertise.[2]

Matáv was the first telecom in the region to invite a strategic foreign investor to restructure its arcane phone system. The government sold off a 30 percent share to a joint venture named MagyarCom formed by Ameritech and Deutsche Telekom in December 1993. Two years later, MagyarCom's ownership stake had reached 67 percent. By the end of 1997, the U.S./German enterprise had sunk nearly $3 billion into Matáv, radically upgrading and expanding the country's telecommunication services, which paved the way for its successful IPO.[3] Foreign direct investment has driven privatization and Hungary's economic revival. In 1995 privatization revenues peaked at $3.83 billion, as did FDI at $4.5 billion.[4] By 1999, privatization receipts were down to $448 million, and FDI diminished to $1.4 billion.[5]

Some of the multinationals that have set up shop in Hungary include technology leaders IBM, Nokia, and Philips. ABN AMRO, Bayerische Landesbank, Société Général, and GE Capital have acquired substantial positions in the country's deregulated banking industry. And in the rapidly expanding auto sector, Audi, Opel, and Suzuki have established key European production centers in Hungary.

By 1999, more than 80 percent of the economy was in private hands, the highest proportion of any country in the entire region.[6] For the decade, the nation had captured $21 billion in foreign direct investment, or nearly one-quarter of all FDI that had flowed into eastern Europe and the former Soviet Union.[7] Privatized companies with foreign backers have established more effective corporate governance and overall operations than their domestically owned counterparts, leading to higher productivity and greater market share.[8]

Austerity Program

Although the initial push to privatize Hungary's state-run businesses dates back to 1991, the 1995 austerity program finally got the economy on track. In addition to triggering the sell-off of the bulk of the nation's corporate assets, proceeds from which have helped pay down the country's large foreign debt, the government made substantial cuts in social spending by laying off 13 percent of the public workforce and freezing wages of the remaining public workers.

To reduce a staggering current account deficit, which had surged to 9.5 percent, the government levied an 8 percent import surcharge, devalued the Hungarian forint by 9 percent, linked it to the deutsche mark and the U.S. dollar (now only the euro), then established a crawling peg that automatically depreciated the currency on a monthly basis to ward off currency speculators and gradually improve the country's external fiscal imbalances.[9]

These macroeconomic improvements coupled with bankruptcy reform helped transform one of the region's weakest economies into one of its strongest. Failing companies were forced to shut down or be bought out, more transparent accounting regulations were adopted, and banks were restructured or privatized.

➤ Between 1997 and 1999, GDP growth expanded by an average of 4.5 percent annually.

➤ Public debt as a percentage of GDP plummeted from 84.3 percent to a Maastricht-qualifying 60.6 percent between 1995 and 1999.

➤ Current account deficit was reduced from a currency-destabilizing 9.3 percent to 4.3 percent over the same time.

➤ Inflation, which had nearly reached 30 percent in 1995, tumbled to a more manageable 11.2 percent in 1999.

➤ The discount rate eased from 29 percent in 1994 to 16 percent in 1999.[10]

➤ In January 1999, yields on 5-year government paper tumbled from

14.5 percent to 11.73 percent.

➤ Industrial production surged from 4.6 percent in 1995 to an average of 11.2 percent between 1997 and 1999, supported by extensive privatization and extensive foreign direct investment.

➤ Exports of goods and services soared by 26.4 percent in 1997 and increased by an average of 15 percent between 1998 and 1999.

➤ Private consumption rose a modest 1.9 percent in 1997, followed by more substantial growth of 4.8 and 5.1 percent in 1998 and 1999, respectively.[11]

By the close of the 1990s, the *Financial Times* reported "Hungary's austerity program has succeeded in putting the country on the path of strong, sustainable growth, consolidating its position as the leading fast-track reformer in central and eastern Europe."[12] And the capital markets seemed to have concurred.

In December 1998, Hungary auctioned off a DM 500 million 7-year bond issue at only 100 basis points above equivalent German paper. Then, a month later, only one day after the Brazilian *real* collapsed, Hungary became the first eastern European nation to float a euro-denominated bond.[13] Secured by the region's highest credit rating (Baa2 from Moody's and BBB from Standard & Poor's), the bond was quickly scooped up by Italian, British, Scandinavian, and Spanish fund managers, who bought 40 percent of the €500 million 10-year fixed-rate issue.[14] By the end of 1999, foreign ownership of Hungarian government bonds hit an all-time high of $1.6 billion.[15]

With nearly all key macroeconomic indicators trending the right way, Hungarian debt is resembling a convergence play—a phenomenon normally reserved for those economies on the cusp of joining common currency.

Equity Performance

On the equity side, the Budapest Stock Exchange has been the best-performing bourse in the region. Between 1995 and 1999, as reform began to set in, the market averaged annualized returns of 26.41 percent in dollar terms, 48.59 percent in forints. The gains would have been even more impressive had it not been for the Russian crisis in 1998, which sent Hungarian stocks tumbling by nearly 9 percent that year in dollar terms. Prior to that, in 1997, the Budapest Exchange had soared by more than 93 percent, and the year before, it was the hottest market in the world, up 103 percent.[16]

According to analysts at S&P/DRI, the strong performance of the bourse has been supported not only by the country's significant economic reforms but also by the stock exchange's "relative transparency and longevity (started in 1990), which helped establish its strong position among eastern European bourses."[17]

More than half of the daily trades on the BSE are executed by foreign investors.[18] While this points out the appeal of Hungarian equities, the market's liquidity and extensive foreign shareholders are also at the core of its risk. Money can move in and out of the market with relative ease. In April 1998, the BUX—the country's leading index—hit its all-time high of 9,016. The election of a new government and subsequent collapse of Russian securities sent the BUX into a tailspin. By early September, the index was down to 4,892. A fourth-quarter rally enabled the index to close the year at 6,308, and by early 2000, it had blown past the 10,000 mark.

Matáv, OTP Bank, and pharmaceutical concern Richter Gedeon are some of Hungary's largest and most liquid issues, all with Global Depositary Receipts that trade in London. They earned some of the top returns in 1999.

Earnings-per-share growth at Matáv, Budapest's largest issue, with a $7.7 billion market cap, expanded at an annual rate of 32 percent between 1995 and 1999, and its shares were up 44 percent in local currency terms in 1999. OTP was the best-performing actively traded stock on the BSE in 1999, rising 37 percent. While its $1.1 billion market cap is relatively small for a bank that's attracting international investors, OTP offers the best access to Hungary's growing financial industry. Richter Gedeon, Hungary's sole independent pharmaceutical company, with a market cap of $1.1 billion, soared 81 percent in 1999.

To help counter the country's chronic retirement deficit, reduce the excessive weight foreign investors have on stocks, and cut turnover and performance volatility, the government has privatized a large portion of the country's pension system. Younger workers are now required to commit three-quarters of their retirement savings into private pension funds.[19] While this exacerbates the current shortfall in the state's own pension system, with 25 percent of all retirement forints now being privately managed, reform will ensure a more secure retirement scheme while fueling equity growth. The Economist Intelligence Unit estimates that by 2005, private pension fund assets will amount to 4.2 percent of the GDP.[20]

A Divided Economy

The primary concern some economists have about Hungary's economic recovery involves the one factor that's most responsible for having turned the country around. Hungary's extensive reliance on foreign businesses has obscured the fact that the bulk of the domestically owned economy has made little progress in restructuring and rationalizing operations. *Business Central Europe* reports that "Hungarian industry consists of a few foreign-owned islands of excellence in a sea of struggling local companies."[21] For instance, many of the large foreign car companies who have set up operations in Hungary, like Audi's big engine plant in Gyor, import the majority of their parts, leaving local manufacturers out of the growth loop. This has minimized the benefits foreign investment has had on the economy, a disappointment given that foreign-owned companies generate one-third of the GDP and three-quarters of all exports.[22]

"This has produced," observes *BCE,* "an economy split down the middle. Some foreign-owned companies are making high-value-added products for export. However, locally owned industries are starved for investment and equipment, competing solely on the basis of low wages."[23]

"If Hungary wants to avoid becoming the EU's Mexico," adds *BCE,* "it must focus on creating a German-style *Mittelstand*"—medium-sized family-run companies that manufacture key value-added parts and become essential niche players in international markets.[24]

Poland—An Emerging Tiger

IT WAS 1939. Several months after Dębica opened up its tire factory in a small town of the same name in western Poland, the Germans marched in. All its machinery was packed up and shipped west to Germany to produce parts for the Nazi war machine. Several years after the war was over, the Polish government tried to reclaim the company's operations, only to see the factory relocated to Soviet Russia. It was not until the early 1990s that all of Dębica's pieces of production were completely returned to Polish soil.

By then the company showed all the troubled inefficiencies of its state-run heritage. Sales per employee were one-eighth of those achieved by multinationals, and a modest commitment to research and development didn't suggest an encouraging future.[1] Dębica countered by trying to convince foreign investors that there was a future under the country's fledgling democracy. But no one was interested.

Then, in 1994, GM, Fiat, Ford, and Daewoo established production facilities in Poland, and that changed everything. Goodyear now owns nearly 60 percent of Dębica, sinking millions of dollars annually in new technology, management, finance, and marketing. And today, the firm is the sole global manufacturer of Goodyear tire tubes and exports half of everything it makes to western Europe.[2]

Although perhaps not a typical Polish corporate story, Dębica does reveal the historic forces that have acted upon Poland's economy—its businesses and its psyche—for more than a half-century. It also provides some insight into the country's entrepreneurial spirit, which has been driving the nation's economic revival, and explains to a large degree why Poland is so eager to gain the protective embrace of EU and NATO membership.

Economic expansion between 1995 and 1999 was impressive.

➤ GDP grew by an average of 5.75 percent a year.

➤ Gross fixed investment increased at an annual rate of 14.3 percent.

➤ Inflation was drastically curbed, from nearly 27 percent in 1995 to under 8 percent in 1999.

➤ The discount rate correspondingly dropped from 25 percent to 19 percent over the same time period.

➤ Public debt shrank from 53 percent of GDP in 1995 to less than 40 percent by the end of 1999.

➤ The budget deficit, which was running at around 3 percent of GDP in the late 1990s, is projected to disappear by 2002.[3]

The result of this metamorphosis is that Poland is increasingly seen as an adjunct to western Europe's developed economies rather than as a fragile emerging market subsisting in the shadow of the former Soviet Union.

Some recent proof of this was seen in 1998 when the Russian ruble collapsed. Unlike other emerging market currencies that substantially weakened in response, the Polish zloty, whose value was linked to a euro/U.S. dollar index, virtually held its ground despite the hit the Polish banking sector took.[4] Why? The economy doesn't depend on commodity exports or the infusion of hot foreign money to support growth.[5] Most important, as the World Bank observes, "Poland is a country with very sound fundamentals."[6]

How did the economy make the transition so effectively from complete state control to free market?

Reformation

Bohdan Wyznikiewicz, vice president of the Gdansk Institute for Market Economics, explains three reasons driving economic reform.

➤ First, soon after it gained its freedom in 1989, the government adopted and stuck with a "shock therapy" approach to reform. The currency was devalued, subsidies pulled, and price controls lifted.

➤ Second, full deregulation of the economy kick-started the country's latent capitalist sentiment. Tens of thousands of businesses opened up overnight, financed by local savings.

➤ And third, privatization didn't happen all at once; it was paced, enabling the country's limited access to domestic and foreign capital to effectively respond to these new opportunities.[7] The London-based Economist Intelligence Unit observed that this approach, often relying on securing strategic foreign investors, "encouraged corporate restructuring rather than just the transferal of ownership," the latter being characteristic of the Czech experience.[8]

As a result, privatization, supported by foreign direct investment, which surged from $89 million in 1990 to $8.2 billion in 1999, has been driving Polish economic growth and reform.[9] The sell-off of state assets steadily increased, from $725 million in 1994 to $3.4 billion in 1999.[10] Whereas only 18 percent of the GDP was generated by the private sector in 1989, more than two-thirds of the economy is now in private hands.[11]

Significant new privatizations include Poland's largest commercial bank, Pekao, which is expected to raise $1 billion, and a 25 to 35 percent stake in Poland's leading telecom provider, TPSA, which promises to generate $4 billion. Also on the block is a tranche of PKN, the state's main oil company; PZU, which controls 60 percent of the domestic insurance market; LOT, the country's national airline; and KGHM, one of Europe's leading metal and mining companies.

Sell-off of state assets accomplishes several key goals.

➤ Proceeds help fill in the shortfall in pension and health care systems.

➤ Size and liquidity of the Warsaw Stock Exchange expands, making it an increasingly viable source for raising corporate capital and attracting hard foreign currency.

➤ Foreign investment flows into the country, bringing with it access to industry expertise and global markets, along with increasing recognition of Polish businesses.

➤ Increased foreign spending in Poland supports the local currency.

Foreign investors have been particularly attracted by the country's banking, retail, and auto industries, which have thrived because of the country's cheap labor, increasingly open trade with EU countries, and a domestic marketplace comprised of more than 38 million residents. With the ratio of bank capital to GDP in Poland only one-third that of the EU average, the president of Citigroup Poland, Shirish Apte, thinks "Polish banking has enormous potential because it remains relatively undeveloped."[12]

This fact has not been missed by international financial institutions, including Bayerische HypoVereinsbank, Deutsche Bank, Allied Irish Banks, and UniCredito, which have helped boost foreign ownership of Poland's commercial banking to nearly 50 percent.

With 94 percent of sales executed by private firms, the retail sector has now become a key force in the country's economic revitalization, right alongside manufacturing and financial services.[13] This renaissance has been assisted by leading European retailers including France's Carrefour, Britain's Marks & Spencer, Sweden's Ikea, Germany's Metro, and Switzerland's Nestlé.

The *Financial Times* reported that with Poles now buying half a million cars a year, the country's auto industry has become a substantial European market and "one of the most important sectors in the domestic economy." German GM subsidiary Opel has invested $360 million, while Italy's Fiat and South Korean conglomerate Daewoo have sunk $1.4 billion each into the sector.[14]

The expanding presence of foreign investors has begun to affect Polish boardrooms, perhaps none more dramatically than at the industrial/telecom conglomerate Elektrim. Inside the company's Warsaw-based headquarters, a foreign-shareholder-led revolt ousted the CEO after he failed to disclose critical events affecting corporate valuation and replaced him with an American venture capitalist, Barbara Lundberg. The first foreigner to be appointed head of a major Polish corporation, Lundberg was quick to sell off dozens of noncore subsidiaries and began assembling stakes in a variety of domestic telecom operators, seeking to consolidate a firm industry hold.

Equity Boom

The upsurge in privatization and FDI has been a boon for the Warsaw Stock Exchange, which has seen its listings expand exponentially, from 9 stocks in 1991 to 119 by April 2000, with a market capitalization of Zl 123.4 billion. Over the 1990s, the main WIG Index rose from 919 to more than 18,000.

Effective regulatory supervision has promoted the exchange's expansion. The securities commission, according to the Economist Intelligence Unit, has "achieved a high level of transparency and avoided the share collapses and trading scandals that have caused setbacks to other exchanges in the region."[15]

Another boost to equities is pension reform, which will eventually channel billions of dollars into the stock market over the coming years, as younger workers are now required to direct 20 percent of their retirement dollars into pension funds. Up to 40 percent of fund assets may be invested in stocks. With only 5 percent of assets permitted to be invested overseas, Polish stocks are likely to be in for a run.[16]

A new electronic trading system was recently adopted, sharing a common platform with the Paris Bourse.[17] This not only facilitates greater international brokerage trading in the WSE (where foreign investors already hold nearly a 40 percent stake in Polish equities) but also suggests that future consolidation with western European markets will be possible.

Still, for all the positive news, investors were treated to a roller-coaster ride during the second half of the 1990s. Between 1994 and 1998, the broad market was down an average of 4.86 percent in local currency terms and off 13.87 percent in dollar terms. Only a phenomenal rally in 1999, in which the market rose more than 54 percent in local currency terms (31 percent in dollar terms), helped Polish stocks regain some of their luster after the 1997–1998 emerging-market crises in Southeast Asia and Russia. This rebound boosted annualized returns from 1995 through 1999 to 18.44 percent in zloty terms (6.54 percent in dollar terms).

How can such strong macro growth be accompanied by such mercurial equity performance?

From a global viewpoint, although more developed than most emerging-market economies, Poland still gets smacked about when Asian or Latin American markets melt down. Just as important, the dollar's long-term rise cuts consistently into U.S.-based investor returns. Since most Polish exports remain on the Continent, where the zloty has been sinking with the euro, there has been no boom for Polish exporters.

From a local perspective, the Polish equity market has struggled because domestic growth is still driven by small- to medium-sized private firms that have been enjoying generally stronger earnings growth than the larger firms that went public.

However, in 1999, some of the country's largest operations took off.

➤ KGHM, a large mining and energy concern, rose 109 percent in local currency terms.

➤ Central and eastern Europe's largest computer manufacturer, Optimus, gained 133 percent.

➤ Poland's second-largest commercial and investment bank, BIG-BG, more than quadrupled in 1999.[18]

Risks

As Poland links up with the EU and its equity market moves closer to resembling the country's underlying economy, the Warsaw Exchange will likely enjoy substantial growth. Still, several significant risks remain.

High current account deficit. Though currently offset by the tremendous influx of foreign investment, the country's current account deficit is dangerously high. By the end of 1999, it hit 7.5 percent of GDP. With the central bank having floated the zloty in the spring of 2000, freeing it from preset monthly devaluation and government support, the soaring current account deficit could now expose the Polish currency to far greater volatility, potentially undercutting returns for foreign investors.

Russia's shadow. Despite Poland's increasing economic independence, Russia's plight will affect domestic investments.

Government economy. More than one-quarter of businesses are inefficient, state-controlled operations; they exert a substantial drag on the economy, and many will be slow to privatize.

Maturing public debt. Substantial public debt, restructured in the early 1990s to help jump-start the economy, will be maturing soon. If there hasn't been an adequate rate of business expansion, this debt could encumber public finances, interest rates, and the economy.

Part Three

Investing
Approaches
and Issues

Chapter Eight

Sectoral Approach

I T WASN'T SO LONG AGO that investors focused on the performance and outlook of domestic economies in Europe. Labor strife in France, the latest government collapse in Italy, or Britain being bounced out of the Exchange Rate Mechanism were enough to send investors scurrying to safer borders.

But deregulation, market reform, and the advent of common currency are steadily eroding the significance of national boundaries. While the passage of sweeping new tax laws in Germany demonstrates that investors can still benefit from broad country exposure, mergers and acquisitions and the creation of multinationals are discounting the import of where corporations are headquartered. Paris-based Suez Lyonnaise des Eaux may have mastered the water business in France, but you buy the stock because of its exposure to an exploding global demand for water services.

Sector-based investing is a reflection of European integration and globalization, key factors that are driving stocks. In fact, one would be hard-pressed to find a stock whose appeal is primarily based on domestic performance. So although economic policy and product specialization still have national faces, Europe's investment environment is increasingly being defined in terms of sectors.

From privatization to corporate restructuring to the development of a shareholder culture, the benefits of Europe's more open and unified economies are exemplified in the five sectors described below.

Sector Performance
(1st Quarter 1995 through 1st Quarter 2000)*

	5-YR ANNUALIZED RETURNS (EUROS)	1-YR RETURNS (EUROS) †
Telecommunications‡	50.72%	86.80%
Insurance§	34.20	17.44
Banking	30.93	2.60
Utilities#	23.64	5.54
Retail°°	21.91	17.28

* Returns are based on market-cap-weighted composite averages of the FTSE industries cited below.
† First quarter 1999 through first quarter 2000
‡ Telecommunication service providers only
§ Insurance and life insurance
# Electricity, gas distribution, and water
°° General retailers, food and drug retailers, and household goods and textiles
Source: "European Company Performance Survey," *Financial Times* Survey of the European Performance League, 23 June 2000, pp. III-IV.

Banking

EUROPE'S HIGHLY OVERCROWDED banking sector has benefited tremendously by the rejuvenation of the region's economic fortunes. In addition to the dramatic fall in interest rates, the big rise in bank stocks has been fueled by industry privatization and deregulation, mergers and acquisitions, restructuring, application of cost-cutting technology, and more effective risk management. At the same time, stronger performing economies are lowering provisions for bad loans, further boosting bottom lines.

From the first quarter of 1995 through the first quarter of 2000, bank shares racked up annualized gains of 30.93 percent in euro terms.[1] Growth was especially strong along the periphery of the Continent—Ireland, Spain, Portugal, Italy, and Greece—where interest rates have fallen the furthest, triggering the rapid expansion of small-to-midsize businesses.

At the same time, diminishing returns on traditional savings accounts are spawning development of an equity culture as household assets are being shifted away from low-interest savings accounts and into stocks and mutual funds, a large percentage of which are sold by banks. So instead of a bottom line relying primarily on the mercurial spread between savings and lending rates, banks are increasingly deriving a greater proportion of their profits from the more steady

Key Findings

> ➤ Industry deregulation and more open markets are inducing domestic consolidation, reducing Europe's surfeit of banks, making firms more efficient and profitable.
> ➤ Bank stocks soared by nearly 31 percent a year in euro terms over the five-year period ending with the first quarter of 2000.
> ➤ Banks are deriving a greater proportion of their profits from the increasing flow of fees and commissions related to asset management.
> ➤ Growth has been especially strong along the periphery of the Continent—Ireland, Spain, Portugal, Italy, and Greece—where interest rates have fallen the furthest, triggering the rapid expansion of small to midsize businesses.
> ➤ State protectionism and incongruous national banking regulations are inhibiting cross-border mergers and the creation of banks that can compete globally.

flow of fees and commissions related to asset management.

However, a key driver of the sector—banking reform—has been proceeding at a sluggish pace in the larger core nations where state intervention still occurs. Governments are trying to be kingmakers. By protecting domestic banking from foreign interests, politicians are hoping to encourage creation of national banking giants through domestic mergers and acquisitions. These new sector leaders, so the argument goes, would then be better positioned to execute foreign acquisitions rather than being the target of one.[2] However, such protectionism tends to perpetuate costly, fragmented banking systems.

For instance, in Germany the country's three big banks—Deutsche, Dresdner, and Commerzbank—retain only 17 percent of the domestic banking market. Nearly 60 percent of the market is dominated by banks controlled by state and local governments.[3] Failure of Deutsche and Dresdner to pull off their planned merger early in 2000 highlighted some of the problems impeding domestic consolidation.

In France, Banque Nationale de Paris's $13 billion hostile takeover of Paribas in 1999 created the world's third-largest bank by assets. But it fell short of BNP's original goal (supported by the government) of snagging Société Générale at the same time in hopes of creating the world's largest bank. More discouraging is that between the two, SG, not Paribas, was a better fit with BNP. So not only did BNP effect a less-than-optimal takeover, it also broke up a friendly, more viable merger that was on the verge of taking place between SG and Paribas.

To lure in strategic partners and direct foreign investment, banking reforms have gone further in Europe's faster-growing peripheral economies where sector activity is less inhibited by the state. There have been far more mergers and acquisitions, which have hastened the pace of restructuring and layoffs. Foreign takeovers have also pushed modernization and the search for shareholder value through consolidation and cost cutting.[4] The result: net interest margins are higher, along with overall profitability. This has reduced the need to pursue riskier ventures into investment banking (like Deutsche Bank's $10 billion acquisition of Bankers Trust) and emerging markets (such as Credit Suisse First Boston's $2.2 billion loss on Russian bonds in 1998[5]).[6]

Profitability is also a function of banking practice. Though the lines are getting increasingly blurred, in part because Europe embraces universal banking rules, the banking sector is divided into the following four basic groups.

Commercial banks. Profit margins have been coming under pressure from the following issues:
➢ client demand for more extensive services,
➢ increasing global banking competition, and
➢ a shift in corporate financing away from bank loans to the debt markets. Over the first half of 1999, corporate debt issued in the bond markets grew by 79 percent.[7]

Investment banks. This more challenging banking environment has been a boon for large, established investment banks that already provide a wide range of sophisticated services:
➢ underwriting debt and equity offerings,
➢ advising on mergers and acquisitions, and
➢ creating and managing a range of financial products, such as mutual and pension funds.

Due to their experience and greater distribution, it has been the big American investment banks, led by Morgan Stanley Dean Witter and Goldman Sachs, that have taken the lion's share of the business in Europe.[8] The two banks together cornered 80 percent ($432.6 billion) of all European M&A activity over the first five months of 2000.[9]

Wholesale banks. This is the most limited group in the banking sector, usually serving as an extension of corporate or investment banking operations, providing loans for the very largest companies—the global 1,000—as well as arranging interbank borrowing. Search for larger margins has led some firms to offer finance for leveraged buyouts, which in turn could generate additional fees from M&A advice.[10]

Retail banks. Often involving a commercial component, retail banks have benefited the most from the structural shifts in European banking for several key reasons.

➤ Throughout deregulation and reform, they have maintained their leading branch networks, against which foreign institutions entering a domestic market cannot easily compete.

➤ Established brand names also help retail banks expand their customer base of households and small-to-midsize businesses.

➤ Their familiarity also promotes individual investor demand for their stocks.

➤ Retail banks enjoy the highest interest spreads, the difference between retail savings and lending rates.

➤ Retail banks are profiting significantly from the rapid expansion in the sale of mutual and pension funds, insurance policies, and the steady cash flow from credit card transactions.

➤ Technological improvements are directly lowering operational costs, especially through expansion of ATMs and Internet banking and investing. According to Carlos Pertejo, banking analyst at J.P. Morgan Securities in London, "banks with a strong focus on retail operations will outperform the sector because of their higher profitability and strong growth."[11]

The sector's most intriguing investment stories involve Europe's peripheral banks. In Italy BIPOP has transformed itself from a small regional bank into one of Europe's leading Internet and e-trading financial groups, propelling shares tenfold between 1998 and 1999. (See Chapter 9 for a more detailed analysis of this company.)

Another Italian success story is UniCredito. Created by the 1998 merger between Credito Italiano and the old Unicredito, the group is fulfilling the promise anticipated by Italy's membership in the common currency. It has become Italy's most profitable bank, with a return on equity of 19.57 percent in 1999, up from a paltry 1.2 percent in 1994. It is also Italy's most efficient bank, with a cost/income ratio of 53 percent in 1999, way down from 86 percent in 1994. This, along with a series of bank acquisitions, has helped spur remarkable EPS growth of 90 percent a year between 1995 and 1999. Shares have soared by an average of 45.5 percent a year between first quarter 1995 and first quarter 2000.[12]

Richard Coleman, banking analyst at Merrill Lynch, sees "UniCredito particularly well positioned to benefit from the Italian banking industry's improving fundamentals and the current momentum in consolidation and cross-border alliances." Anticipating further enhancements in "revenue flow, cost and quality control, and asset management," Coleman expects bank profits to rise substantially over the next three to five years, through 2004. And he ranks "UniCredito among the top banks in southern Europe."

Allied Irish Banks is Ireland's largest bank, controlling a 40 percent banking share in Europe's fastest-growing economy. It was the first Irish company to exceed pretax profits of €1 billion in 1998. A diversified portfolio has helped reduce risk while supporting strong earnings growth. Nearly one-third of AIB's profits are generated from U.S. operations, 10 percent from the United Kingdom, and 6 percent from Poland—one of the strongest emerging-market economies around.[13]

Although competition and lower interest rates drove net interest margins down from 3.82 to 3.27 percent between 1995 and 1999, AIB responded by becoming a more efficient bank, reducing its cost/income ratio from 66 percent to 57 percent. A compound annual earnings per share growth rate of 18 percent over the five years through 1999 helped propel shares up nearly 27 percent a year over the same time.

David Poutney, banking analyst at Panmure Gordon in London, expects the bank's future to remain bright. The bank's main markets remain strong, reducing the need to lend in more risky business segments.[14] And its dependence on interest revenue is steadily declining as the group increasingly relies on a more steady flow of fees from asset management and other financial products.

Between 1995 and 1999, the National Bank of Greece was the top-performing bank stock in Europe, rising an astonishing 66.30 percent annually in local currency terms. The bank pursued massive restructuring between 1995 and 1997, focusing on bad debt, asset and risk management, cost containment, leadership strategy, and corporate culture. The result, according to Charalambos Papademetriou, banking analyst at Intersec International Securities in Greece, is the transformation of NBG into the unchallenged market leader, controlling 41 percent of Greek banking deposits.[15]

Reform has made the bank more efficient. Its cost/income ratio fell dramatically, from 85.6 percent in 1997 to 45 percent in 1999. The bank's nonperforming loan ratio dropped from 14 percent in 1996 to 8 percent in 1999, while return on equity increased from the low teens to over 25 percent during the same period.[16] These improvements, coupled with broad growth of the Greek economy, have contributed to annual triple-digit EPS growth. Despite the huge appreciation in share price over the last half of the 1990s, Edward Fryer, banking analyst at ING Barings in London, believes the NBG's "long-term operational outlook is very positive."[17]

Run-up in NBG shares has also been part of the overall appreciation of Greek stocks in anticipation of the country's membership in the eurozone. Preparing for common currency sent interest rates down dramatically, converging toward European Central Bank rates and increasing the flow of foreign direct investment into Greece. This in turn has been a boon for banks, which have benefited from increased borrowing and strong growth in stock and mutual fund sales as investors continue to shift assets out of low-yielding savings accounts and into equities and bonds. EMU membership is also expected to speed up consolidation of the country's fragmented banking sector, favoring the country's largest banks.

In addition, NBG is benefiting from increased globalization of its shares. In December 1998, the stock became part of the FTSE Eurotop 300 Index, triggering automatic acquisitions by mutual fund managers tracking the index. The company's decision to adopt U.S. accounting standards is making its financials more transparent, while having paved the way for listing on the New York Stock Exchange in 1999—a move that has increased corporate news coverage and share ownership.

While the current economic environment augurs well for the continued growth in bank stocks, investors should keep their eyes on the following risks.

➤ The combination of European Commission directives and adoption of common currency should facilitate further domestic and cross-border consolidation; however, the resulting increase in competition will drive margins down.

➤ Accumulating larger market share through mergers and acquisitions and alliances will offset lower profits, but it will also expose banks to new, unfamiliar issues and risks associated with more open markets. Among the most blatant is the lack of harmonization between countries' basic banking regulations, especially in the retail sector.

➤ Threat of currency exchange loss within the eurozone is eliminated, but EMU has cut into a major source of revenue. According to consultants at the McKinsey Group, foreign exchange and deposits account for $100 billion in industry revenue. They estimate that while hardly eliminating the need for currency exchange, introduction of the euro will reduce foreign-exchange-related revenue by 25 percent.[18] Making up for that loss will be a challenge.

➤ Banks must also respond to the steady erosion of their base of inexpensive funding resulting from individuals continuously shifting assets out of savings accounts and into mutual funds and stocks. This will force banks increasingly to rely upon asset management—the fortunes of the stock market—to generate revenue.

➤ Europe's larger banks will feel the impact of upstarts like Italy's BIPOP-Carire that provide the convenience and cost savings of Internet banking and e-trading. Their own move into Web banking will subsequently cannibalize their branches as well. How this will pan out over the long run is a big unknown.

Perhaps the most significant risk is whether European banking can pull off a fundamental change in the way it does business. European banking culture has traditionally been driven more by "relationships" than by the American focus on the bottom line. In many instances, there is an incestuous connection between banks and corporations. Many banks hold large, often inefficient positions in clients' equity. This has led to preferred lower lending rates to finance corporate

Major Banking Acquisitions

($5 Billion and Greater—January 1998 through May 2000)

COUNTRY	COMPANIES (ACQUIRERS & TARGETS)	DATE	ANNOUNCED PRICE°
U.K.	Royal Bank of Scotland & NatWest	February 2000	$32.4 B
Switzerland	Union Bank of Switzerland & Swiss Bank	June 1998	$23.3 B
Spain	Banco Santander & Banco Central Hispano	May 1999	$16.6 B
France	Banque Nationale de Paris & Paribas	August 1999	$12.5 B
Germany	Bayerische Hypotheken und Wechselbank & Bayerische Vereinsbank	September 1998	$12.3 B
Spain	BBV & Argentaria	October 1999	$11.3 B
Belgium	Fortis & Générale de Banque	June 1998	$11.0 B
Italy	Credito Italiano & Unicredito	October 1998	$10.9 B
U.K./France	HSBC & CCF	April 2000	$10.5 B
Germany/ U.S.	Deutsche Bank & Bankers Trust	January 1999	$10.0 B
Italy	San Paolo Bank & IMI	November 1998	$8.5 B
Italy	Banca Intesa & BCI	July 1999	$8.4 B
Italy	Banca Nazionale del Lavoro & Banca di Napoli & Istituto Nazionale delle Assicurazione	June 1998	$6.4 B
Belgium	Kredietbank & CERA Bank	June 1998	$5.0 B

° For more recent deals, acquisition values may have changed

Sources: John Willman, "Fear of Becoming Takeover Candidates," *Financial Times* Survey of Banking in Europe, 26 May 2000, p II; and "European Banking Sector," Merck Finck & Co., 1998.

operations and expansion.

As we are witnessing in Germany, some of these relationships will be cut as tax reform enables corporations to unwind such large cross-shareholdings and reinvest capital more productively.

Still, this won't happen overnight. As banks further privatize, consolidate, and become more focused on shareholder value, greater profitability will be necessary to further propel Europe's banking shares.[19]

Insurance

FEW SUBJECTS GENERATE less excitement than insurance. Maybe it's because unlike all other businesses, insurance is inherently linked with bad news: car accidents, houses being blown apart by a tornado, death. And as Woody Allen put it in the closing scene in *Love and Death*, spending an evening with an insurance agent qualifies as one thing in life that's worse than death. It's hard to get folks interested in the sector—that is, until they see the kind of returns European insurers have been racking up over the past few years.

Between first quarter 1995 and first quarter 2000, insurance stocks generated total annualized returns of 34.2 percent in euro terms, and that's in spite of a slowdown over the previous twelve months, when the sector rose by 17.44 percent.[1] Then consider that insurers control nearly 50 percent of all financial assets in Europe.[2]

Several distinct forces have been driving up insurance shares through the mid and late 1990s. On the macro side, consider these two points:

➤ Insurance firms generally do well during periods of strong growth. Market penetration increases, as does the degree of coverage, because firms and individuals feel richer and have a greater need to protect their assets.

➤ A surge in private pension funding has opened up a steady flow of cash under management as well.

On the business side, there have been a number of operational improvements:

➤ Spread of information technology and reliance on more advanced communications are helping companies function more efficiently across larger regions.

➤ Enhanced speed and productivity have promoted aggressive expansion of European insurers beyond the region's borders into more profitable markets. ING, AEGON, and Fortis recently invested $17 billion in the U.S. insurance industry.

Key Findings

➤ Insurers control nearly 50 percent of all European financial assets, with the biggest European insurers being among the largest and most profitable in the world.

➤ Annualized 5-year returns through the first quarter of 2000 topped 34 percent in euro terms.

➤ The insurance sector is more volatile than the broad market, with recent behavior suggesting insurers are significantly affected by the bond market.

➤ Common currency and large foreign acquisitions are diversifying insurers' investment portfolios as well as their risks.

➤ European cross-border expansion has been limited to commercial nonlife products; the lack of tax harmonization has inhibited creation of a Pan-European life industry.

➤ The life industry is widely recognized as the sector's fastest-growing and most profitable segment, driven by the growing demand for private pension products in anticipation of underfunded government retirement programs.

➤ Insurers are restructuring and downsizing, spinning off unprofitable divisions, and consolidating core functions. These moves have specifically improved the balance sheet by reallocating the buildup of capital toward acquisitions, share buybacks, and increased dividends.

➤ Sales have been greatly enhanced through lower-cost bank distribution networks.

The bottom line is that industry deregulation and intensifying competition have focused attention on shareholder value, forcing insurers to become more profitable. Return on equity has virtually doubled since the early 1990s, ending the decade between 10 and 15 percent.[3]

Share prices have also been buoyed by insurers' increasing exposure to equity markets. And this is where the story gets particularly interesting.

"Contrary to the traditional view of insurance being a ho-hum play," observes Tim Dawson, insurance analyst at Credit Suisse First Boston in London, "insurance stocks are decisively more volatile than the broad market, especially during times of financial disturbance."

Why?

Dawson attributes it to "the sector's inherent gearing [or nondebt-related leverage] to the stock market, wherein a 10 percent shift in an insurer's balance sheet can translate into a 40 percent movement in shareholder capital."[4]

Whereas this exposure has generally translated into good news for many insurers, it's also a point of confusion for investors, as many believe these securities are driven instead by interest rates and the bond markets.

A brief look at the basics. Insurers make money two ways.

➤ One is through their core business based on premiums paid for life and nonlife (property and casualty) policies. If their actuarial tables predicting the frequency of accidents, natural disasters, and death are not too far off the mark, then insurers pocket the difference between what they've collected and what they've paid out.

➤ The second source of income is generated by the investments they make with policyholders' premiums and their own profits, the latter otherwise known as shareholder capital.

To make sure they can cover claims at any given time, insurers are pretty much committed to investing premiums, especially from far less predictable property and casualty policies, in secure fixed-income instruments—nothing exotic. Before the 1990s, insurers tended to reinvest life insurance premiums and their own profits in much the same way.

However, with the boom in equity markets across Europe and the collapse in interest rates leading up to common currency, insurers have dramatically increased their equity exposure. This has helped them realize huge capital appreciation—ergo, the concept of "gearing."[5] So we have a sector that profits from movements in both the bond and the stock markets.

The proportion of profits coming from core operations versus investments varies widely from insurer to insurer. A look at the 1997 profit-and-loss statement of the big, highly profitable Dutch insurer AEGON gives a sense of how important shareholder capital is to bottom-line performance. Nearly one-third of its pretax operating profits of 2.8 billion Dutch guilders was derived from its own investments.[6] It's this kind of exposure that scares the market out of the insurance sector during times of economic volatility.

But then, as mentioned earlier, there is the other school of thought that believes the market judges insurance stocks as mere proxies for the debt market because their operations are linked with bonds. It's little help to investors that such a pronouncement also comes from the same folks at Credit Suisse who told us about how leveraged insurers are to the stock market.

Their point is based more on market reaction than fundamental principle. For example, when long-term interest rates rose by nearly 20 percent in the first half of 1999, insurance stocks collapsed by a comparable amount. A CSFB sector report explained that "despite all arguments to the contrary, the insurance sector has time and again shown that the most important determinant of its performance appears to be interest rates and their impact on bond yields. Insurance stocks that do not appear to us to be particularly interest-rate sensitive have performed as if they were nothing but bond proxies."[7]

The previous comment is clearly focused on the impact of declining bond values on insurers. But since insurers usually select bond maturities to correspond with the time frame of specific liabilities, the issue of interim price fluctuations should be a relatively moot point. "But it hasn't been," explains Credit Suisse's Dawson, "because the market has pretty much been ignoring the complex relationship between insurers' real economic values and their market values." Actually, higher rates improve returns being earned on property and casualty premiums and enhance the spread between guarantees being paid on life policies and the interest actually earned by insurers.

The first-half 1999 market bailout also discounted the fact that insurers' own stock portfolios hadn't been particularly hurt by a rise in interest rates. Many analysts argued that the rate adjustment, in fact, helped set the stage for a renewed rise in equity values.

Another hole in the "bond proxy" argument was evident during the Russian economic crisis of 1998. With most major insurers maintaining only 5 percent exposure in the region, one might have expected that as bond proxies, insurance stocks would have held up as defensive plays, like the interest-sensitive utilities that did well during the summer and fall of 1998. Instead, insurance stocks got pounded, some losing up to half their value. By the end of the year, however, insurance stocks returned to their record highs as the market recognized its mistake.

Confusing? Absolutely.

But this is the bottom line for investors:

➤ The market has clearly decided to punish insurance shares during short-term spurts of volatility.

➤ However, over the long run, insurance stocks seem to offer uniquely positive exposure to both the bond and the equity markets.

➤ With the introduction of the euro having opened up securities markets in which European insurers can now invest (which had been largely limited to securities sold in an insurer's own currency), and with global acquisitions funneling in profits from faster-growing markets, insurance portfolios are becoming more diversified and profitable.

To make the smartest insurance play, it's essential for investors to understand the sector's underlying industries: property and casualty, reinsurance, and life insurance. Most insurers provide a combination of services. But diversity is not necessarily what investors should seek. As explained below, the best investments are those most heavily focused on life.

Property and Casualty

Property and casualty has been a highly competitive industry due to its inherently slow growth rate (comparable to a nation's GDP growth) and its highly fragmented character. There are simply too many insurers bidding after a finite amount of business. This condition was substantially triggered by the 1994 EU Insurance Directive, which opened up cross-border opportunities, and substantial appreciation of insurers' and shareholders' capital. This helped finance price wars, which resulted in unprofitable premiums.

Richard Urwick, head of Schroders Salomon Smith Barney European Financials group, says insurers racked up 40 percent annual returns in the early and mid-1990s. By the end of 1999, "property and casualty operations were actually losing €0.25 on every euro in premiums they were collecting."[9] This has proven very costly to firms that were heavily into property and casualty. The Italian insurer SAI is 81 percent weighted to property and casualty, and its stock appreciated by the paltry total of 19 percent in local currency terms over the five years preceding the end of first quarter 2000.[10]

The big insurers with significant property and casualty business, such as Europe's largest insurer Allianz, can better manage the industry's highly cyclical nature, explains Urwick, through geographic diversity and cross-subsidization from other activities and investments. Though it generates 57 percent of its premiums from property and casualty, Allianz has been able to maintain strong double-digit earnings growth, which propelled its shares by nearly 30 percent annually over five years through the first quarter of 2000.[11]

Smaller, undercapitalized firms tend to become takeover targets. Subsequent consolidation will ease competition, permitting premiums to return to more economic levels. But for the foreseeable future, most analysts do not recommend significant investment exposure to property and casualty.

Reinsurance

The reinsurance industry is dominated by large, sophisticated firms that insure specific pieces of an existing policy originally underwritten by a primary insurer. The purpose: to help reduce overall risks to primary insurers.

A primary carrier typically needs reinsurance when it provides coverage to a huge corporation, such as a major automobile company. Because of a car company's size, this kind of coverage exposes the insurer to a concentrated industry liability. To reduce this risk, the primary would insure a portion of its own liability by securing selective coverage from a reinsurer. Reinsurers may also directly insure one-time projects, such as a satellite launch.

Although some large insurers, such as AXA and Zurich Financial Services, have reinsurance operations, four companies dominate the European reinsurance market: Swiss RE, Munich RE, Hannover RE, and France's SCOR.

Like the rest of the insurance industry, reinsurance shares experienced accelerated growth in 1997 and through much of 1998. But they plummeted by an average of 20 percent in the wake of the Russian financial crisis. During the first half of 1999, the steady rise in long-term interest rates further cut into valuations.

During the five years through the first quarter of 2000, reinsurance shares performed very well. Munich RE and Swiss RE paced the way, having soared by an annualized rate of 41.6 and 32 percent, respectively, in local currency terms. SCOR shares rose by an average of 28.4 percent a year, while Hannover RE shares gained nearly 25 percent annually.[12]

However, Goldman Sachs is cautious about the industry's long-term outlook. The firm sees consolidation and asset expansion of primary insurers reducing their need to outsource risk. In addition, primary insurers' experimentation with policy securitization—a means of re-allocating risk and raising capital during volatile times when credit markets threaten to choke off the flow of funds to primaries—may further cut into reinsurers' growth.[13] Analysts at Credit Suisse First Boston have more confidence in the big reinsurers, projecting five-year-earnings growth to remain strong, in the low double digits.[14]

Life Insurance
The sector's top-performing stocks have a strong concentration in life insurance. Analysts recommend that portfolios with insurance exposure be overweighted in these stocks.

From the first quarter of 1995 through the first quarter of 2000, life insurance shares generated annualized returns of 46.09 percent in euro terms.[15] Sweden's Skandia led the way with five-year gains that challenged the earth's gravitational pull, rocketing nearly 80 percent a year. Dutch insurer AEGON didn't do quite so well; its highly rated shares appreciated a mere 57.5 percent a year. And the Italian *bancassurance* company Mediolanum rose by more than 92 percent annually during its first three years after going public in June 1996.[16]

Broad economic growth has increased underwriting premiums and the rate at which investors have been saving. At the same time, industry consolidation has been generating enhanced economies of scale.

However, the life insurance industry has been booming primarily as a result of two fundamental factors affecting global as well as European markets:

➤ The first is demographics. Baby boomers are in the prime money-making stage of their careers, stimulating demand for insurance products.

➤ The second trend involves the rush to create private retirement plans. With the likelihood that traditional government pension systems will be severely underfunded by the time baby boomers retire, many have started to plow savings into their own private retirement accounts, largely managed by insurers. According to the brokerage firm Dresdner Kleinwort Benson, if governments pursue pension reform, private plans could generate an additional flow of $4 trillion into Europe's capital markets by the year 2010.

Life insurers are also benefiting from a shift in the life insurance plans that clients are setting up. The traditional "discretionary management" program, which still predominates in Europe, involves insurers guaranteeing a minimum return (3 to 4 percent) plus the potential of an annual bonus that's generated from invested premiums. On average, policyholders would keep approximately 90 percent of net investment returns; insurers would keep the rest.[18]

Insurers are exposed to substantial market risks not only because their earnings are linked to the performance of the securities markets but also due to industry regulations that require them to put a minimum of 4 percent of their own assets into the same investments purchased by their policyholders' premiums. However, insurers are bene-

Premium Income Split of the Largest European Insurers

INSURER	COUNTRY	LIFE INSURANCE*	NONLIFE INSURANCE*	5-YEAR CUM. RETURNS THRU 3/31/00†	MARKET CAP 3/31/00
AEGON	Netherlands	85%	15%	787.1%	€55.8 B
ING	Netherlands	84	16	350.0	54.7 B
AXA	France	73	27	367.5	52.8 B
CGNU	U.K.	52	48	183.9	19.2 B
Munich RE	Germany	47	53	468.5	60.5 B
Swiss RE	Switzerland	29	71	301.2	26.7 B
Allianz	Germany	34	66	267.7	104.4 B
Zurich Fin. Serv.	Switzerland	32	68	279.2	46.7 B

Source: Robin Buckley, Credit Suisse First Boston; and "European Company Performance Survey," *Financial Times* Survey of the European Performance League, 23 June 2000, p. IV.

* Premium income split as of year-end 1999   † Returns are in local-currency terms

Major Insurance Acquisitions

(Greater than $5 Billion—1998 through May 2000)

COUNTRY	COMPANIES (ACQUIRERS & TARGETS)	DATE	ANNOUNCED PRICE*
Netherlands/U.S.	AEGON & Transamerica	February 1999	$11.81 B
U.K.	CGU & Norwich Union	February 2000	11.58 B
U.K.	CGU & General Accident	March 1998	10.64 B
U.K.	Lloyds TSB & Scottish Widows Fund and Life	July 1999	10.60 B
Germany/France	Allianz & Assurances Générales de France	February 1998	10.30 B
U.K./U.S.	ING & ReliaStar Fin.	May 2000	6.10 B
U.K.	Sun Life and Provincial Holdings & Guardian Royal Exchange	February 1999	5.46 B

Source: Bloomberg

* For more recent deals, acquisition values may have changed.

fiting from an increasing shift to life policies backed by variable annu-ities. In the United Kingdom, 70 percent of life policies now use VAs, but on the Continent the percent is much less. In Germany, for instance, by the end of the 1990s only 15 percent of life policies involved variable annuities. But the proportion is changing rapidly.

Variable annuities are reducing insurers' risk by eliminating the need to put up investment capital, which boosts their return on equity. What's more, income based on a more steady flow of flat management fees is increasing economies of scale: revenue increases with minimal additional cost through asset appreciation, additional contributions to variable annuities, and acquisitions of competing life insurers.[19]

Simply put, the critical need for individuals across Europe to devel-op their own retirement plans is transforming life insurance into a growth industry. With market penetration still very low in southern and eastern Europe, the prospects for substantial industry expansion appear very bright.

However, there are two caveats. First, the lack of tax harmonization across Europe is preventing life insurers from effectively reaching across borders. This condition will sustain inefficiencies and prevent consumers from locking into the most profitable policies. Second, investors can only keep up the current pace of savings if European economies remain strong.

Retail

ON THE SURFACE, retailing may seem to be an unlikely sector to generate big stock returns. Operating margins are traditionally in the single digits. A continuous barrage of domestic and cross-border mergers is intensifying an already competitive marketplace, squeezing margins even further. And to add just a dash more pessimism to the profit picture, Wal-Mart—the true beast of discount retailing—has locked its focus on Europe, securing beachheads in Germany and England, directly challenging retailers' basic business models.

Some companies are scurrying into acquisitions out of sheer fear of being outmaneuvered in their own markets. Yet, remarkably, the sale and consumption of European retail goods over the last half of the 1990s generated very solid returns. Through the first quarter of 2000, general retail stocks gained nearly 19 percent annually in euro terms over the previous five years: food and drug shares appreciated by nearly 21 percent, and household goods and textiles climbed an average of 27 percent a year.[1]

Some of the reasons behind retail's strong performance will sound like the familiar virtuous circle. Stores have been gaining greater efficiency through corporate restructuring and a clearer focus on core activities. Acquisitions are sewing up domestic markets for the biggest players, enhancing cash flow and economies of scale as they break into fractured foreign markets. As they evolve into global players, European retailers are seeing their shares rerated at higher multiples. Rising market capitalization has subsequently pushed some of these stocks into major equity indices. Also, with retailers' increasing focus on shareholder value, demand for these shares has risen substantially.

Retailing's strong performance is testimony to European economic rejuvenation, not just in terms of enhanced efficiency and geographic reach of some of the world-class retail operators but also in the increasing spending power of households across much of the region. Two of the eurozone's largest economies, France and the United Kingdom,

Key Findings

➤ Five-year annualized returns of this low-margin sector were an impressive 21.91 percent through March 2000.

➤ Major trends: consolidation of domestic market share, mergers and acquisitions, cost cutting, and globalization.

➤ Extensive domestic and international acquisition has transformed European food retailers into nine of the world's ten largest operations.

➤ Wal-Mart's initial foray into Europe is triggering significant restructuring and consolidation.

➤ Retailers remain largely indifferent to the potential and threats of e-commerce, despite projections that 15 percent of all sales will be generated through the Web by the year 2015.

➤ Recommendations: Intense competition will leave only the largest and most efficient retailers on top; conglomerates offer some of the strongest plays in the sector, led by PPR and Kingfisher, while smartly run niche players, such as Sweden's Hennes & Mauritz, will also continue to excel over the long term.

saw domestic retail spending rise by an annual average of 2.8 percent and 4.7 percent, respectively, through most of the 1990s.[2]

However, because of the sector's diversity, investors need to understand retailing's constituent industries: food, department stores, apparel, electrical goods, do-it-yourself (home improvements), furniture, and conglomerates that deal in a variety of these businesses. Each industry also has distinct margins and supply chain issues.

Investors then need not only to target the best-run companies in the fastest-growing industries but to identify those that are also consolidating domestic market share and showing ability to expand profitably abroad. The latter is no easy task given the inherent cultural differences that have traditionally inhibited cross-border ventures. Mastering the French market hardly assured success when in 1991 Galerie Lafayette decided to open in New York City. In fact, just several years after setting up shop on 57th Street, the venerable Gallic department-store giant was gone.

A brief look at some of the top-performing European retailers and their respective industries reveals some of the basic features that can help a stock take off.

Food

The food industry is the largest segment within the retail sector, accounting for approximately €793 billion, one-third of total annual retail sales.[3] Nine out of the ten largest food retailers in the world are European.[4]

While the industry has among the lowest profit margins in retailing, topping out at 5 to 6 percent, its huge scale and additional economies gained through mergers have triggered extensive consolidation. The most notable deals in 1999 were Wal-Mart's $10.7 billion acquisition of Britain's third-largest supermarket group, Asda, adding to the group's already monstrous economies of scale; and the $17 billion merger of France's leading players, Carrefour and Promodès, forming the world's second-largest food retailer.

Quietly building up a highly profitable global portfolio has been Netherlands-based Ahold, with 1999 global sales of €33.6 billion and net earnings of €766 million. EPS growth was up 21.4 percent. This was well ahead of the company's historic earnings expansion rate of 15 to 20 percent, driven by its aggressive acquisition strategy both at home and abroad.[5]

Sidestepping western Europe, where individual country markets are often difficult to break into due to high valuations and an already large degree of domestic consolidation, Ahold has built up a substantial stake in the United States, where the industry is more fragmented. Unknown to most Americans, Ahold has become the country's fourth-largest food retailer, with U.S. sales of $18.5 billion.

Recent U.S. acquisitions included Giant and US Foodservice, reflecting Ahold's strategy of buying into established, undervalued franchises and generating greater economies and improved cost efficiencies. The result: U.S. sales now account for 55 percent of total sales and almost 63 percent of operating profits.[6] This helped propel Ahold's stock price 28.1 percent annually in euro terms for the five years through March 2000.[7]

Electronics

A new generation of TV, video, and audio electronics is providing a boost to this €100 billion industry, which is expected to push sales growth well above the average retail rate over the next several years.[8] Unfortunately, there are a limited number of publicly traded companies focused on electronics.

Dixons of the United Kingdom is among the industry's top stock plays, having turned in one of Europe's best returns of all stocks over the five-year period through March 2000, soaring 51.42 percent annually in local currency terms.[9]

A key driving force behind the company's meteoric rise was its flotation of the United Kingdom's first free Internet access service, Freeserve. However, the IPO's subsequent volatility in response to the launch of other free service providers has made shares in Dixons track more like an Internet stock.

Nevertheless, Dixons's shares are ultimately underpinned by the company's dominance in Britain's electronics market. Sales nearly doubled between 1995 and 1999, exceeding £3.15 billion. Profits rose even faster, up 122 percent to more than £200 million, as margins moved up from 5.5 to 6.4 percent.[10]

Despite its lack of foreign ventures and Wal-Mart's incursion into its own home market, Dixons's shares are likely to continue to excel. The company's 27 percent industry share, coupled with what Morgan Stanley Dean Witter describes as an insightful and proactive management, should help the company profit significantly from consumer transition from analog to digital products and the run-up in mobile phones and Internet-driven computer sales. This will assist Dixons to weather the deflationary forces that are cutting far more dramatically into smaller electronic retailers.[11]

Apparel

The apparel industry is the second-largest segment of the retail sector in western Europe, with annual sales of €250 billion.[12] Like the electronics industry, there are few publicly traded apparel stocks on the

Continent. The bulk of industry shares are U.K.-based stores. Their domestic focus reflects the difficulties of exporting designs elsewhere and their limited growth potential.

Despite those impediments, in the late 1990s there was one extraordinary European apparel story: Sweden's Hennes & Mauritz. As the *Financial Times* explains, "H&M is benefiting from a Wal-Mart-like virtuous circle: an everyday low-price strategy fueling market share gains, which in turn feed unmatchable economies of scale."[13] Its stock soared 69.15 percent annually for the five years through March 2000 (making it the sixth-best-performing stock in the FTSE Europe Index), having propelled its market cap beyond €21 billion.[14]

The company has hit it huge by focusing on the latest top designs for the thirty-five-and-under crowd, sourcing them out to low-cost foreign manufacturers and bringing them to market quickly and inexpensively. Its basic strategy is to move into a niche market and dominate it. Toward this end, H&M does two particularly unusual things to pump up sales: it relies on supermodels to promote its latest runway designs, and it shifts buying decisions away from a centralized source to the individual stores, which can respond quickly to the latest consumer demands.

Analysts are likening H&M's success to that of the GAP in its ability to export a well-focused business model to key international markets, reflecting a key retail phenomenon: the globalization of fashion trends. In 1995, 73 percent of sales were foreign; by 1999, the figure was up to 84 percent and will go higher with current expansion into the U.S. and Spanish markets.[15]

With foreign margins actually larger than those in Hennes' & Mauritz's home market, total operating margins broke through 15 percent in 1999—extraordinary for a mid-to-low-end retailer. This helped push profits up nearly 260 percent between 1995 and 1999, to SKr 4.76 billion.[16]

However, in the second quarter of 2000, the stock plummeted. The cost of aggressive expansion, a substantial foreign-exchange-rate hit, a fashion miss in women's wear, and perhaps the market's wariness of supporting a P/E rating that resembles a high-tech start-up ended up knocking nearly 50 percent off its share price.[17] (See Chapter 9 for further information on H&M.)

Conglomerates

The appeal of investing in multi-industry operations, or conglomerates, is their ability to alter their exposure to the fastest-growing segments of the market. And since conglomerates are large-cap stocks, they have the ability to corner significant industry share across a sizable region. However, two key problems confront European investors:

➤ conglomerates are not known for individual unit transparency, making it difficult for analysts to accurately discern specific performance trends; and

➤ the playing field is limited to three choices: Metro, Pinault Printemps Redoute (PPR), and Kingfisher.

Metro. German-based Metro is Europe's dominant diversified retailer, with 1999 sales of €43.8 billion. When it was first privatized in 1996, its shares rose steadily, more than doubling through the middle of 1998. But since then, the stock has been on a slide, having lost half its value in less than two years.[18] To halt the collapse and gain greater focus and efficiency, management began slashing away at one-third of Metro's turnover. The goal: to consolidate fourteen business segments down to five core units: cash-and-carry (wholesale—33 percent of sales), food (20 percent of sales), department stores (12 percent), electronics (12 percent), and do-it-yourself (DIY) (9 percent). Despite these changes, falling margins and flat sales in both its food and its DIY operations have kept pressure on Metro's shares. While this has led to a fairly inexpensive-looking stock, market uncertainty continues to expose shares to further hits.

Pinault Printemps Redoute. Paris-based PPR has been an extraordinary performer. The share price of the €23 billion conglomerate—involved in professional electronic products, leisure goods, furnishings, mail order, and luxury goods—soared 535 percent over the five-year period through the first quarter of 2000.[19] Since its subsequent victory in the battle for Gucci, analysts have been increasingly bullish on the stock, citing support for the company's continued commitment to high-margin luxury goods acquisitions, e-commerce, the spin-off of mature businesses, and its increasingly global market share. More than half of PPR's sales are outside France.

"One of PPR's major strengths," observes retail analyst Eric Biassette of ING Barings in Paris, "is its ability to acquire companies with substantial growth prospects, such as Rexel in 1990 and FNAC in 1994."[20] PPR has a strong track record of adding value to such investments through improved capital management—that is, shifting excess cash generated by one unit to help support development of another.[21] And this strategy helped propel EPS by more than 26 percent a year between 1995 and 1999.

Kingfisher. An unfamiliar name outside of Europe, Kingfisher ranks among the world's top ten retailers, focused on do-it-yourself (DIY), electrical, and general merchandising. FY 1999 sales reached nearly £7.5 billion, a figure that appeared likely to rise by nearly 50 percent in the following fiscal year as a result of acquisitions.[22]

Among the most notable deals, Kingfisher consolidated its lead in the DIY segment of its business by pulling off a creative acquisition. By agreeing to sell its own successful DIY unit, B&Q, to French industry leader Castorama in exchange for 58 percent of the enlarged French company, Kingfisher created a company twice the size of the nearest competitor, with annual sales of €5.5 billion. With new huge economies spread over a much larger market place, Castorama should see profits rise substantially.

Recent electrical unit acquisitions in the Benelux region and Germany have propelled Kingfisher into the Continent's top spot in the industry. This has led Merrill Lynch to conclude that "the real excitement with Kingfisher shares is the growing realization that the group is laying the foundation for a credible Pan-European business in both DIY and electrical retailing."[23] This helped drive shares up 265 percent during the five years through March 2000.[24]

The largest immediate risk to the stock is Wal-Mart's entrance into its home turf. As it restructures Asda to compete more directly with Kingfisher's general merchandising and electrical stores, Wal-Mart will most likely be able to exploit its huge scale advantages. According to Richard Edwards, retail analyst at Salomon Smith Barney in London, this prospect "presents a long-run strategic challenge to Kingfisher's businesses that will be hard to avoid."[25]

Some Additional Issues

While Wal-Mart's move into Europe may bring about some of the most significant changes in European retailing, investors should also be mindful of the effects the euro, e-commerce, and information technology will be having on retail operations and bottom lines.

Euro. In 2002, investors should expect retail margins to weaken as the result of the one-time costs associated with final conversion of local currencies to the euro. Sector analysts at Deloitte Consulting expect the costs of conversion to range from 1.3 to 2.6 percent of sales. Some international retailers will be hit by price transparency, revealing not just their individual countries' high tax rates and labor costs but also their own significant markups.

On the plus side, supply costs should fall as wholesale price transparency increases retailers' ability to bargain shop throughout the twelve eurozone nations. Currency risks and exchange transaction costs associated with payables and receivables will be eliminated for those dealing with eurozone-based companies.[26]

Yet the biggest benefit brought by EMU to the retail industry is substantially lower interest rates, especially in the area's peripheral higher-growth countries. This has not only reduced retailers' operating and expansion costs but significantly improved the credit environment for shoppers as well.

Internet commerce. As we are seeing in the United States, e-commerce is fundamentally changing the way retailers are looking at the Internet. E-commerce is realizing the potential of trading in the traditional high bricks-and-mortar expense for this far more efficient means of selling. At the same time, the Internet also offers managers a means to shop more efficiently for their own inventory.

Yet retailers at this time seem more concerned about Internet sales cannibalizing their own in-store turnover. As Keith Wills of Goldman Sachs in London sees it, "European retailers have shown a real lack of willingness to accept the Internet as an alternative channel to the consumer."[27]

This sets up a huge competitive problem for retailers holding back from the Net. Foreign players are beginning to enter into their domestic markets, unencumbered by high rents, offering consumers tremendous savings on a full range of everyday products that don't require shoppers' in-store presence. While Internet penetration in western European households in 1999 was less than one-third of that in the States (11.6 percent versus 38.5 percent), European retailers are already beginning to lose sales to the likes of Amazon.com, CDNow, and Gap Inc.[28] They will also see their margins squeezed by pending

Recent Large Retail Mergers and Acquisitions
(January 1998 through March 2000)

ACQUIRER	INDUSTRY	TARGET	ACQUISITION VALUE*	ANNOUNCED
Carrefour (Fr.)	Food	Promodès (France)	$17.00 B	Aug. 1999
Wal-Mart (U.S.)	Food	Asda (U.K.)	$10.70 B	June 1999
Ahold (Neth.)	Food	US Foodservice (U.S.)	$3.60 B	Mar. 2000
Ahold (Neth.)	Food	Giant Food (U.S.)	$2.60 B	May 1998
PPR (Fr.)	Conglomerate	Gucci Group (Italy)	€2.68 B	Mar. 1999
Numico (Neth.)	Food	Gen'l Nutrition (U.S.)	$2.49 B	July 1999
Ahold (Neth.)	Food	ICA Group (Sweden)	$1.83 B	Dec. 1999
KBB (Neth.)	Conglomerate	Vendex (Netherlands)	$1.10 B	Feb. 1998
PPR (Fr.)	Conglomerate	Guilbert (France)	FF4.69 B	Jan. 1998

* For recent deals, acquisition value may have changed.

price wars and the need to spend more money on customer service to entice shoppers into their stores. Investors, therefore, need to watch not only the pace of Internet penetration into various European markets but also how retailers respond to this challenge to their core businesses.

Just how real is this threat? Analysts at Goldman Sachs project European Internet sales to escalate from negligible levels in 1999 to 15 percent of the retail market by 2015.[29]

Information technology. Retail earnings growth depends upon two simple factors: cost cutting and market expansion. And the adoption of information technology is playing a critical role in both matters.

With profit margins in the single digits, reducing the cost of doing business is just as critical as expanding market share. New IT systems are helping in a variety of ways. Increasing use of loyalty cards helps retailers track and correlate consumer spending patterns and demographics. Better inventory control ensures a faster rate of turnover and less waste. In addition, new data-sharing between retailers and suppliers, even with manufacturers, is helping the industry respond more efficiently to consumer demands, thus driving up sales.

Exporting a business model to new foreign markets—that is, setting up new shops run by local management—has always been handicapped by the slow flow of information back to the home office. All

Growth in Consumer Spending in the
Eurozone and the United States: 1996–2000

	1996	1997	1998	1999	2000*
Eurozone	1.5%	1.5%	3.0%	2.5%	3.1%
Belgium	0.7	2.2	3.8	2.0	2.7
Germany	0.7	0.8	2.1	2.1	2.6
Netherlands	4.0	2.6	4.1	4.2	3.5
Spain	2.0	2.9	4.1	4.4	3.4
France	1.3	0.1	3.4	2.3	3.0
Italy	1.2	3.0	2.3	1.7	2.3
United States	3.2	3.4	4.9	5.3	5.7

* Estimates

Source: ING Barings

that is beginning to change as new IT systems are keeping top management homed in on the latest sales, costs, and inventory figures almost as soon as they are generated in each venue. In addition to ensuring that local management is following company strategy, data sharing helps retailers maximize economies of scale by coordinating purchases from their suppliers.

What does this all mean to investors?

IT networks reveal that smart, profitable retailing is as much about information, and what one does with that information, as it is about products. It's no surprise, then, to find that Wal-Mart is the master of such technology. Other big competitors are beginning to follow. Companies that don't have the resources to install such systems or that don't believe in such aggressive oversight are probably stocks best avoided.

Telecommunication Services

TELECOMMUNICATION SERVICES WAS the second-hottest-performing sector on the Continent for the year through the first quarter of 2000, soaring 86.8 percent in euro terms. Only the telecom-related Information Technology Hardware shares, including the likes of Nokia, Ericsson, and Alcatel, did better.

An extraordinary year. But nothing new.

European telecoms averaged returns of 50.72 percent over the five-

Key Findings

➤ Deregulation, breakup of state-run monopolies, perforation of national barriers, and technological innovation have transformed telecommunication services into one of Europe's top-performing sectors.

➤ Between the first quarter of 1995 and the first quarter of 2000, the sector registered annualized gains of 50.72 percent in euro terms.

➤ Although mergers and acquisitions are increasingly blurring this division, the sector is comprised of three basic parts: incumbents (former state monopolies), alternative carriers (a hybrid group of fiber-optic service providers, resellers, industrial conglomerates, and foreign competitors), and mobile operators.

➤ Telecommunications is being increasingly driven by the demand for data and Internet access, especially through mobile networks, which are expected to dominate the sector in the coming years.

➤ Topping off its acquisition spree with buyouts of AirTouch Communications and Mannesmann, Vodafone has clearly established itself as the dominant wireless player worldwide; its shares soared by more than 68 percent a year over the five years through the first quarter of 2000.

year period through the first quarter of 2000, establishing Europe's service operators as among the world's best telecom investments.[1]

Even better, there's nothing on the horizon to suggest an end to the good news. As an article in *Euroweek* aptly put it, "The telecom industry has captured the hearts and minds of international investors in a way not seen since the railway boom of the late nineteenth century."[2]

As markets continue to liberalize and technology is unleashed across Europe's increasingly more open and competitive marketplace, demand for voice, cable, and data transmission services—especially via the

Internet—will likely outpace growth in other sectors. "Demand is not merely growing, it is exploding," explains a Morgan Stanley Dean Witter industry report, "and costs are not just falling, they are collapsing."[3]

The Yankee Group Europe, an industry consulting firm, expects Internet access to expand by 186 percent between 1998 and 2001 and mobile subscribers to increase by 113 percent over the same period, with market penetration of more than half the population of western Europe as of the millennium. Meanwhile, data traffic, which has been expanding by 50 percent a year,[4] has already overtaken voice usage, with data revenue expected to do the same by 2003.[5]

Although technological innovation drives the sector, the key to its explosive performance dates back to January 1, 1998. That's when the European Commission required member countries to begin deregulating their telecom markets. Save for Portugal, Greece, and Ireland, who required additional time to liberalize, this has meant the end of state-controlled monopolies, the creation of more open and competitive markets, and cheaper service.

This was a radical change, for European governments have traditionally run most essential services.

But now, industry giants like Deutsche Telekom and France Telecom no longer hold exclusive control over their respective markets. Not only are they required to sell line access to competitors at regulated prices that afford new carriers ample room for profit, but national borders no longer shield them from foreign competitors, who may now qualify for domestic operating licenses in any country. Telecoms based in London can now service residential customers in Rome; those in Madrid can provide Internet access to companies in Brussels.

What all this will mean to Europe has been foreshadowed by the British experience—the first national system to deregulate back in 1984. Though the former monopoly, British Telecom, was forced to lay off tens of thousands of workers to compete in an increasingly more aggressive marketplace, phone service improved and rates fell drastically. Rapid growth in telecom traffic opened up opportunities for all sorts of new players, generating jobs, revenues, and profits that have more than made up for the losses associated with BT's restructuring.[6] Among the new participants was a mobile operator named Vodafone.

What has this meant for British Telecom and its investors? *The Economist* says it has enabled BT to be one of the first incumbents to "make the change from a plodding giant to an agile service provider."[7] The company's stock returns have soared. BT was the best performing of all the former state monopolies, with annualized returns of 33.16 percent for the five years through the first quarter of 1999.[8]

However, since then, through the first quarter of 2000, many of the other national incumbents have caught up, led by Dutch KPN (up 231 percent), France Telecom (up 145 percent), Deutsche Telekom (up 126 percent), and Tele Danmark and Spain's Telefónica (both up 110 percent).[9]

It now requires a scorecard of sorts to understand the expanding number of players and services of a sector that was recently limited to state-run operators delivering simple voice transmission. According to Jason Holzer, portfolio comanager of AIM's European Development Fund, telecommunication services can be broken down into three basic parts: incumbents, alternative carriers, and mobile operators.

Incumbents

The former state monopolies, commonly referred to as incumbents, lost up to 30 percent of their long-distance revenues within the first year of deregulation. Nevertheless, the likes of Deutsche Telekom, France Telecom, and British Telecom have remained the big boys on the block, with distinct competitive advantages:

➤ comprehensive networks of voice, data, and mobile services,
➤ superior access to customers,
➤ trusted brand names,
➤ long-standing business relationships,
➤ political influence,
➤ strong cash flow, and
➤ experience.

All of these benefits were the result of the incumbents' previous monopolistic positions in the market.[10] As a result, five of the six top-performing telecom shares from the first quarter 1999 through the first quarter 2000 were former state monopolies.

Still, many of these giants are handicapped by leaden government roots. Risk-averse bureaucracies with bloated payrolls are characteristics that will persist as long as governments retain influence over operations. Perhaps it's little surprise that in a sector where swift decision-making is essential—especially when it comes to committing to the latest technology and corporate alliances—new private telecoms are emerging as sector leaders.

No one single event signified the changing of the guard more dramatically than Olivetti's audacious, highly leveraged takeover of Italy's former state phone operator. Telecom Italia was the fifth-largest fixed-line and mobile group in the world, five times the size of this formerly also-ran computer maker, with the largest market capitalization of any Italian stock.

In October 1997, when the Italian government sold off shares of TI, the deal was regarded as "the mother of all privatizations." But the failure to secure a strategic investor to exercise substantial control over the company resulted in a highly diverse and fractured shareholder base, leaving it vulnerable to outside players.[11]

Management had already begun to restructure operations, making TI more competitive. But the company was struggling with the transition from government to private telecom operator, lacking strategic focus and a sound long-term business plan. Specifically, it was slow in revamping an expensive, complex, and inefficient cost structure. Leadership turmoil made TI resemble the Italian government more than a corporate powerhouse. Over a period of twelve months between 1997 and 1998, the company went through three chairmen.[12]

The company's last chief, Franco Bernabe, was appointed in November 1998. He seemed like the right man for the job, having proven himself as an expert in turning around underperforming assets. But Olivetti pounced before Bernabe barely got his seat warm.

In restructuring Olivetti from a mediocre manufacturer of computers and office equipment into an increasingly profitable cellular and fixed-line provider, CEO Roberto Colaninno saw the opportunity to instantly transform the company into a major integrated telecom operator in one dramatic step. His successful $33.3 billion bid, choreographed by a network of U.S. investment bankers and supported by Italy's key power brokers and bankers, woke up corporate Europe to the fact that it indeed had crossed the Rubicon. The Continent's accustomed order was turned upside down. Even huge former state industries are now fair game for corporate raiders of any size—a reality that has since fractured a number of uneasy telecom alliances and partnerships that evolved in the aftermath of deregulation.[13]

Alternative Carriers

In contrast with the rather homogeneous character of former state telephone companies, alternative carriers are comprised of a diverse group of operators. These include firms that are building their own new fiber-optic Pan-European networks, such as Colt and Global TeleSystems, and other companies known as resellers, such as MobilCom, that own virtually no infrastructure of their own and instead lease line space from incumbent telecoms or from new carriers.

Alternative carriers also include big conglomerates, such as France's Vivendi Universal and Germany's Mannesmann (now Vodafone), that restructured their complex mix of industrial operations, having sold off loss-making ventures and moved into the more profitable telecom industry through joint ventures and acquisitions.

Then there are large foreign competitors, such as MCI WorldCom, that are buying out existing operators, then funding their expansion and subsequent integration with other acquisitions.

While the diversity of this group makes it difficult to generalize about their characteristics, there are a few common traits.

➤ Alternative carriers usually benefit from reliance on new, cutting-edge systems, unencumbered by older, slower lines.

➤ Because many of these new networks are being built around the specific needs and commitments of new clients, financial risks are minimized.

➤ However, without proven cash flow and with limited industry recognition, start-up debt is often of "junk" status, requiring high yields to attract investors.

Similarly, on the equity side, investors demand fast growth and high multiples to justify the risk. In response, carriers, in turn, often pursue aggressive ventures to significantly alter their bottom lines. Olivetti pulled this off in one highly charged move. Before being bought out by Vodafone, Mannesmann was demonstrating how an alternative carrier could become one of Europe's most important telecoms through a more methodical strategy.

By acquiring majority positions in Germany and Italy and minority holdings in France and Austria, "Mannesmann had assembled the most strategically important set of telecom assets in Europe," according to Merrill Lynch telecom analyst Christopher McFadden.[14] This helps explain why Vodafone was so eager to absorb and remove Mannesmann from the scene, especially after the German conglomerate established a foothold in Vodafone's home turf through the purchase of successful U.K. mobile operator Orange.

Mobile Operators

With mobile usage expected to more than double over the next several years and with penetration to exceed 50 percent of western European households, mobile operators will potentially experience the greatest growth within the telecom sector. "The mobile industry is expanding exponentially," observes John Jensen, telecom analyst at Salomon Smith Barney.[15] And a *Financial Times* industry survey projects that "soon most people's primary phone service will be mobile."[16]

Technological innovation and market deregulation are dramatically cutting the cost of usage. But several other structural factors are also driving expansion.

➤ Unlike the United States, western Europe has adopted a single standard platform, GSM, integrating mobile operations across the Continent.

➤ There are also fewer mobile operators, reducing the complexity of network integration.

➤ Along the periphery of Europe, in the less developed regions of Portugal, Greece, and southern Italy where there are poor or no fixed lines, mobile has become a more efficient means of providing basic telephone service. Its infrastructure costs are one-third less than fixed-line networks, taking one-third the time to build.[17]

Rapid expansion of mobile usage has led to the proliferation of mobile investment opportunities. France Telecom's acquisition of U.K. mobile operator Orange (formerly a part of Mannesmann but demerged after Vodafone acquired the German telecom) now makes the Gallic incumbent the Continent's second-largest mobile service provider, with $110 billion in wireless assets. A planned spin-off of FT's entire mobile operations will create a very well financed player with a projected market capitalization of $150 billion.[18]

But there's no more intriguing wireless story than U.K.-based Vodafone.[19]

The company catapulted from regional mobile player to world

Telecommunication Services Performance
(Through March 31, 2000)

COMPANY	COUNTRY	1-YEAR RETURNS°	5-YEAR CUM. RETURNS°	MARKET CAP 3/31/00
KPN	Neth.	231.4%	790.5%	€57.2 B
GN Store Norden	Denmark	202.4	686.9	3.5
France Telecom	France	144.5	NA	184.4
Deutsche Telekom	Germany	125.6	NA	255.1
Telefónica	Spain	109.9	934.8	86.1
Tele Danmark	Denmark	109.6	486.2	19.8
Telecom Italia Mobile	Italy	108.1	NA	85.1
Telewest Comm.	U.K.	103.0	NA	18.3
Netcom	Norway	78.1	NA	2.5
Cable & Wireless	U.K.	72.6	378.1	47.9
Vodafone	U.K.	71.5	1,239.0	356.3
Cable & Wireless Comm.	U.K.	68.9	NA	26.3
Portugal Telecom	Portugal	65.2	NA	14.0
Telecom Italia	Italy	60.7	891.3	82.1
Olivetti	Italy	42.1	343.3	17.8
Telecel	Portugal	40.5	NA	4.4
Hellenic Telecom	Greece	35.5	NA	15.0
British Telecom	U.K.	32.2	488.2	127.4
Panafon	Greece	29.2	NA	7.9
Equant	France	23.3	NA	17.5
Swisscom	Switz.	13.1	NA	29.5
Sector Performance		**86.8%**	**677.7%**	

° Returns are in euros.

Source: "European Company Performance Survey," *Financial Times Survey of the European Performance League*, 23 June 2000, p. IV.

leader first through its 1999 acquisition of AirTouch Communications for $62 billion, followed by its $70 billion linkup with Bell Atlantic, creating Verizon Wireless. Then it cemented its global position with the $183 billion takeover of Mannesmann in 2000, which pushed annual company sales to $27 billion.

Vodafone secured the following benefits from these deals:

➤ Enhanced purchasing power,

➤ Geographic diversification of revenue flow, and

➤ Increased systems linkage, further eliminating connect costs of outside operators.

Most impressive about the buyouts is what they do for Vodafone in Europe—the world's largest cellular market. Combining its established position in northern Europe with AirTouch's and Mannesmann's strong positions in southern Europe transformed the new company into the Continent's largest and most complete mobile operator. This will enable Vodafone to more aggressively pursue additional alliances and acquisitions, further insuring its dominant market position, especially as it moves into Internet access.[20]

Vodafone's shares have responded like those of any world-beater. Annualized returns for the five years through the first quarter 2000 exceeded 68 percent, tops in the industry by a very wide margin, and have pushed Vodafone's market capitalization beyond €350 billion.[21] (For further analysis of Vodafone, see Chapter 9.)

Utilities

CONTRARY TO WHAT MOST INVESTORS would expect, European utilities have been generating solid returns. Electricity shares gained 22.72 percent annually in euro terms for five years through the first quarter 2000. Gas distribution stocks did even better, rising 27.6 percent annually. U.K.-dominated water stocks appreciated annually by a not-too-shabby 18.26 percent. Meanwhile, large diversified industrial/utility stocks nearly tripled over this time, with annualized returns of 24.53 percent.[1] Not too bad for investments that have traditionally been thought of as defensive plays.

However, unlike some other sectors whose broad gains were based on clear fundamental improvements, the near-term outlook for utility stocks is far less certain, for two basic reasons:

➤ Key factors responsible for recent strong gains are no longer extant.
➤ Current efforts to deregulate the sector will continue to distort the revenue and expansion picture of many utilities over the next several years.

The rise of utility stocks was significantly linked to the steady decline in interest rates associated with European economic and monetary

Key Findings

➤ Privatization and market liberalization are transforming utility stocks into very solid investments.

➤ Electric, gas, and water shares have collectively generated annualized returns of more than 23 percent over the five years through the first quarter of 2000.

➤ The varying pace of deregulation across Europe's electricity markets has inhibited industry consolidation and the creation of regional leaders.

➤ Utilities are beginning to benefit from moves into the New Economy, including creation of a common Internet procurement platform and investment in telecom services that run along existing electricity lines.

➤ Despite the limited number of publicly traded stocks, natural gas shares have become very attractive because of rising energy prices, an abundant supply of gas in Europe, and environmental standards that are demanding cleaner-burning energy.

➤ Tremendous demand for improved water distribution will drive industry growth worldwide.

➤ Diversified utilities, such as Suez Lyonnaise and Vivendi Environnement, offer the greatest growth potential.

union. In this environment, interest-rate-sensitive stocks (which includes a large numbers of utilities) rose as investors chased after their higher yields. As interest rates fell by 50 percent (which they did, and more, in many European countries), interest-rate-sensitive stocks correspondingly shot up by 100 percent as their yields converged with broad market rates.

For example, dividend yield on Belgium's dominant electricity and gas giant, Electrabel, fell from 7.3 percent in 1994 to 4.2 percent in the first quarter of 1999 (paralleling the decline in 10-year German government bonds from 6 to 3.5 percent), contributing to the stock's five-year annualized gain of 21 percent. Spain's largest private sector electricity utility, Iberdrola, tracked a similar history: its 1995 yield of 7 percent was cut in half by a stock price that also appreciated 21 percent annually over the trailing five years.[2] (See the table on page 175 for more dividend/price comparisons.)

Flight to quality during the emerging market crises of 1997 and 1998 also added to the sector's substantial returns. As markets reeled from first the collapse of the once formidable Southeast Asian economies and then Russia's currency mismanagement and default on foreign debt, many investors (especially institutional) sought protection from further capital erosion through shelter in utilities—known for their price stability and yield.

Although European business expansion and increasing consumer affluence have been steadily driving up demand for electricity, gas, and water (the industries that comprise the sector), ongoing liberalization of utility markets and the maintenance of regulatory pricing controls leave a murky profit picture. True, companies are now freer to operate more efficiently and in larger and more diverse markets. Endesa, Spain's primary electricity utility, has embarked on a major restructuring program that will cut costs by 40 percent by 2003. This will enhance profitability, propelling the sell-off of government-owned shares.[3] Centrica, the trading arm of British Gas, is now using its residential connections to sell a variety of non-utility-related financial services, including credit cards and insurance, which have inherently higher margins.[4]

At the same time some governments are finding it necessary to regulate prices to promote competition while ensuring fair returns on investments. Spain cut gas rates in 1999 by 2 to 4 percent partially in response to a higher than anticipated uptick in inflation. This eroded support for shares of the formerly high-flying Gas Natural, the country's dominant gas distributor. In the United Kingdom, after permitting electricity prices to rise between 1990 and 1995 to help offset the costs associated with privatization, regulators subsequently cut tariffs by nearly 25 percent between 1995 and 2000 in light of declining operating costs.[5]

Complicating matters further, observes Chris Rowland, lead utility analyst at Merrill Lynch in London, is an inconsistent regulatory framework spreading across western Europe as each EU country grapples in its own way to meet the European Commission's phased open-market standards. Incongruous operating rules are inhibiting cross-border expansion, restraining the pace of mergers and acquisitions.[6]

Among the worst culprits is the French government, whose electricity and gas markets are dominated by Eléctricité de France—Europe's largest energy producer—and Gaz de France, both of which are state owned. Although EdF is open about its ambitions to add to its foreign holdings, which now include London Electricity, outside power generators and suppliers remain hard-pressed to make effective inroads into France's still highly regulated electricity market. (However, investors should note that the likelihood that France will privatize a portion of both utilities over the next few years could generate two very attractive IPOs.) Regulatory inconsistency has also blocked creation of some formidable sector players that would themselves be strong investment opportunities while also helping secure the Continent's future energy needs.

For investors, this is the bottom line.

➤ The European utility sector is experiencing what Christos Papoutsis, energy head of the European Commission, describes as "a profound change from rigid, monopolistic, and separate markets toward a vibrant, competitive market."[7]

➤ Near-term implications of the sector's restructuring are far from clear.

➤ E-commerce strategies will generate substantial cost savings, improve client development, and enhance revenue flow from fees and trading. A dozen utilities have recently established an Internet platform for capital spending.

➤ Technological innovation will enable utilities to provide telecommunication services along the same lines that deliver electricity, giving these power companies a strategic advantage.

➤ The utilities likely to end up on top after the dust settles are those that are the most efficient with the largest customer reach, especially those that are developing stakes in more than one type of service across various geographic markets.

Consolidation is building up some national giants, especially in Germany, but Paris-based Suez Lyonnaise des Eaux and Vivendi Environnement remain Europe's largest and most diversified utilities.[8] Both have restructured themselves into diversified high-growth operations with significant international exposure. Suez has been selling off noncore activities to become a more fully integrated utility company. Vivendi Environnement, on the other hand, is a spin-off from its parent company, Vivendi Universal.

The question this restructuring poses is whether Vivendi Environnement can continue its impressive earnings growth rate on its own. Before the demerging, the company expected profits to expand at an annual rate of 20 percent, 5 percent larger than was projected for Suez.[9] Vivendi's numbers were based on a financial model in which nearly 30 percent of earnings were generated from media and telecom activity.[10]

Still, both companies are expanding much faster than traditional utilities. And according to Pierre Coiffet, utility analyst at BNP Paribas in Paris, "Vivendi Environnement and Suez Lyonnaise are recreating themselves into a new equity hybrid: the 'defensive growth stock.'" (See Chapter 9 for a more detailed description of Suez Lyonnaise des Eaux.)

To understand the potential value of investing in European utilities, and specifically in Vivendi Environnement's and Suez Lyonnaise's cross-industry expansion strategy, we need to look at the electricity, gas, and water markets and the issues affecting their growth both domestically and abroad.

Electricity

The electricity industry in Europe is a $200 billion-a-year market, with tremendous price and regulatory variations from one country to another. Between first quarter 1995 and first quarter 2000, industry stocks returned nearly 23 percent a year, despite being virtually flat over the preceding twelve months.[11] The industry is comprised of the following players:

➤ Generators (the companies that produce the power),
➤ Transmission companies (utilities that operate and maintain nationwide power grids),
➤ Distribution companies (the folks who physically link the grids with consumers), and
➤ Suppliers (the nonhardware companies that arrange the sale of electricity to commercial, industrial, and residential consumers).

In countries where government control has been dominant and competition limited, these four functions have been "bundled" within a single company, like Scottish Power in the United Kingdom, Electrabel in Belgium, and Eléctricité de France.

Where open markets are flourishing, generators and suppliers enjoy the most competition. In these places, according to Merrill Lynch utility analyst Sam Brothwell, investors will find the greatest risk and the largest returns. Although extensive infrastructure requirements of transmission and distribution are most efficiently served by monopolies, regulators are careful to limit their profitability.[12]

To promote cheaper power and greater competition, the European Commission ordered phased industry deregulation. As of February 1999, 25 percent of each country's customers are now permitted to openly select their power supply. Initially, this involved only the largest power consumers—primarily large industry. By 2003, one-third of the market is to enjoy free choice, and by 2007, European electricity markets are to be completely open.

The Commission has left nations with near total discretion in how to deregulate their markets. A key issue is how to unbundle functions. Whereas France has been slow to legislate the required changes, Norway, Finland, Sweden, and the United Kingdom took a fast track and now offer fully open electricity markets.

Investors must discern which functions (generation and/or supply) and which national markets offer the greatest opportunity for growth and profitability. Potential will vary from country to country, based on the particular regulatory environment, pricing, and government policy. An example of the latter: government control of the electricity market in France is supported by a social contract with EdF that emphasizes jobs, wages, and the subsidy of poor customers who are delinquent in paying their utility bills.

The United Kingdom offers some of the most promising utility investments because of the country's early commitment to privatization and deregulation. Besides offering higher dividends than their Continental counterparts, U.K. utilities benefit from regulators focused on price rather than on the rate of return. This has meant utilities have been able to profit more from cost-cutting moves and efficiency improvements, which permit more of their revenues to pass down to the bottom line. With extra cash, many utilities are diversifying and becoming more attractive investments.

A good example is the regional utility Scottish Power, which has been expanding into gas, water, and telecommunications. In 1999, it made the first foreign acquisition of a U.S. power utility when it purchased PacifiCorp, an Oregon-based electric company, for $6.5 billion.[13]

While they've pulled back recently on a portion of their investments, U.S. companies have gobbled up two-thirds of Britain's dozen privatized electric utilities.[14] The latest move was by Texas-based TXU, which acquired the Eastern Energy Group for $10.5 billion in mid-1999. That's a rich fourteen times the company's earnings. But it's not nuts. Eastern's earnings are growing 8 percent a year, whereas TXU's domestic unit growth is a paltry 1 percent. Eastern was projected to contribute nearly 30 percent to TXU's bottom line in 2000.[15]

Gas

The $118 billion European gas market, although significantly smaller than its electricity market, is growing at a faster rate due to deregulation, greater energy efficiency, and environmental directives pushing utilities to cleaner power sources.

The potential of deregulation and subsequent consolidation of the industry is most evident in the dramatic variations of gas prices across Europe, which are on average 40 percent higher than those in the United States.[16] With the demand for gas projected to rise from 22 percent of the European energy market in 1997 to 30 percent by 2020, the largest and most efficient operations are poised to benefit.[17] This outlook has helped send gas utility shares sharply higher. In 1998, industry stocks shot up nearly 75 percent; in 1999, they rose another 19.3 percent. Over the five years through the first quarter of 2000, gas shares returned an average of 27.6 percent a year.[18]

While proceeding at a bit slower pace, gas deregulation has been following a similar pattern to electricity liberalization, with comparable problems and potential. A key driver of growth is the need for power generation, which HSBC utility specialist Steve Turner regards as "the foundation of the new gas markets."[19] With nuclear power being phased out of many countries and coal power plants simply unable to meet the EU's increasingly stringent environmental regulations, there is already a demonstrable shift in usage from conversion of existing stations and new construction to new gas-powered electricity generating plants.

How sizable has this shift been? According to Nick Antrill, gas analyst at Morgan Stanley Dean Witter in London, only 5 to 7 percent of European electricity was generated from gas in 1980. By 1999, that figure was approaching 25 percent in some countries.

Being 50 percent more efficient than coal, in abundant supply around Europe, and with its prices collapsing by the end of the 1990s, natural gas has become increasingly more popular in both business and residential markets. In Germany, for instance, gas sales to the industrial power market now account for nearly one-third of all energy consumed. More than 70 percent of the new housing built in Germany relies on natural gas for space heating.[20]

Unfortunately, while supplies, prices, industry deregulation, and environmental laws are pushing demand for gas, investors have limited direct access to the gas market. Most gas operators are either government controlled or are subsidiaries of oil and diversified utilities. Only four gas utilities are open to investors. Two were split off from the former U.K. monopoly: British Gas (a transmission company that has performed exceedingly well, up 26.81 percent annually over the five years through first quarter 2000) and Centrica (BG's new trading arm, which soared 143.6 percent for the year ending March 31, 2000). Italgas, a small, diversified Italian gas distributor, also locked in big gains over the five-year period through the first quarter 2000, up 26.3 percent annually. And then there is Gas Natural, Spain's dominant distributor and supplier, who turned in the industry's best returns over the same period, with annualized gains of 33.07 percent.[21] Even though its stock price corrected by nearly 30 percent during the year through the first quarter of 2000 (due to regulated price cuts and an acceleration in the timetable for deregulation in Spain), Nick Antrill still believes Gas Natural is strongly positioned to take advantage of the long-term growth in demand for natural gas.[22]

However, Antrill believes that the best way to invest in the gas market is through multi-utilities that have the ability to exploit the deregulatory potential of both gas and electricity. These companies can increase gas sales to power plants at the same time that broad economic growth will trigger increased demand for electricity from the largest and most efficient utilities. Further, established brand name utilities that embrace this diversification enjoy economies of scale in all facets of business.

Water

With annual revenues of $46 billion, Europe's water industry is the smallest among the major utilities. Nevertheless, it possesses perhaps the greatest growth potential. This is due to the continuing pace of urbanization coupled with accelerating need for water purification and wastewater treatment in both emerging and industrialized economies. Globally, water is a $400-billion-a-year industry—and it's getting bigger.[23]

The urgency of action underpins the industry's investment appeal. Over the five years through the first quarter of 2000, water stocks appreciated by more than 18 percent a year.[24] With both industrialized and emerging governments turning to private utilities having financial and technical expertise, further investment gains are likely.

In Europe, a 1991 EC directive requires all towns of 15,000 or more to have a water treatment facility. By 2006, towns of only 10,000 must meet the same standard. At the same time, more stringent water standards are requiring replacement of thousands of kilometers of lead pipes. Altogether, western Europe is expected to spend $80 billion to $100 billion on infrastructure improvements between 1995 and 2010.[25]

Such systemwide changes are leading to rising water prices across Europe, reflecting greater reliance on customers rather than taxpayers to finance such improvements.[26]

Potential expansion into the United States—where only 15 percent of municipal water systems have been privatized, leaving nearly 60,000 operations available to private bidders—is very strong. Local authorities generally grant rational rate increases to cover expenses. With new laws extending the time frame of management contracts from five to twenty years and beyond, utilities will be more assured of achieving adequate returns on their investments. This has led Gerard Mestrallet, CEO of Suez Lyonnaise des Eaux, to conclude that there is "great opportunity in the fragmented U.S. water market." Suez and Vivendi Environnement have responded by establishing significant presence in the States, where they are collectively generating annual water revenues in excess of $7 billion.[27]

Emerging markets are also quite ripe for privatization. The United Nations estimates that urban populations in Asia and Africa will expand from 23 percent in 1970 to 54 percent by 2025. Latin American urbanization will be even more intense, moving from 58 percent to 86 per-

Dividend Yields and Price Appreciation of Sample Utilities: 1992–1999

COUNTRY	1992 YIELD	1999 YIELD	1992-1999 DIVIDEND GROWTH	1992–1999 CUMULATIVE PRICE RETURN
Iberdrola (Spain)	8.5%	3.3%	28%	232%
Electrabel (Belgium)	8.4	4.2	31	152
Endesa (Spain)	3.8	2.6	193	332
Italgas (Italy)	3.6	1.9	50	181
Powergen (U.K.)	4.8	4.1	128	287
VEW (Germany)	4.8	2.9	41	135

All figures are calculated as of the X-dividend dates, 1992–1999.

Source: Bloomberg

cent. Yet access to clean drinking water in urban areas worldwide fell from 50 percent to less than 40 percent between 1980 and 1994.

Supported by funding from the World Bank, the International Finance Corporation, and other supranationals, emerging-market governments are following one of two models to address their water needs. There's the U.K. model, based on full infrastructure privatization, overseen by centralized, regulated management. And there's the French paradigm, which maintains public ownership of water systems and opts instead to privatize management.

Utilities that venture abroad often rely on profits from their industrialized operations to help support their emerging-market projects. However, there is the promise of profitability through cheap infrastructure acquisition, favorable development rights and management terms, and inexpensive local financing. Further, utilities will likely be able to find value by plugging leaky systems, reducing illicit tapping, and improving metering and bill collection. Such improvements in places like New Delhi can increase receivables by 75 percent.[28]

Investors can gain limited exposure to the diverse water market through the dozen or so integrated utilities in the United Kingdom, where the equity gains among the top four companies have been roughly comparable. United Utilities, Thames Water, Angilan Water, and Severn Trent generated total annualized returns ranging between 15.39 and 21.87 percent over the five years through the first quarter of

2000.[29] As they are slow-growth operations, with high dividend yields, most of their capital appreciation has been due to falling interest rates during the late 1990s and periodic shifts to defensive stocks.

But Suez Lyonnaise and Vivendi Environnement are virtually the only two European investments capable of exploiting the global water market. As in the gas industry, most other players are either state owned or wrapped within larger diversified companies. This leads Michael Cohen, water analyst at Schroders Salomon Smith Barney in London, to conclude that "the water market is best played through multi-utility companies who are in position to participate in the increasing trend of privatization and contract management."[30]

Chapter Nine

Model Stocks

W HEN SELECTED IN LATE 1999 and early 2000, the stocks featured below would have made up a great mutual fund. They still may.

These companies are among the Continent's most prominent growth stories, describing the various kinds of investment opportunities restructuring now offers. Each stock is a compelling example of the new European business model. They offer exposure to the Continent's leading sectors while being geographically diverse, including companies from nine different countries.

The list features established industry leaders, such as Dutch insurer AEGON and U.K. telecom giant Vodafone. It also includes innovators: Sweden's smart fashion retailer Hennes & Mauritz; Europe's low-fare airline leader, the Dublin-based Ryanair; and the Swiss global temporary-staffing giant, Adecco.

A common feature of all these stocks is their focused operations. No highly diversified conglomerates here. Each company has achieved significant—if not dominant—market share in its respective industry. Carrefour's series of acquisitions, culminating in the purchase of Promodès, has poised the French retailer to challenge Wal-Mart's global leadership. Paris-based Suez Lyonnaise des Eaux is among the largest water suppliers in the world. Vodafone's successful acquisition of Mannesmann has given the U.K. telecom service provider the largest mobile footprint around, while Helsinki-based Nokia is the worldwide mobile phone manufacturing leader.

Another common trait: all the firms aggressively embrace technology and the Internet to drive profits, none more so than the upstart northern Italian bank BIPOP. It was one of the first financial institutions in Europe to gain brand leadership in Internet banking and securities e-trading as part of its strategy to redefine the meaning of regional banking. Rule of thumb: When looking to invest in European securities, find the industry leaders, making sure of their capacity to exploit Europe's more open and competitive markets.

At the same time, keep in mind that Europe is changing at an intense pace. Industry leaders that have found their way into this book may have their status challenged by the time you start reading about them. So while the stocks listed below give you a good place to start searching for European investments, make sure you practice due diligence before spending a single euro.

Adecco

Ticker: ADE (NYSE)
Country: Switzerland
Industry: Employment Agency

" *With labor markets deregulating globally and with both business and government realizing the benefits of temporary staffing, Adecco offers investors top-quality exposure to this fast-growing industry.... It outpaces its competitors both in terms of sales penetration and profitability, and is likely to continue its delivery of superior earnings growth.* **"**

DRESDNER KLEINWORT BENSON[1]

AT FIRST GLANCE, a temp agency does not seem to be a natural way of playing Europe's economic recovery. But that's exactly what it does.

A closer look into this $140 billion global industry reveals that businesses worldwide are relying increasingly on the use of temporary labor to help meet demand in a wide variety of sectors. As *Business Week* reported, "From semiconductor clean rooms in France to mobile phone factories in Finland and jet engine research labs in

Key Findings

➤ More flexible business practices and government policy are propelling the rapid growth of the temporary staffing industry.

➤ Swiss-based Adecco is the market leader, capturing a 12 percent share of global demand.

➤ Since the 1996 merger that created the company, annual revenue has been increasing by more than 23 percent, annual operating profit increased by 29 percent through 1999, and shares soared 200 percent through 1999.

➤ Three key purchases in 1999 will further propel growth and expand EBITA margins, likely fueling additional acquisition.

➤ High share valuation, cyclical character of the industry, additional share offerings, and the lack of geographic transparency are likely to contribute to price volatility.

Germany, companies are filling thousands of empty posts with temporary workers."[2] And Adecco has a 12 percent share of this global market.[3]

From a strategic point of view, use of temps helps businesses perform more efficiently, utilizing labor in a "just-in-time" manner. Just as important, a more flexible workforce enables companies to more deftly respond to new opportunities with fewer full-time employees and reduced financial burden. Large multinationals are increasingly consolidating their search for temporary needs through a single global concern—like Adecco. And this is at the heart of the industry's potential profitability.

For example, Adecco has an exclusive hiring agreement with a large U.S.-based computer manufacturer with operations in twenty-two countries, from Argentina, France, and Turkey to New Zealand. In a typical month, Adecco filled nearly 4,200 professional, industrial, and administrative positions for this firm. The company generated $110 million in sales from this single client in 1998. And this kind of contract is typical of more than one-third of Adecco's business.

The boom in temporary staffing and more flexible business policy has been triggered by government deregulation of labor markets. This propelled annual industry growth of 18 percent during the 1990s,[4] anchoring Adecco right in the middle of a major European restructuring story.

With temporary work traditionally having been seen as the antithesis of real jobs, policy makers, especially in Europe, are realizing that nonpermanent employment is the most effective means of reducing perennial double-digit unemployment rates. And with more than 10 percent of European jobs now being temporary or fixed-term contracts, even unions are finding it difficult to challenge the positive role the industry is having in helping workers find jobs.[5]

Equally important, the majority of European governments have embraced the industry because it is helping them meet several fiscal requirements of monetary union and the New Economy.

➤ With unemployment benefits running as high as 50 to 75 percent of a worker's former wages, getting the jobless back to work relieves state budgets of a substantial financial burden while, in turn, generating additional wage tax revenues.

➤ Efficiency and flexibility of temporary labor is credited with curbing inflation rates.[6]

➤ Temporary staffing has become a key component of the New Economy, which demands quick responses and more aggressive compensation packages, especially for high-tech professionals.

Having established itself as the global leader of an industry that's still in its nascent stage, Adecco is well positioned to profit from the temp trend that is weaving itself through the economies of Europe and much of the world. And the stock market has recognized this as well, having driven the company's share price up 200 percent in local currency terms from the end of 1996 (the year Adecco was created by the merger of French and Swiss concerns) through the end of 1999.

Between 1996 and 1999, net service revenues increased from CHF 8.52 billion to CHF 18.47 billion. Net income (before amortization) climbed similarly, from CHF 241 millin to CHF 526 million, helping boost EPS from CHF 14.46 to CHF 30.5.[7]

Helping to drive expansion has been Adecco's success in acquiring and efficiently integrating complementary operations, which account for approximately one-third of the company's annual increase in sales. The company made a series of significant deals in 1999.

➢ In the spring, it purchased the U.K.-based Delphi—an IT staffing, training, and solutions group with annual sales of nearly CHF 583 million—for around $270 million. This pushed Adecco's overall higher-margin IT sales up to 10 percent of total revenue and boosted 1999 EPS by about 3 percentage points.[8]

➢ In May 1999, the company acquired Career Staff, a Japanese concern with CHF 544 million in annual sales.[9] In making Adecco the third-largest temporary agency in Japan, the deal positions it to exploit the increasing liberalization of the country's temporary work laws. At the same time, wide-scale corporate restructuring is turning increasingly away from lifetime work agreements and toward more flexible arrangements. Currently, temp jobs in Japan account for only 0.5 percent of all jobs—the lowest percent in the industrialized world.[10] However, over the next several years, increasing demand is expected to accelerate the industry's annual domestic growth from 5 to 13 percent and boost its perennially low EBITA margin of 2.3 percent.[11]

➢ In August 1999, Adecco made its largest deal yet, acquiring one of the United States' leading temporary services, Olsten, for $1.45 billion. With Olsten's annual sales of $3.1 billion and nearly 1,300 offices, the deal instantly transformed Adecco into the market leader in the United States, the United Kingdom, and Scandinavia and pusheed it into the second spot in Germany. The acquisition also made Adecco the largest IT staffing specialist in the world.

By the end of 1999, these acquisitions propelled Adecco into the top spot in ten of the world's thirteen largest staffing markets. This includes market shares of 30 percent or more in France, Italy, Spain, and Switzerland, along with the top spot in the United States, the United Kingdom, Canada, and Australia.[12]

Adecco's long-term goal: a 20 percent global market share and the first or second position in the world's thirteen largest markets. The strategy is simple. By building critical mass, both organically and through acquisitions, Adecco hopes to attract a greater share of both talent and clients. Cost synergies associated with a larger scale will enable Adecco to more efficiently service domestic as well as multinational contracts, triggering further growth.[13]

"What should frighten its competitors," observes Paul Ginocchio, industry analyst at Deutsche Bank in London, "is that Adecco may be on the verge of becoming the employer of choice for the brightest staffing executives, helping the company to sustain its comparative advantage."[14]

The latest full-year financials seem to indicate that the company is indeed achieving just that. In 1999, when Belgium and Japan market growth was virtually flat, Adecco's revenues there grew by 28 and 14 percent, respectively. In France, where the market expanded by 9 percent, company turnover increased by 13 percent. And in Germany, where movement towards a less restricted market pushed up industry sales by 18 percent, Adecco's revenue grew by 28 percent.[15]

Adecco is also seeking to enhance profitability by increasing margins. In 1998, with 85 percent of its workers categorized as generalists, the company's EBIT margin was an industry-average 4.2 percent. By purchasing companies with strong technical staffing (such as information technology workers, for whom margins and growth rates are twice those of administrative and blue-collar positions), Adecco intends to increase the amount of total profits derived from specialty staffing from between 20 and 25 percent to 50 percent. The results of such acquisitions were already evident a year later, in 1999, when the EBIT margin was up to 4.5 percent, with subsequent increases projected to be 10 basis points a year.[16]

Moving quickly into newly deregulated markets is also driving company growth. For example, in 1998, Italy introduced temporary work to the marketplace. By the end of 1999, Adecco had 190 branches in operation. It had consolidated a leading 31 percent market share and was already operating in the black. And by 2002, analysts at HSBC project that the Italian temp market will exceed €1 billion.[17] Down the road, the company expects similar performance gains in Germany and Japan, where deregulation will create comparable potential for huge growth.

Do Adecco shares face any material risks? While the company is striving for consistent performance through geographic diversification and a steady shift toward greater technical staffing, 85 percent of its

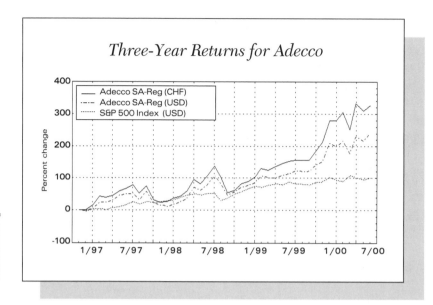

Three-Year Returns for Adecco

— Adecco SA-Reg (CHF)
--- Adecco SA-Reg (USD)
····· S&P 500 Index (USD)

Percent change

Source: Bloomberg

business is GDP-geared, making it a cyclical play. But it's not rated like one. "What is somewhat unnerving," observes Deutsche Bank's Paul Ginocchio, "is that the shares are trading near the multiples of non-cyclical business services stocks."[18]

Some analysts are concerned by the company's refusal to isolate performance by national markets, which makes it more difficult to discern specific trends and forecast impacts of acquisitions. Adecco breaks down performance into four regions: France, Europe (minus France), North America, and the Rest of the World.

This lack of transparency is of particular concern when it involves mature, low-unemployment markets, such as the United States, where the company derives nearly one-third of its sales. Because temp agencies are not like headhunters, fewer unemployed people means fewer positions to be filled. However, the States' single-digit growth rate is somewhat enhanced by increasing specialty-staffing fees and higher salaries due to the tighter market.

Countering exposure in the tight U.S. market is Adecco's substantial position in the French jobs market, which is booming despite talk of a disincentive temp tax and a government tilted toward traditional union concerns.

Finally, there is talk about price and earnings dilution. What if Olsten shareholders are quick to sell off their CHF 560 million worth of high-priced Adecco shares received in the transaction? Funding for the deal also required a secondary offering of CHF 510 million and a convertible bond issue that raised an additional CHF 530 million. At the same time, Adecco's cochairmen announced they were substantially reducing their positions in the company. Still, most observers feel dilution is only a marginal concern, as these actions will actually improve the stock's liquidity, pushing up its free float from 49 to 65 percent.[19]

First-Half 2000 Highlights

➤ *Superb financials*—Revenues climbed 45 percent, and net operating income soared 49 percent.

➤ *Smooth merger*—Integration of Olsten is proceeding on schedule.

➤ *Strong market growth*—U.K. sales increased by 30 percent, French sales by 31 percent, North American sales by 50 percent, and European sales (minus France) by climbed 53 percent; outside of these core markets, Adecco sales nearly doubled.

➤ *Increase in higher-margin business*—More lucrative specialty contracts increased to 37 percent of revenue.

AEGON

Ticker: AEG (NYSE)
Country: Netherlands
Industry: Insurance

66 *With strong, shareholder-driven management and strategic focus forging a remarkable track record of judicious acquisitions, rigid cost controls, and strong earnings growth, AEGON has achieved phenomenal share appreciation through the last half of the 1990s. And the Dutch-based insurer continues to be one of the best plays on the accelerating demand for managed savings accounts in Europe and the U.S., positioning the stock for continued growth.* 99

J.P. MORGAN[1]

THAT'S CERTAINLY NOT the kind of praise one would expect of an insurance company. But the markets have changed, especially for life insurers, who have seen their industry transformed into a growth busi-

Key Findings

➤ Life insurance has become a growth industry as a result of the increasing wealth of baby boomers and their need to fund private retirement plans in response to escalating state pension deficits.

➤ AEGON anticipated this increasing demand and profitability of life insurance before many of its competitors, and is benefiting from the explosion in virtually risk-free asset management fees.

➤ Strong management, a focus on shareholder value, a superb record of acquisitions, and broad fiscal discipline sent AEGON shares soaring 54.73 percent annually over the five years through the first quarter of 2000.

➤ To propel continued strong earnings growth, AEGON needs to move into Europe's two largest life insurance markets, Germany and France, and maintain its pace of acquisitions.

ness. Whereas pretax earnings in AEGON's small accident-and-health unit are projected to increase 9.3 percent annually between 1999 and 2002, profits in the company's life insurance division are slated to grow by 19.24 percent a year.[2]

The reasons driving the life industry are basic, and AEGON's success is attributable to its having seen change coming early on.

First, with strong economic growth and the baby-boom generation in the prime of its income-making years, household wealth has significantly increased, along with the need to insure it. Second, with state pension systems unlikely to fund their long-term obligations across nearly all of Europe, workers are rapidly setting up their own retirement accounts, driving sales of life insurance products. According to research specialists at Intersec, private pension assets in Europe rose from $1.22 trillion in 1993 to more than $2 trillion in

1998. By 2003, Intersec projects this figure to rise by an additional 50 percent.[3]

Another key development: as European interest rates declined in preparation for common currency, insurers benefited from the corresponding rise in their bond holdings—the predominant security type in their portfolios. At the same time, with life insurers' liability spread out across a longer investment horizon than nonlife insurers', many companies began shifting assets into equity markets, which have rapidly appreciated.

As if all of that weren't enough good news for life insurers, the increasing popularity of unit-linked accounts (variable annuities, as we know them in the States) has created an almost risk-free flow of management fees. ULAs are quickly catching up in euro terms with traditional discretionary managed accounts, the latter requiring a commitment of shareholder equity. The result of this shift is sending life insurers' returns on equity soaring, making assets under management an increasingly critical measure of financial performance.

What has all this meant for AEGON and its investors?

Over the five years through the first quarter of 2000, AEGON rose an amazing 54.73 percent a year in euro terms.[4] With the acquisition of Transamerica, AEGON became the third-largest life insurer in America and the second largest in all of Europe, with a market cap of €54 billion.

AEGON generated about 12 percent of its 1999 pretax earnings (before interest and other charges) from banking and accident, health, and general insurance. But the lion's share of earnings, 88 percent, came from its life insurance operations in the United States, the Netherlands, and the United Kingdom—the company's core markets. And that percent is projected to rise even further, providing investors with about the most focused play available in this rapidly growing industry.

Between 1994 and 1999, AEGON's life premiums and related investment income rose 22.6 percent a year, to €19.11 billion. Reflecting economies of scale and AEGON's focus on cost cutting, EBIT grew even faster, increasing by nearly 30 percent a year, to €2.13 billion in 1999. This led to a steady climb in pretax margins on gross premiums from 12.8 to 16.6 percent over the same period.[5]

Overall, total gross insurance premiums increased by almost 19 percent annually between 1994 and 1999, reaching nearly €15 billion by the end of 1999. Investment income grew at an even faster rate, climbing 20.87 percent a year to €6.69 billion in 1999. And assets under management soared from €58 billion to €222 billion.[6]

The bottom line: AEGON's net income after taxes appreciated by 24.64 percent annually between 1994 and 1999, ending the decade at €1.57 billion. Because acquisitions boosted capital needs and the number of shares outstanding, EPS rose at a slightly slower pace, on average 20.21 percent a year, with 1999 earnings of €2.56 a share.[7]

In addition to industry trends that are pushing up shares of all life-oriented insurers, AEGON's success has been predicated on several key business strategies.

➤ The company knew early on the advantage of focusing on life insurance and made sure that Wall Street understood its business plan. According to Angus Runciman, insurance analyst at J.P. Morgan in London, "AEGON came to the market and said, 'Look, these are economics of life insurance and this is how we make money; here's our top line and here's our bottom line.' It was all very clear and compelling."[8]

➤ Besides its transparency, AEGON understands the need not to disappoint Wall Street. "The company tends to understate cost savings and projected revenues and frequently delivers better-than-expected earnings," observes Nicholas Byrne, industry analyst at Merrill Lynch in London.[9] Consistent positive earning surprises keep sentiments toward the stock on an upward bias.

➤ AEGON was among the first European companies to compensate its employees with stock options.

➤ In addition to generating substantial organic earnings growth (averaging 17.5 percent a year),[10] AEGON relies on a disciplined acquisition policy that emphasizes profitability over market share. Specifically, AEGON goes after deals that will give it economies of scale, sound management, and returns of at least 10 to 12 percent on investment.

Since 1986, the company has averaged nearly one deal a year to build up operations in the United States, the United Kingdom, Hungary, Mexico, and Germany. And unlike other insurers who are concerned with expanding their own branding, AEGON maintains the local names and management of their acquisitions, understanding the domestic-oriented nature of insurance. At the same time, AEGON adds value by extending its vast financial and technological resources and experience to acquired operations in fragmented, less mature markets. Overall, according to Jason B. Zucker, an insurance analyst at Banc of America Securities in New York, "AEGON maintains an unblemished acquisition record supported by superior execution and financial management skills."[11]

In 1999 came the biggest deal ever—the $9.7 billion acquisition of San Francisco–based Transamerica. Besides generating cost savings conservatively estimated at $150 million to AEGON's existing U.S. operations, the deal adds 3 percent to the company's earnings and $58.5 billion of assets to its balance sheet.

Even though AEGON paid a high price for Transamerica and may not immediately generate a double-digit return on investment, the deal increases AEGON's U.S. pretax earnings by 50 percent, improves its U.S. product line and distribution, and reduces domestic borrowing costs because of Transamerica's AAA rating. Ultimately, this expanded client and financial base will support further acquisitions and joint ventures.

The Transamerica deal also highlighted a unique asset of AEGON: Vereniging AEGON, a foundation that holds a large minority of the company's shares for the express purpose of increasing shareholder value. In addition to being completely off the insurer's books and maintaining 30 to 40 percent of the company's equity in friendly hands, VA offers AEGON access to these shares for acquisitions. In the Transamerica deal, VA sold AEGON 20 percent of the shares that were eventually transferred to the American insurer. This reduced EPS dilution by cutting back on the number of new shares AEGON needed to issue to close the deal. Further, the foundation is self-regenerating. After selling the shares to AEGON, it is slowly replenishing its position, using stock dividends to repurchase shares. And this in turn helps support the share price.[12]

AEGON is not afraid to divest assets that are either unprofitable or no longer complement its core life focus. It sold off its insurance operations in Belgium and Greece, its auto insurance unit in Hungary, and up to 40 percent of Transamerica's nonlife assets.

Controlling costs is a key component of AEGON's rising profitabili-

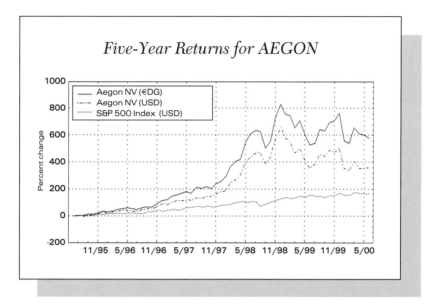

Five-Year Returns for AEGON

Aegon NV (€DG)
Aegon NV (USD)
S&P 500 Index (USD)

Source: Bloomberg

ty. Between 1992 and 1999, as the company pursued acquisitions and joint ventures, increased efficiency and productivity helped drive its expense-to-revenue ratio from 21 to 13 percent.[13]

Although AEGON shares will excel over the long term, several intermediate-term risks may cause volatility. Share prices of most insurers have taken a hit since interest rates began to rise in 1999. Although higher rates will increase insurers' profitability on discretionary accounts, the market sees the trend as a big negative for the sector. It sees the value of insurers' bond holdings declining and overall sentiment for stocks turning neutral. (See the description of the Insurance Sector in Chapter 8 for further discussion of this issue.)

AEGON's high multiple (ending 1999 with a P/E of 25.7) is far greater than those of other Dutch and U.S. insurers. But most industry observers think it is merited given the quality of management, profitability (the highest among European insurers), and related demographic and industry trends.[14] Nevertheless, the market may wait for greater earnings before further driving up the stock.

There are two fundamental concerns that are a bit more troubling: one, the company's near-invisible presence in Europe's two largest life insurance markets, Germany and France; and two, the likely need for continuous acquisitions to drive share price. As the life insurance industry consolidates, good deals that meet AEGON's standards will be harder to come by. Cross-border deals in Europe are hamstrung by high insurance share prices, complex shareholder structures that complicate the acquisition process, and the domestic diversity of insurance markets (that is, different governments tax retirement contributions at very different rates).

Nevertheless, projected pretax earnings growth between 1999 and 2002 in AEGON's three main markets indicates a company that's thriving. In the United Kingdom, where AEGON generates nearly 10 percent of its profits and where the company recently acquired the life insurance arm of Guardian Royal Exchange for $1.13 billion, life premiums and profits are expected to rise by more than 26 percent a year. In its home Dutch market, where AEGON generates 35.5 percent of its earnings, life insurance profits are expected to rise by 11.5 percent annually. After the Transamerica acquisition, U.S. operations now account for more than one-half the company's profits, which is particularly good news as U.S. life insurance earnings are projected to increase by 21.5 percent a year. AEGON's total earnings are projected to grow 17.5 percent annually between 1999 and 2002. Share dilution, however, is expected to reduce EPS growth to 12.4 percent.[15]

First-Half 2000 Highlights

➤ *Strong growth continues*—Consolidation of Transamerica operations sent revenues soaring 64 percent, to €15.36 billion, and net income climbed 29 percent, to €1.01 billion; premium income was up 63 percent and investment income skyrocketed 79 percent; and the strong dollar and sterling added 8 percent to EPS.

➤ *Transamerica integration proceeding well*—The merging of Transamerica and AEGON's operations is moving ahead of schedule; however, AEGON has so far been unable to sell off Transamerica's nonlife operations. Due to the strong dollar, Transamerica's lending, leasing, and real estate activities are expected to boost AEGON's bottom line for the year.

➤ *Stock split*—In May, AEGON shares split 2 for 1.

➤ *Poor share performance*—Dragged down by market indifference toward many financials, AEGON shares were off by more than 22 percent despite continued strong performance.

BIPOP-Carire

Ticker: BIP (Milan Stock Exchange)
Country: Italy
Industry: Banking

> **"** *BIPOP's strong revenue growth generated by innovative products and unique low-cost distribution channels is creating the lowest cost/income ratios in European banking. This fact, coupled with the Continent's healthiest loan books and an industry-leading on-line banking and trading strategy, gives BIPOP one of the brightest profit growth outlooks in our European universe.* **"**

MORGAN STANLEY DEAN WITTER[1]

IT TAKES SOME GUMPTION to consider a bank stock whose name sounds like the latest music craze, even more intestinal fortitude to do so when its trailing P/E is on the edge of triple figures. But as the market has come to realize, BIPOP is not your ordinary Italian bank.

Although small in comparison to Europe's venerable financial institutions, BIPOP is arguably the Continent's most exciting banking story. It is revolutionizing the industry. That's why, despite caveats flashing that at its current price the stock carries extraordinary risks, I decided to feature it.

In the mid-1990s, as it was reconfiguring itself from a traditional cooperative retail bank (Banca Popolare di Brescia) into a joint stock company, BIPOP saw that its future would be better served by pushing beyond traditional banking and into a wide variety of financial services, distributed through a diverse sales network. The strategy sought to exploit the changing economic environment sweeping over Italy as the country prepared itself for monetary union.

BIPOP saw that traditional banking would take a double hit from Italy's formerly double-digit interest rates descending and converging with the European Central Bank's far looser monetary policy. First, lower rates would dramatically squeeze lending margins, and second, it would discourage Italians, who are among the Continent's best savers, from plowing earnings into low-rate savings accounts and bonds. In fact, there was the likelihood of a flow out of savings accounts and into

Key Findings

➤ Based in Italy's affluent northern region, BIPOP is among the most innovative and profitable banks in the industry.
➤ Its success is based on offering a wide variety of financial services, focusing on asset management, and developing a low-cost sales network that will increasingly rely on the Internet.
➤ Between 1998 and 1999, BIPOP was one of the top-performing stocks in Europe, increasing tenfold in value, which left its shares extraordinarily valued at the beginning of 2000.
➤ Long-term success requires the bank to leverage its current momentum to gain market share and to strategically position itself to compete against the country's largest banks, especially as cross-border consolidation begins.

alternative investments. These changes threatened the industry's prime source of cheap capital.

As a retail bank, BIPOP saw the best opportunity to regain profitability would be in offering clients better access to the country's burgeoning equity culture. By the late 1990s, asset management began driving profits as the bank shifted its focus from smaller-margin interest income activities to higher fees and commissions associated with the sales and management of mutual funds, asset allocation, and private banking services. And by the end of the decade, BIPOP became the fastest-growing asset gatherer in Italy, with more than €25 billion of assets under management.[2]

At the same time, the bank saw ways of relieving the drag bricks and mortar and staffing traditionally have on earnings. By selling its products and services through exclusive and nonexclusive commission-based sales agents, through other banks, and via the Internet, BIPOP has been able to significantly reduce its reliance on expensive branch offices and full-time workers. Less than half the bank's income is now generated through its branches. And this shift has helped reduce the company's cost/income ratio to below 50 percent, versus an Italian banking average above 58 percent. By 2001, BIPOP's ratio is expected to drop even further, to 42 percent.[3]

What BIPOP has done—unique to the industry—is to develop a matrix of diverse financial services (current accounts, credit cards, leasing, securities trading, mutual funds, and life insurance) and various low-cost channels in which to sell them. This strategy expands the reach of the bank exponentially as it opens up new means of picking up new clients and substantially increases the frequency with which its products and services are cross sold.

The result has been astonishing growth. From 1997, the year the company legally restructured itself, through 1999, revenues grew 143 percent, from €381 million to €925 million. Reflecting increasing efficiencies, profits soared 394 percent, from €52 million to €257 million, while the bank's cost/income ratio declined from 53.44 percent to nearly 44 percent. Declining lending margins and the company's shift from traditional banking to higher-value-added financial services have decreased interest income as a percent of total income (from 38.23 percent to 29.55 percent). However, this has enhanced return on equity from a sickly 12.31 percent to an industry-leading 22.39 percent.[4]

Even though the bank still isn't on everyone's radar screen, this kind of performance hasn't escaped the market's attention. From the end of 1997 through 1999, the stock jumped tenfold, ending the year at €87.85. And in the spring of 2000, the stock split 10 to 1. This no-name little bank, with assets of less than €11 billion—only the thirteenth-largest bank in Italy—closed the century as one of the hottest stocks in Europe.

With a market cap approaching €15 billion, BIPOP shares are getting a further push by making it into MIB-30, Italy's leading index, and three of the Continent's key benchmarks: the FTSE Europe 400, the Dow Jones STOXX (590 companies), and the EURO STOXX (294 companies).

However, what's disconcerting about BIPOP's stock rise was its performance particularly over the last month of 1999, when it nearly doubled. Already straining credulity before the run-up, BIPOP's shares then left the Earth's atmosphere; most of its ardent fans are scratching their heads. As one analyst put it, "despite how much we like the company, we cannot overcome our traditional bias, which would allow us to recommend a bank stock trading at 51 times our expected 2000 earnings."[5]

In January, as shares surged into the €90s, BIPOP's P/E broke into triple figures while its price-to-book value was over 11, versus Italian banking averages of 17 and 1.8, respectively.[6] Even when assessing a 25 percent premium due to unusually high levels of cross selling generated by the company's distribution network, Goldman Sachs came up with a valuation that was still several billion euros short of BIPOP's market cap, leaving the brokerage firm to wonder, "Does valuation matter?"[7]

One of the bank's underwriters, Morgan Stanley Dean Witter, came out with a note entitled "Take.A.Break.Com."[8] But perhaps the analysts at Société Générale captured the sentiment of the market most accurately: "When at a Feast, Don't Give Up Your Seat at the Table."[9]

What drove the year-end spasm in BIPOP shares? Just as important, can it be remotely justified?

With 60 percent of BIPOP's income generated through financial services, the market appears to be rerating the company more as an asset manager than as a bank.[10] Milan-based Société Générale banking analyst Alberto Gaddi observed that BIPOP, "in becoming Italy's number-one financial services provider, has more in common with Italian asset managers like Fideuram and Mediolanum than with the average Italian bank."[11] And this is borne out in comparing financial ratios—P/Es, price-to-book value, and return on equity.

But the predominant explanation for BIPOP's soaring share price lies in the fact that the stock got caught up with the craze for all things Internet. And we can see three key developments that sparked this connection.

First is the bank's rapid expansion into e-trading. Its online trading operations have grown at a torrid pace since they started up in 1999. Instead of ending a year with only several thousand clients, as originally projected, FIN-ECO, BIPOP's online bank and trading service, attracted 25,000 clients. This amounted to half the Italian online market. And on average, these investors were trading €100,000 worth of securities a month.[12]

Never mind the fact that net income from e-trading operations was in the red for 1999 and that it was expected to contribute no more than 11 percent to 2001 profits.[13] And never mind the fact that subsequent waves of new traders will be less active. The market seems focused on the demographics:

➤ The number of Italian shareholders is expected to double, to 7 million by 2002;[14]

➤ Internet penetration is likely to expand even faster, reaching into more than 15 percent of Italian households by 2001; and

➤ There will be 1.3 million Internet brokerage accounts in Italy by 2003.[15]

The second event: BIPOP struck a nonexclusive deal with Telecom Italia Mobile—the country's leading mobile service provider and one of Europe's major players—that could dramatically expand FIN-ECO's client base. The company, at no charge to TIM cell phone users, is offering to upgrade handsets to permit proprietary online trading. Capturing even a fraction of 1 percent of TIM's 18 million customers could be explosive for sales.

Third, and most intriguing, BIPOP acquired a 68 percent stake in DataNord Multimedia, one of only two Italian Internet and e-commerce consultants. "This gives BIPOP a portal into the huge untapped potential of e-commerce," observes Simone Concetti, Merrill Lynch banking analyst in Milan.[16] By helping retailers and wholesalers wire themselves for online business, DataNord could in turn encourage clients to make BIPOP the source of underlying debit or credit, giving the bank a stake in every sale it transacts.

From an earnings standpoint, although these three events cannot justify the level the stock hit in January 2000, they clearly suggest how BIPOP's unique network of products and distribution could boost sales and profits at a far greater pace than that of traditional banking. And that's what the market is responding to.

BIPOP's strategy of penetrating multiple levels of the economy, breaking through the limitations of traditional banking, could increase demand for its various products with each new industry it services. The key to all this: leveraging the Internet and the low-cost means it provides to integrate ostensibly disparate operations. One way we can see how this works is by looking at the number of bank products sold per client. In 1999, the average was 2.4. By 2001, the company expects the figure to reach 4.[17]

But what prevents other banks from adopting BIPOP's innovative strategies and cutting substantially into its growth? This is already happening. Three of Italy's largest banks, Banca Intesa, UniCredito, and San Paolo IMI, are developing competitive e-banking and e-trading networks supported by far greater capital and client bases. Because it is not weighed down with a lot of branches (only 238), BIPOP will retain a key efficiency advantage. And whereas most of BIPOP's Internet customers are new clients, the large banks are quite fearful of cannibalizing their own banking systems and seeing customers shift from higher fee and commission transactions to much less profitable e-rates. And unless they begin to shut down branch offices, e-banking will actually prove to be quite costly.

While its 50 percent market share in e-trading will substantially decline as the market for online trading expands, BIPOP's more sophisticated platform will also help it maintain its market leadership. Currently it's the only Italian e-trader offering access to the Paris, Frankfurt, New York, and Nasdaq exchanges, and soon, the Madrid exchange.

BIPOP is also well positioned to continue exploiting the current boom in the Italian mutual fund industry—a key driver of its asset management business. The hottest mutual funds market in Europe is in Italy, which is projected to expand at an annual rate of 22 percent through 2002. That's nearly twice the U.S. growth rate.[18] Its two fund companies, Cisalpina Gestioni and Azimut Gestione Fondi, are among the industry's top performers by asset class, having returned 31.1 percent and 24 percent, respectively, in 1999.[19] And through its joint venture with Putnam International, the Boston-based asset management firm, BIPOP is able to offer clients the most progressive range of domestic, European, international, and sector funds, with the largest exposure to equity markets available in Italy.

With over half its funds being stock or hybrid plays—twice the industry average—BIPOP is exposed to above-average market risks. However, indicative of how well it can manage during a correction, net sales in BIPOP funds actually increased by €1.2 billion during the last quarter of 1999, when Italian mutual funds suffered a cash outflow of €15.2 billion.[20]

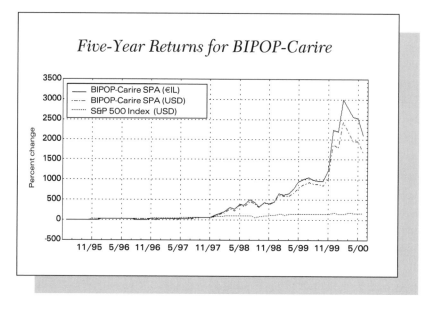

Five-Year Returns for BIPOP-Carire

BIPOP-Carire SPA (€IL)
BIPOP-Carire SPA (USD)
S&P 500 Index (USD)

Percent change

Source: Bloomberg

Investors should keep the following concerns in mind:

High cost of borrowing. To attract savers, the bank pays a high interest rate, especially on Internet accounts (3.5 percent), resulting in a negative deposit margin. The bank has turned to more expensive debt for funding, which is expected to account for one-third of BIPOP's interest-bearing liability in 2001.[21]

Above-average mutual fund costs. Despite providing investors with sound performance, increasing competition and transparency will force BIPOP to reduce front-end loads that run as high as 4 percent and management fees that average 2 percent on its equity funds.[22]

Ultimately, BIPOP's long-term success hinges on its ability to exploit its current momentum, leveraging its highly rated stock for strategic acquisitions and alliances. In several years, the playing field will level out among banks in terms of services and products, and BIPOP's subsequent size will prevent it from achieving today's eye-catching growth rates.

Therefore, it is essential that BIPOP soon carry enough financial weight to take on the industry leaders head-on. If it fails to achieve that status, it will be most challenged in the next growth phase in European banking—cross-border consolidation—which has already begun.

First-Half 2000 Highlights

➤ *Phenomenal growth*—Income grew by 57.4 percent, to €672.9 million, and earnings soared by 61.7 percent, to €186.2 million; heavy mutual fund activity helped push assets under management up by 71 percent, to more than €42.6 billion.

➤ *Shares have corrected*—Caught up in the spring Internet sell-off, BIPOP shares are off by more than 30 percent from their peak.

➤ *Soaring online brokerage service*—The number of clients doubled from the end of 1999, to more than 50,000; FIN-ECO now executes more than 7 percent of all transactions performed daily on the Italian Stock Exchange.

➤ *A major acquisition*—Plans to purchase Germany's leading online bank, Entrium Direct Bankers, for €2.5 billion will nearly double BIPOP's customer base, giving the enlarged enterprise a substantial foothold in Europe's largest banking market. Analysts at ABN AMRO believe "the two banks complement each other perfectly, with easily achievable synergies."[23]

Carrefour

Ticker: CA (Paris Stock Exchange)
Country: France
Industry: Retail Food

" *With complementary retailing expertise, increased purchasing power, and enhanced global market share generating greater efficiencies, lower costs, and higher margins— likely accelerating the rate of acquisitions—the merger of Carrefour and Promodès has created one of the most formidable retail operations in the world.* **"**

LEHMAN BROTHERS[1]

WITH PRAISE LIKE THAT being sung throughout the investment community celebrating the merger of two of France's top food retailers into the world's most geographically diverse operation, second only in size to Wal-Mart, Carrefour would appear to be the quintessential model of the New Europe and an automatic inclusion in this section.[2]

The financials are indeed overwhelming: projected sales for 2000

Key Findings

> ➤ The merger of two leading French food operators has created the most internationally diversified retailer in the industry, second in size only to Wal-Mart.

> ➤ The companies are a strong fit in terms of market share and management expertise, making Carrefour the first Pan-European food retailer and giving it significant market share in a variety of store formats.

> ➤ Projected three-year financials: cost savings are expected to exceed €1 billion, margins will likely rise by 200 basis points, and annual EPS growth should approach 30 percent.

> ➤ Main risks: the market is already comparing Carrefour to Wal-Mart—big expectations for a merger that only recently received regulatory approval; pace and effectiveness of corporate integration are unknowns; as is the question: Will Wal-Mart expand into France?

were nearly €62 billion and gross merger synergies were expected to top €1 billion, pushing EBITDA margins up two full points, from 6.1 to 8.1 percent, generating 3-year annualized earnings growth of nearly 30 percent.[3] Neither Europe nor the rest of the world has ever seen anything like this.

There's an immediate caveat. In mid-2000, only months after regulatory approval and with only a single joint financial under Carrefour's belt, no one could know how efficient or effective the new company will be. However, there wasn't a single analyst who doubted the long-term outcome of this $17 billion merger. Not one observer even questioned its logic. Despite my reservations about featuring a newly created company with a minimal track record, considering such universal confidence and given what is at stake, I must tell you about Carrefour.[4]

Since opening its doors in 1963, Carrefour has become France's number-one food retailer, with 1998 sales of €27.41 billion and net profits of €647 million. Its success has been driven by its expertise in hypermarkets (the European equivalent to superstores that combine food and nonfood products), superior merchandising, and marketing. Organic growth both in France and abroad has enabled it to maintain complete control over operations and has revealed Carrefour's remarkable ability to quickly learn what works in different cultures.

By the end of 1998, it operated 351 hypermarkets in twenty countries across Europe, Latin America, and Asia. Then, to accelerate expansion, it made an uncharacteristic move: an acquisition. It purchased the French supermarket chain Comptoirs Modernes for $6 billion, securing Carrefour's leading position in France and Brazil and second place in Spain.[5] Just as important, it provided Carrefour expertise in a second food format, giving it diversity essential for international expansion.[6]

By mid-1999, Carrefour had grown into the world's sixth-largest food retailer by sales and the third-biggest by market cap, which exceeded €26 billion. It had racked up a 5-year annualized earnings growth rate of 19 percent through 1998.[7] And its stock performance was, as Alberto Montagne of Lehman Brothers put it, "nothing short of spectacular," up more than 30 percent a year over the five years preceding September 1999.[8]

Promodès opened up shop two years before Carrefour, in 1961, in the Normandy town of Caen. This smaller operation had 1998 sales of €19.5 billion and net profit of €293 million.[9] Within the food retail industry worldwide, it ranked sixteenth in sales and thirteenth in market cap.[10]

However, Promodès excelled in two key ways. First, it operated a wide diversity of formats: hypermarkets, supermarkets, and convenience and discount stores, as well as wholesale outlets in Europe, Latin America, and Asia. Second, it consolidated the industry's first Pan-European food network. It achieved significant market share in Belgium (30.6 percent), Portugal (18.1 percent), Greece (18 percent), Spain (13.6 percent), and Italy (4.5 percent) through its willingness to pursue joint ventures, demonstrating its strengths in franchising and logistics (coordinating efficient product movement from suppliers to warehouses to shelves).[11] According to Jaime Vasquez, lead retail food analyst at Salomon Smith Barney in London, Promodès was "probably the best-positioned food retailer in Europe, capable of negotiating the best purchasing terms from suppliers, helping to eliminate cross-border wholesale pricing differentials."[12]

The result of aggressive expansion across the Continent was an annual earnings growth rate of 22 percent from 1994 through 1998. That's about as good as it gets in the industry. And the stock market rewarded its shares accordingly, boosting their value by 30 percent annually from the first quarter of 1994 through the first quarter of 1999.[13] Between April and the end of August 1999, when the merger was announced, Promodès's shares soared an additional 60 percent, giving it a market cap of €18 billion.

Since Carrefour paid a hefty price for Promodès (a 20 percent premium on top of an already inflated price), the first obvious question about the deal is whether it made financial sense. By every analyst's account, the answer is a resounding yes. Strategically, it provided Carrefour four key benefits.

> The merger put Carrefour center stage, immediately making the French retailer the dominant European player, making possible cross-border economies of scale and further Continental expansion.
> With intense industry consolidation going on, led by Wal-Mart's foray into Germany and Britain, the merger protects Carrefour from corporate raiders who might have been eyeing its superior position and its vulnerable 70 percent share float.
> It enhanced its international position beyond the likes of any other player, preparing it to exploit global supplier discounts.
> It positions the company to funnel its strong European cash flow into additional emerging markets, which are themselves quickly consolidating and maturing.

Besides the advantages of being a same-country merger, which eliminates a whole host of cultural, linguistic, and political complications that come with cross-border deals, the deal makes sense from an asset point of view. The holdings of each company should meld well together, offering synergies and enhanced valuation that more than make up for Promodès's high cost. Salomon Smith Barney explained it simply: the present value of all its synergies far exceeds the premium Carrefour paid for Promodès.[14] The group's new earnings power will increase Carrefour's P/E multiple, pushing up its market value beyond the premium it paid for Promodès.

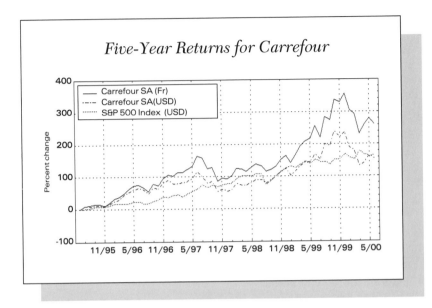

Five-Year Returns for Carrefour

Source: Bloomberg

Here are some financial projections for the years through 2002:

➤ Purchasing and supply chain savings should total €760 million,

➤ Advertising and marketing expenses should be cut by €152 million,

➤ Administration costs should decline by the same amount,

➤ Integration is expected to cost €229 million plus an additional €76 million to upgrade the group's information technology system, and

➤ Net synergies are projected to be €765 million.[15]

The deal's bottom-line impact on earnings appears to be truly remarkable. Food retail analyst Amita Gulati at Morgan Stanley Dean Witter in London projects Carrefour's organic earnings growth will continue to expand at an annual rate of 14 percent through 2002. Margins will see an annual improvement of 3 percent, and synergies will add 13 percent to earnings each year. Total EPS growth is therefore projected to increase on average by 30 percent a year through 2002.[16]

How big will Carrefour then be? Even after selling off some stores to satisfy monopolistic concerns of regulators, Carrefour still operates 10,082 stores in twenty-seven countries across four continents. It has the leading market share in France (24 percent), Spain (21.9 percent), Portugal (21.3 percent), Belgium (30.6 percent), Greece (19 percent), Argentina (13.8 percent), Brazil (5.4 percent), and Taiwan (3 percent). It is Italy's second-largest food retailer and has emerging market positions in Indonesia, Poland, Turkey, China, the Czech Republic, Chile, Columbia, Mexico, Malaysia, Singapore, and Thailand. It also has stores in Hong Kong and Korea.[17]

So what can get in the way of this solid-looking merger?

➤ Even before the ink had dried on the deal, the market began valuing Carrefour as if it were Wal-Mart. That makes for some pretty hefty expectations.

➤ Smooth integration of operations is never a sure thing, especially given the two companies' past managerial differences: Promodès being comfortable with franchising and sharing power, Carrefour needing to be in control.

➤ Risk of direct competition from another global player remains possible. At this moment, Wal-Mart and Carrefour are only going head-to-head in Mexico and Brazil. If the U.S. giant (with twice the market cap of Carrefour) is able to establish a French beachhead in conjunction with its German and U.K. operations, Carrefour's margins and cash flow could be threatened, along with expansion plans essential for propelling earnings growth. Keep in mind that achieving 15 or 20 percent annual earnings growth on a sales basis of €30 billion (Carrefour's former size) was a lot easier than on the current basis of €62 billion.

As of year-end 1999, the consensus was that Carrefour is indeed in the same league as Wal-Mart. On a global basis, many analysts believe Carrefour could be an even stronger play. Regulatory approval had minimal impact on the company's overall structure. Integration is going rather smoothly. And as for Wal-Mart, European regulation—especially in France—makes it difficult for companies to expand organically. There are limited large-scale acquisitions that will suit Wal-Mart's tastes. And outside of western Europe and the United States, Carrefour has a superior performance record, frankly making it the player to beat in key emerging markets.

First-Half 2000 Highlights

➤ *Positive initial postmerger results*—With revenues of €30.68 billion, sales growth of the new Carrefour group climbed 27.7 percent versus the combined pre-merger first-half 1999 revenues of Carrefour and Promodès. EBIT grew 36.7 percent, to €831 million. However, the effects of goodwill amortization and nonrecurring expenses limited net profit growth per share to 4.3 percent.

➤ *Stock correction*—After soaring by more than 70 percent in 1999, Carrefour shares pulled back more than 20 percent. Increased debt, necessary to finance consolidation moves in Greece, Italy, Belgium, and Argentina, pushed up interest costs, slowing earnings growth in 2000. Still, the company is on target to double earnings between 1999 and 2002.

➤ *Retail's first worldwide online supply marketplace*—Sears, Carrefour, and Oracle are creating a multibillion-dollar business-to-business alliance that will reduce purchasing expenses and enhance supply chain efficiencies. GlobalNetXchange, as it's called, will initially serve the two retailers' $80 billion supply-chain purchases from 50,000 suppliers, partners, and distributors.

Hennes & Mauritz

Ticker: HM B (Stockholm Stock Exchange)
Country: Sweden
Industry: Retail

❝ *Hennes & Mauritz is one of the most successful cross-border retailers around, delivering consistent growth in sales, profits, and returns in the industry. Strong management does a good job containing costs and generating earnings surprises on a regular basis. And the company's expansion into the U.S. offers massive potential for long-term growth.* **❞**

HSBC SECURITIES[1]

THE INVESTMENT PREMISE of the Sweden-based clothing retailer Hennes & Mauritz is a simple one: appeal to the thirty-five-and-under crowd looking for affordable designer-style fashions. Not just GAP khaki or dress-down casual, H&M creates clothing that's runway stylish as well. It keeps prices down by generating huge turnover, which it achieves by setting up shops in prime high-street locations: the Kuhdamm in Berlin, the Rue de Rivoli in Paris, and Fifth Avenue in New York City.

Few retailers address this market niche, and none better than H&M, which saw sales double from SKr 13.52 billion in FY 1994 to SKr 26.65

Key Findings

➤ Swedish-based Hennes & Mauritz was the top European retail story in the last half of the 1990s, with shares soaring 69.16 percent annually in local currency terms over five years through the first quarter of 2000.

➤ Sales more than doubled between FY 1995 and FY 1999, ending the decade at SEK 27.89 billion; operating margins hit 16.4 percent, boosting profits to SEK 3.08 billion by the end of 1999.

➤ H&M achieved the rare retail feat of successful cross-border expansion, with 84 percent of FY 1999 sales generated in foreign markets.

➤ Keys to the company's success: creating affordable clothing, a superb record of responding to changing consumer tastes, a rapid production process, and individually managed stores.

➤ Main risk: a trailing P/E of 50—exorbitant for the retail sector—and a first-half 2000 slowdown; yet continued foreign expansion could help the company quickly regain its footing.

billion in FY 1999. Profits rose even faster, from SKr 1.07 billion to SKr 2.29 billion.[2] And this performance propelled shares up a staggering 69.16 percent annually in local currency terms over the five years through the first quarter of 2000, making H&M among Europe's top-performing stocks.[3]

Here are some of the keys to Hennes & Mauritz's success.

➤ Thirty designers are very good at capturing the latest fashion trends.

➤ An efficient production process enables H&M to get these designs into stores weekly, whereas most retailers introduce new clothing lines three, maybe four times a year. "Every time you walk into one of their stores, there are new products; there is a real freshness," observes Keith Wills, retail analyst at Goldman Sachs in London.[4]

Not only does this keep customers coming back to the store frequently to see what's new, but such rapid turnover encourages even casual shoppers to make purchases sooner rather than later. As a result, H&M has been able to generate same-store annual growth that's consistently in the double digits.

➤ H&M hires supermodels and celebrities to promote its latest fashions in order to enhance the image of the clothes and the company.

➤ Each of the company's 600-plus stores are individually run; managers respond to their own particular clientele, which cuts down on administrative inefficiencies.

➤ H&M's information technology systems feed back sales data to its design and manufacturing groups daily, enabling them to quickly react to the latest buying trends. Just as important, such information enables H&M to decide which stores require expansion and which should be shut down.[5]

Ultimately, H&M's success has been founded on a new design phenomenon: globalized fashion trends. *The Economist* reported that "national tastes are disappearing due to feeding the MTV generation—from Tokyo to London—the same diet of satellite television, movies, and music, with the Internet shrinking the world further."[6]

Started as a small women's clothing store in Västerås, Sweden, in 1947, expanding into menswear with the 1968 acquisition of Mauritz Wildfoiss, and subsequently moving into the teenagers' and children's markets, H&M has regularly looked toward foreign outlets for growth. This completely counters the industry dictum that distinct domestic tastes make it difficult for retailers to successfully cross borders.

In the 1960s, H&M opened stores in Norway and Denmark. In the 1970s, it ventured into the United Kingdom and Switzerland, then into Germany and the Netherlands in the 1980s. Recognizing the consolidation of high-style fashion, especially among the younger generation, H&M made its most aggressive moves in the 1990s, opening stores in Belgium, Austria, Luxembourg, Finland, and France.[7] And in 2000, H&M opened shops in Barcelona and New York City.

One of just a handful of highly successful multinational retailers, H&M relies on its foreign share of sales, which hit 85 percent in 1999.[8] With its international profits actually higher than those the company is earning at home, H&M's operating margins hit 16.4 percent in FY

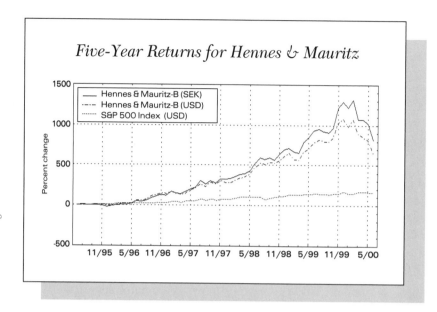

Five-Year Returns for Hennes & Mauritz

Source: Bloomberg

1999—extraordinary for a mid-to-low-end retailer. And this helped total profits soar 34.5 percent in FY 1999.[9]

This kind of growth led to a stratospheric multiple of 75 by the end of 1999.[10] For a retail stock that's outrageous, clearly indicating delusional market expectation—which was subsequently deflated in spring 2000 when growth began to slow. On March 23, H&M shares fell by more than 30 percent when the company issued a profit warning and its chief executive, Fabian Mansson, resigned. The key problems:

➤ Higher inventories and greater markdowns,

➤ A weak euro accounting for 50 percent of the first-half 2000 shortfall,[11] and

➤ High initial costs of expanding into New York and Spain.

Although the current stumble hit H&M's shares hard, it was not necessarily unexpected given the inherent whimsy of the fashion industry. And many analysts believe that long-term the company should be able to regain its strong growth rate. Mal Patel, Merrill Lynch's lead retail analyst in London, explains that H&M's high valuation "is justified due to the rare combination of sustained momentum, visibility, and the dearth of alternative growth stories, which is likely to keep a correction at bay for some time."[12]

Then there is the issue of liquidity. With a market cap of $17 billion,

Hennes & Mauritz is Sweden's third-largest stock. But as Louise von Blixen, retail analyst at SG Securities in London, points out, H&M's size makes it "a core holding in any Nordic portfolio. That demand, in combination with a limited supply [its free float is only 58 percent], helps to drive the share price."[13]

But perhaps the most compelling support for a multiple that's still double that of Gap, Inc., is H&M's ability to export its store brand without a hitch—a rare feat in the retail world. Between FY 1995 and FY 1999, while the number of its stores grew from 357 to 613, sales per store increased cumulatively by nearly 45 percent. Profits per store more than doubled.[14]

But is there much more room for expansion? There seems to be. H&M's retail share in Germany—the company's largest market, with more than 190 stores—is only around 2 percent. In the more challenging U.K. market, H&M's 45 stores have accumulated less than 1 percent of the country's retail business.[15] H&M has captured only a 1.2 percent share of the $250 billion European apparel market.[16]

H&M has barely ventured into southern Europe, whose markets—especially in Italy—would appear to be a natural fit. Eastern Europe, with its younger generation's enthusiasm for things western, is virgin territory for H&M. And until it opened its Fifth Avenue store in New York City in 2000, H&M hadn't even touched the vast (albeit highly competitive) American market, which potentially stands to be the largest part of this remarkable growth story.

First-Half 2000 Highlights

➤ *Disappointing results*—Sales growth slowed to 10 percent, and earnings were off 11 percent due to a combination of inventory, expansion, and currency-related issues.

➤ *Major loss*—H&M's chief executive, Fabian Mansson, suddenly resigned without explanation.

➤ *Huge price correction*—Shares were down as much as 50 percent from their peak in early 2000.

➤ *Weakened brokerage support*—Analyst recommendations have been tempered.

➤ *Successful U.S. opening*—Three new stores opened in the New York metropolitan area, including its flagship on Fifth Avenue, with sales running ahead of expectations.

Nokia

Ticker: NOK (NYSE)
Country: Finland
Industry: Telecommunications

" *Coupling a prescient vision of exploding wireless markets with flawless execution by its management and conservative guidance on earnings growth, we regard Nokia as the premier growth stock in Europe.* **"**

GOLDMAN SACHS & CO.[1]

THE CONVERSION OF FINNISH-BASED NOKIA from a sprawling, unfocused conglomerate into a worldwide leader in mobile telecommunications is a remarkable story of restructuring and market deregulation, showing the potential of European companies when they shed their risk-averse nature. "What Intel is doing for microprocessors, Nokia is doing for mobile," exclaims European management specialist Robert Heller.[2] This comparison is no better in evidence than in the meteoric rise of Nokia shares. Between the first quarter of 1995 and the first quarter of 2000, the stock rose a mind-boggling 103.44 percent a year in local currency terms, making it the second-best-performing European equity over that time.

This kind of appreciation may rightfully leave many to wonder if the stock has much octane left in its tank. The broad market consensus is that it does. Nokia has the technology, manufacturing capacity, and marketing acumen to exploit the industry's increasingly open standards and geometric expansion. Most impressive, observes Goldman Sachs, is an evolving business model that "combines elements of Dell [working-capital lean and high-volume manufacturing] with those of Microsoft [long development cycles giving way to high gross margin license sales] and Cisco [enhancing core activities through the integration of niche technologies secured through a series of small, strategic acquisitions]."[3]

One could hardly imagine the company's current state given its roots as a paper and pulp manufacturer that opened up shop in 1865. By the turn of the century, with the addition of a rubber works and chemical division, Nokia was forming one of Europe's earliest conglomerates. Its strategy: exploit its isolated Scandinavian geography to offer business and consumers an early version of one-stop shopping, gaining a domi-

Key Findings

➤ Nokia is one of Europe's top growth stocks; shares soared 103.44 percent annually in local currency terms over the five years through the first quarter of 2000.

➤ The company has become the world's largest manufacturer of mobile phones, which generate 66 percent of total sales and nearly 80 percent of profits, and is well positioned to exploit the explosive demand projected for mobile phones through 2002.

➤ Nokia's infrastructure group has been involved in developing nearly 29 percent of all GSM digital infrastructure networks worldwide; business is expected to expand in concert with worldwide telecom deregulation.

➤ The stock's high proportion of institutional ownership and sky-high valuation expose shares to substantial volatility, with the risk of sharp downturns on news of even minor performance slips. This occurred one day in July 2000, when the stock collapsed by 26.5 percent on news of product delays.

nant position in a variety of essential markets. Then in 1912, foreshadowing where the company would go, Nokia expanded into electronics and telephone cables.

After surviving two world wars, the company took a major step in its evolution when in the 1960s it became the first company to successfully transmit voice and data digitally over cable. This led to further expansion and acquisitions in technology, with an increasing focus on electronics and telecommunications.

By the 1980s, the company's diversity—and its lack of focus—was no better in evidence than in what was found in its employee store: rubber boots, snow tires, toilet paper, televisions, audio speakers, and first-generation cellular phones. However, by this time, it was becoming clear that the cost of conglomeration was sluggish growth.

Then in 1992 the head of Nokia's fledgling cellular-phone division, Jorma Ollila, was catapulted to the top of the company. Having witnessed firsthand Europe's move toward a digital standard for mobile phones, Ollila gambled that a restructured firm focused on mobile communications could transform Nokia into an industry leader in a new and potentially explosive market.

Between 1995 and 1999, sales increased by more than 33 percent a year, ending the decade at nearly €20 billion. Over this time, operating profit margins grew from 13.6 to 19.8 percent, commitment to research and development soared from €426 million to €1.76 billion, and return on equity rose sharply, from 31.2 to 41.3 percent.[4]

Sharp financial gains have been achieved by rebuilding the company around two core groups: mobile phones and telecommunications (infrastructure networks).

Mobile Phones

In 1998 Nokia became the world's largest mobile phone manufacturer, selling more than 40 million units in 120 countries, achieving a 25 percent global market share. Sales topped €8 billion. In 1999, mobile phone sales topped €13 billion. In the first half of 2000, operating margins reached 24.5 percent, well above the industry average, while inventory turnover was approaching single digits.[5] Mobile phones generated 66 percent of company sales and nearly 80 percent of its operating profits.

Although phone unit margins are expected to come under increasing competitive pressure, projected rapid expansion of mobile phone penetration globally (from 6.2 percent in 1998 to 19.2 percent in 2003), coupled with a corresponding explosion in total handset sales from 165 million in 1998 to 446 million in 2002, will more than offset any decline in unit profitability.[6] Name-brand recognition is especially valuable, with more than 40 percent of the market involving upgrade sales. The company also agilely addresses diverse market groups (from teenagers up through CEOs) by successfully spinning off variations of core models. This effectively reduces research and development costs per unit, further sustaining profitability.

Jan Dworsky, telecom analyst at Crédit Agricole Indosuez in Paris, projects Nokia's mobile phone sales to climb 113 percent between 1998 and 2001, exceeding €17 billion, with operating margins expected to rise to 21.4 percent.[7] Two big contracts secured in June

1999 that are helping Nokia reach these goals include a $165 million CDMA digital phone order from Telefônica Celular in Brazil and a dual-band order placed by Sprint PCS worth up to $500 million.

Infrastructure

Nokia Networks develops and manufactures infrastructure equipment and systems for mobile, fixed-line, and Internet protocol networks. From 1995 through 1999, annual sales grew by more than 34 percent, to nearly €5.67 billion. With operating margins of nearly 18.1 percent, the group has helped develop ninety-four operating systems across forty-three countries. This has given Nokia a 28 percent market share of all GSM digital infrastructure networks worldwide.[8]

Growth is being driven by worldwide telecom deregulation, which is opening up new markets, especially across Europe and Asia. New operating licenses increase the need for expanded and more competitive infrastructure by both incumbents and new service providers. Some examples: a $160 million contract with Primatel to set up Hungary's first nationwide GSM network; a $180 million mobile network ugrade for Omnitel, a leading Italian mobile telecom company, the second-largest GSM network operator in Europe; and a $300 million–plus GSM expansion for network service provider Fujian in China.[9]

Nokia is relying on small strategic acquisitions to enhance its infrastructure technology and its position in Internet protocol telephony. Among the $500 million in corporate acquisitions made between 1997 and 1999 were Ipsilon (routing platforms), Vienna Systems (voice, fax, and video distribution), and Diamond Lane (high-speed Internet access).

These purchases are part of Nokia's overall strategy, which is fundamentally altering mobile telephony. No longer just a means of wireless voice communications, the mobile phone in Nokia's vision will be an interactive extension of the desktop computer, having complete integration with the Internet. In fact, Nokia predicts that by the end of 2004, more mobile devices than fixed terminals—including PCs—will be connected to the Internet.[10]

Toward this end, Nokia is working with other major telecom competitors to develop a new generation of open industry standards. Some of the new software sports unusual names, such as Bluetooth, Symbian, and WAP (Wireless Application Protocol).

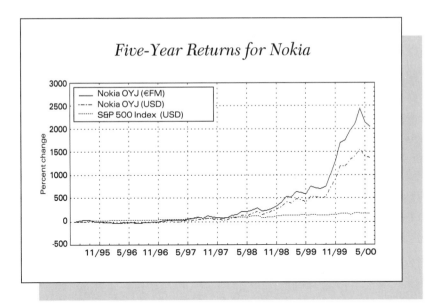

Five-Year Returns for Nokia

- Nokia OYJ (€FM)
- Nokia OYJ (USD)
- S&P 500 Index (USD)

Source: Bloomberg

Cooperating in technological innovation to shape a common operating standard is not a new strategy for Nokia. The company's success in both mobile phone and infrastructure sales has been based on the spread of a common digital platform for cellular communication—first across Europe, and now expanding across the States and throughout much of Asia. The logic: a uniform market offers far greater potential for profit than a fractured one based on various proprietary standards. The risk: well-financed, technologically innovative competitors could claim substantial market share. Indeed, Nokia will find itself competing directly or peripherally with the likes of Ericsson, Motorola, Alcatel, Lucent, Nortel, and Microsoft.

However, by being a complete telecommunications supplier, offering a full range of hardware and services—from infrastructure development to the phones that bring the network into the customer's hands—Nokia is betting it will be able to exploit the exploding market for mobile communications. Based on an expanding commitment to research and development (8.9 percent of 1999 sales) and a remarkable track record in reading and timing market trends, odds are that Nokia will continue to outperform the market.

The risk is that if Nokia slips at all in the face of increasing competition, the market could punish its shares as quickly as it has rewarded them. This concern is made more acute by the fact that institutional investors, known more for their trading than their long-term holds, control 90 percent of Nokia's free float.

First-Half 2000 Highlights

➤ *Terrific results*—Net sales rose 61.6 percent, to €6.98 billion; operating profit increased by 65.4 percent, to €1.41 billion; operating margin hit 20.2 percent; and EPS soared by more than 77 percent.

➤ *Shares rise and split*—Shares were up nearly 19 percent through June, after having split 4 to 1 in February.

➤ *Huge infrastructure contract*—Nokia secured its largest network contract—a $900 million deal to upgrade and expand a GSM network for Telsim, a leading Turkish mobile operator.

➤ *Frighteningly prescient*—As if on cue, shares collapsed 26.5 percent one day in July due to anticipated delays in product development. The day after, Nokia announced plans to buy back up to 36 million shares.

Ryanair

Ticker: RYAAY (Nasdaq)
Country: Ireland
Industry: Airlines

" *Ryanair is the largest and most profitable player in Europe's rapidly expanding low-fare airline market. Having established a proven low-cost structure, annual revenue growth of 25 percent, strong margins, and substantial financial resources, Ryanair will continue to aggressively develop new routes across Europe's recently deregulated market. And this should help ensure continued strong share performance.* **"**

SALOMON SMITH BARNEY[1]

IF YOU REGRET not having gotten into Southwest Airlines when it was a young upstart, Ryanair offers you a second chance.

Ryanair's story mirrors many of the features driving the region's financial renaissance: corporate restructuring, market deregulation, and increasing integration of economic activity across Europe. Specifically, the airline is a paradigm of what happens when a company intro-

Key Findings

➤ Modeled after Southwest Airlines, Ireland's Ryanair has become the largest and most profitable low-fare carrier in Europe.

➤ It is the best airline play in Europe, redefining the industry from cyclical to growth with sales that are rising 28 percent a year, operation margins of 23 percent, and EPS growth averaging a non-airline-like 21 percent a year.

➤ After it went public in spring 1997, shares rose more than 300 percent in local currency terms through the first quarter of 2000.

➤ The company's relatively small size (market cap of €3 billion) and large degree of float expose its shares to short-term volatility.

➤ But over the long term, the market for low-fare air service is poised to expand dramatically, ultimately minimizing investment risks.

duces an essential service at an affordable rate for customers who are used to paying nearly the same fare to travel within Europe as to cross the ocean.

After initially stumbling out of the block in the mid-1980s, this small Dublin-based also-ran remade itself in 1991 as a low-fare no-frills airline. Company founder Tony Ryan knew Southwest chairman Herb Kelleher, and with his then tax consultant Michael O'Leary by his side, he ventured to Texas to see how things were done. "It was like the road to Damascus," Ryan recalled, "and we quickly realized that this was the way to make Ryanair work."[2]

The keys to Southwest's low-fare model, which Ryanair has embraced:

➤ Use of a single plane type (737) reduces operation and maintenance costs and maximizes pilot flexibility;

➤ Flying only into secondary airports reduces landing/departure charges, and the airports' lower levels of congestion promote fast (twenty-five-minute) turnarounds and therefore more flights per plane per day;

➤ No-frills service keeps costs down and also minimizes turnaround times;

➤ Point-to-point travel (without transfers) eliminates passenger- and baggage-related delays and enables transparent analysis of a route's profitability;

➤ Low administrative costs means all support operations are efficient and nonluxurious, right down to the furniture; and

➤ Safety is the first priority, because low-fare airlines have a difficult time recovering from accidents.[3]

Soon after his visit to Texas, Ryan put O'Leary in charge of remaking the company into Europe's low-fare airline. The fleet was revamped, multiple classes of service were eliminated, and the travel network was slashed from more than twenty routes to four, focusing on the Dublin-to-London run, the twin hubs of the airline's network.

By the end of the 1980s, a typical one-way ticket cost I£ 169. Then between 1993 and 1997 came industry deregulation, paving the way for the airline's explosive growth by eliminating the bulk of Europe's competitive flight restrictions. By early 2000, Ryanair was flying 6 million passengers a year on twenty-six planes to thirty-five destinations in ten countries. The Dublin-to-London run has become the most traveled international route in the world, traversed by 4 million passengers a year. It represents nearly one-fourth of Ryanair's business, with fares as low as I£ 19.

In classic supply-side fashion, replacing Europe's traditionally high, regulated rates with low fares is rapidly expanding the market for air travel. In June 1999, just six weeks after launching service from its London hub in Stansted to Frankfurt, Ryanair was carrying more passengers than Lufthansa.[4] Some were crossovers from existing carriers, but the majority were new travelers enticed by fares 20 percent below the lowest coach rates. And this is how Ryanair is redefining a cyclical business into a growth story.

Between FY 1996 and FY 2000, Ryanair revenues grew 27.5 percent a year, from €140 million to nearly €370 million. Operating profits climbed slightly faster, increasing 28.3 percent a year, while after-tax profits rose by nearly 35 percent a year.[5] And the future looks just as bright.

Between FY 2000 and FY 2003, it is a good bet that Ryanair will be able to sustain these same lofty numbers by averaging the addition of more than six new planes and five new routes every year. This will nearly double the size of its fleet and expand capacity by 150 percent while reducing the fleet's average age from a mature 15.4 years to a more youthful 11.2 years.[6]

Compared to those of the European airline industry as a whole, Ryanair's financials are simply stunning. Its sales growth is eight times the industry average. Its EBIT margins have been expanding four to five times faster. And where Ryanair's EPS has turned in consistent double-digit gains, earnings at most major carriers have been contracting.[7]

While the stock's small size (market cap of €3 billion) and large degree of float exposes it to volatility, the company's strong performance has helped Ryanair shares rise dramatically since its 1997 IPO on the Dublin and Nasdaq exchanges. In nearly three years, through March 2000, the stock was up 307 percent in local currency terms.

Ireland's continued strong growth, rising household incomes, and declining corporate tax rate, coupled with the company's increasing reliance on Internet sales (40 percent of all bookings) and a declining depreciation schedule, should significantly boost bottom-line profitability over the next few years. But what makes Ryanair a truly intriguing investment story (even more so than Southwest Airlines) is its huge market potential.

Unlike the United States, where the airline industry is a mature, deregulated market, Europe is virtually virgin territory. Low-fare airlines in the States carry 24 percent of all passengers, generating 17 percent of total domestic industry revenue. In Europe, only 2.8 percent of all passengers are flying on low-fare airlines, and they account for only 1.5 percent of all airline sales.[8]

Industry analysts do not expect low-fare airlines in Europe to capture anywhere near the same market share as in the States because of generally shorter travel distances that make alternative services viable (e.g., trains and ferries). But they do project that low-fare airlines will eventually attract 10 to 15 percent of all air passengers and revenues. And that speaks of tremendous near-term growth potential.

Although much of this expansion comes from an enlarged passenger

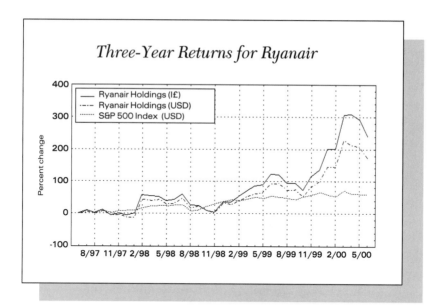

Three-Year Returns for Ryanair

— Ryanair Holdings (I£)
-·- Ryanair Holdings (USD)
······ S&P 500 Index (USD)

market, Europe's former state carriers—Lufthansa, British Airways, Alitalia, and Air France—are taking direct hits. They still dominate most intra-European travel, but they are losing their monopolies. And their response over the next several years to this more competitive environment will determine just how deep low-fare airlines will be able to penetrate the market.

The current price war has so far cost incumbents a relatively small portion of their existing passengers. But where the big carriers are getting hurt the most is in their growth rates, which have been cut in half.[9] Ultimately, in a sustained fare battle, the majors will lose money on many of their routes due to their high structural costs borne from the days when they were inefficient government-owned operations.

Perhaps indicative of where all this may be leading was British Airways' strategic policy change announced in 1999 that seeks to reduce the airline's intra-European service, shrinking its overall business and refocusing operations on more profitable full-fare transcontinental routes.

If this proves prescient and other majors follow, then this will be a boon to Europe's low-fare carriers. And given its dominant position, Ryanair seems extremely well positioned to profit from this fundamental industry shift.

Ryanair does face several basic risks, however.

Growing competition. Although it is the largest and most profitable low-fare airline in Europe, competition will intensify. London-based EasyJet and British Airways' start-up, GO, are the ones to watch. They currently compete directly with Ryanair on only a few routes, but that will change.

Airport fees. Secondary airports offer very low landing charges to low-fare operators initiating routes. But once operations are established at an airport, these fees rise. In fact, coupled with increasing ground charges, airport costs are now growing at twice the rate of revenue, amounting to 10 percent of total expenses, and are pushing down operating margins.[10] Ryanair is still small and flexible enough to move out of an airport that pushes up charges too quickly. However, as the airline's operations mature and become more profitable at certain locations, it may not be able to respond as nimbly.

Fuel costs. Ryanair is among the most aggressively hedged airlines against rising fuel prices, maintaining rolling twelve-month contracts for 70 to 90 percent of its fuel needs. This contained the dramatic rise in oil prices in 1999. But as its contracts are exercised, and if fuel prices remain high, the company will eventually be hit by this escalating cost.

Currency exposure. With more than half its business generated in the United Kingdom and 60 percent of its costs in British pounds and U.S. dollars, Ryanair has substantial currency risks. This will continue as long as Great Britain remains outside of the euro (of which Ireland is a part).[11] The company mitigates a part of this risk by matching revenues and costs by currency. When this isn't possible, Ryanair purchases future dollar contracts to cover aircraft purchases, fuel, and insurance expenses.[12]

First-Half 2000 Highlights

➤ *Continued strong performance*—Second-quarter results, ending June 30, 2000, showed passengers up 32 percent, to 1.67 million, revenue gains of 37 percent, to €115.0 million, and earnings after taxes climbing 29 percent, to €18.1 million .

➤ *Shares rise*—Though hit by profit-taking at the end of the second quarter, shares were still up by more than 14 percent.

➤ *Recognition*—Ryanair earned industry accolades as the "Best Managed National Carrier" for the second consecutive year and was named

"Most Efficient Operator" by *Aviation Week & Space Technology*.
➤ *Index boost*—Demand for Ryanair shares received a boost by the stock's inclusion in the Dow Jones STOXX Index in March.

SAP

Ticker: SAP (NYSE)
Country: Germany
Industry: Software

66 *SAP's superior profitability, earnings outlook, and leading blue-chip status make it among our top European stock picks. And the company's increasing reliance on the Web—as a more flexible and affordable delivery platform and as a means of providing electronic business-to-business marketplaces—is encouraging the market to rerate SAP as an Internet play.* 99

WARBURG DILLON READ[1]

ASK THE AVERAGE INVESTOR to name a non-American software maker. He likely can't. Software is not a typical European enterprise. Then again, SAP's cochairman and CEO, Hasso Plattner, is not your typical executive.

Leaving IBM with four other colleagues in 1972 after Big Blue was unable to see the point of their new prototype program, Plattner and his friends subsequently went on to capture nearly 40 percent of the $20 billion global market for enterprise resource planning (ERP) software. This has helped transform SAP into the third-largest software maker in the world, giving Plattner something of a cult status in the Continent's burgeoning tech culture. As *The Wall Street Journal* put it, "whether jamming on an electric guitar at a gathering of SAP customers or dropping his pants during a yacht race to moon minions of Larry Ellison of software rival Oracle, Plattner is capturing the fancy of a new generation of entrepreneurs."[2]

So what is ERP? It's the total integration of back-office functions, from order entry to manufacturing, inventory control, accounting, and staff compensation. The point: to increase efficiency and profitability, management must be able to thoroughly track and understand business operations—the flow of products, services, and cash

Key Findings

> ➤ German-based SAP is the world's largest manufacturer of enterprise resource planning software (ERP), with a 39 percent market share.
> ➤ Shares soared more than thirteenfold between 1995 and 1999, pushing the company's market capitalization to more than $56 billion.
> ➤ The stock is a core technology holding in most European funds.
> ➤ The company's belated adoption of an Internet-based operating and delivery platform is refocusing growth on supply-chain management and the explosive potential of business-to-business e-commerce.
> ➤ As a result, the market is rerating the stock as an Internet play, vastly increasing SAP's valuation and risk.

from the beginning of the pipeline to the end. No more tail wagging the dog or the left hand not knowing what the right forefinger is up to. So when a sale is made, not only does the company know it has the merchandise in stock and the price it paid for it, but it knows that inventory will be automatically replenished whenever it drops below a critical level. Ultimately, the appeal of ERP is that it can enable companies to focus their attention on the very essentials of business: developing ideas and selling them.

ERP has become common procedure in most of the world's leading multinationals, and as the *Financial Times* reported, "SAP's flagship R/3 software has become the de facto standard."[3] It has been installed in 60 percent of *Fortune* 500 operations. And this has helped propel group sales by 270 percent, from €1.38 billion in 1995 to €5.11 billion in 1999. Net profits nearly tripled, from €211 million to €602 million. And shares of SAP have soared, from €44.89 to €598.

But it hasn't been all smooth sailing, especially toward the close of 1999, when the stock took a roller-coaster ride. After peaking in the third quarter of 1998 at €672, the stock slid tumultuously over the next several months, bottoming out at €269 in the first quarter of 1999. The reasons behind the skid: some were a matter of timing; but the market also identified some fundamental flaws in SAP's business model.

First: R/3 can take up to eighteen months or longer to install. As early as mid-1998, clients began expressing concern that the prolonged programming period would run right into Y2K, and that cut into orders.

Second: The Asia-Pacific market, SAP's third largest, was hit hard by the lingering effects of the 1997 currency and securities crisis, the Russian debt crisis of 1998, and especially by recession in Japan, which cut deeply into the country's capital spending.

Third: Because R/3 was so successfully licensed to global-sized clients, SAP developed the reputation of being user-unfriendly for small-to-midsize companies, leaving a sizable market pretty much untapped.

Fourth: SAP was slow to recognize several significant industry shifts.

➤ The high-end multinational market for ERP is becoming saturated. There's a finite number of large-scale clients that can afford the time and money required to implement R/3. SAP had already achieved substantial market penetration, and R/3-related sales alone can no longer be expected to sustain the company's 30 to 40 percent revenue growth, an expansion rate the market is demanding of SAP.

➤ Whereas R/3 was a watershed in back-office management, it failed to exploit the potential for front-office management and to focus on customer relations.

➤ SAP was late in developing the Internet as a more flexible and less expensive operating platform for delivering its software.

➤ The company was reluctant to offer employees what Silicon Valley had long ago recognized as essential compensation for maintaining its staff: stock options. As a result, SAP went through several years of talent drainage, especially in its key U.S. sales force, before introducing what it still believes to be a very un-German form of compensation.

But the ship has been righted, and the potential of SAP has been greatly enhanced. New Dimensions and mySAP.com are two new broad strategies comprised of product offerings that can be sold as independent modules or as add-ons to existing ERP infrastructure. Designed to address the above-mentioned deficiencies, they are also expected to play a key role in significantly expanding SAP's market reach.

Two of New Dimensions' key products focus on supply-chain and customer relationship management (SCM and CRM). Both solutions rely on the Internet to help automate the link between a client's various manufacturers (products, prices, and availability) and its marketing, sales, and customer service divisions. Business Intelligence is another key component of New Dimensions, offering advanced strategic planning for both front- and back-office analyses, going beyond the normal capacities of ERP.

Merrill Lynch anticipates the market for SCM to more than double between 1998 and 2003, hitting $13.7 billion. It projects demand for CRM to grow even faster, from $1.6 billion to $8.7 billion over the same period. Merrill expects SAP to capture 10 to 15 percent of these two markets.[4] SAP plans New Dimensions to generate 30 percent of the company's total revenues within the next several years.[5]

MySAP.com is a new delivery strategy, enabling clients to access all of the company's products. But as Charles Elliott, technology analyst at Goldman Sachs in London, points out, mySAP.com is not just about selling ERP over the Web but is a means of "reengineering a customer's entire technical architecture and business processes to support e-business."[6]

The main components of mySAP.com: trading exchanges designed around nineteen individual industries; Internet delivery of R/3 applications to more workstations (where ERP has already been installed); projections and analyses based on various business scenarios; and application hosting.[7]

This last solution is expected to help SAP reach small and midsize operations that could not otherwise manage the costs or intricacies of R/3. ERP software is installed, maintained, and upgraded at a third-party location. A company's operational data flows through this external network and is analyzed on an as-needed basis. Cost to the company is based on frequency of access.

But what's driving SAP's Internet initiative is the creation of an e-commerce platform. And that's what's exciting the heck out of Wall Street.

As the *Financial Times* explained, "SAP's Internet-based strategy integrates ERP functions with the electronic marketplace, effectively allowing companies to do all their purchasing and selling in the virtual marketplace while at the same time managing internal business processes."[8]

What's the size of this potential marketplace? Warburg Dillon Read projects total B2B Internet transactions could reach $5 trillion dollars by 2004.[9] To get to that level, demand for software and services to access this trading network would be phenomenal.

Recovery in SAP shares was confirmed when the company released its 1999 fourth-quarter results. Whereas year-over-year sales figures for R/3 licenses showed a decline of 10 percent, to €1.62 billion, fourth-quarter R/3 sales were up 17 percent. This ended three consecutive quarters of substantial decline and suggested that companies were getting past their Y2K concerns.

Even more telling was strong acceleration in New Dimensions and mySAP.com sales of €316 million, which more than compensated for the decline in R/3 sales and helped pushed total product revenue for the year up 14 percent, to €3.1 billion. Consulting revenues, the company's second most important revenue source, climbed 38 percent, to €1.55 billion, boosting total annual revenue growth by 18 percent, to €5.11 billion.[10]

For the year, operating earnings fell 12 percent, to €797 million. Only an investment gain of €235 million helped lift 1999 pretax profits 5.5 percent, to €981 million. And a substantial decline in SAP's tax rate propelled EPS 16 percent.

While SAP's 1999 year-end rally was largely driven by the initial success of the company's Web-based business strategy, a great deal of expectation now accompanies SAP's new rating as an Internet play. For the company to sustain this momentum, subsequent revenue growth will have to double 1999's sluggish performance. SAP can no longer risk being behind the product development and delivery curve, especially now that its valuation is based on a triple-digit trailing P/E.

Near term, investors also need to focus on the revenue-generating shift away from high-margin R/3 licensing and installation income to more streamlined Internet-based sales. To what degree will SAP's core product sales be cannibalized by more piecemeal sales and third-party leasing, and ultimately, how will that affect bottom-line margins? This change in sales strategy may indeed be essential as the high-end mar-

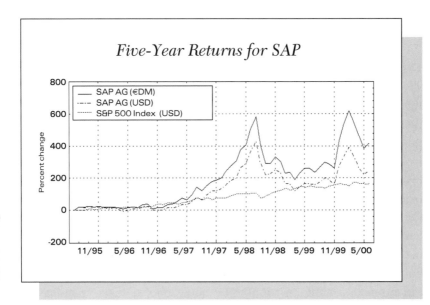

Source: Bloomberg

ket for R/3 becomes increasingly saturated. But it does change the company's financial model, and the market is presuming it will be doing so for the better.

Another consideration that begs watching is SAP's unique stock compensation plan. The company's Stock Appreciation Rights (STAR) program must be paid out annually and expensed quarterly—assuming a rise in the stock beyond the strike price. Due to the stock's strong surge in 1999 above the €337 strike price, SAP paid out €157 million in 1999 in equity-related compensation and allocated more than €300 million for 2000.[11] According to Alla Gorelova, technology analyst at Oppenheim Finanzanalyzse in Frankfurt, STAR cut more than 3 percentage points from the 1999 EBIT margin, reducing it to 15 percent. And she expected the program to have an even greater impact in 2000.[12]

To help offset future STAR costs, SAP will continue taking capital gains from its investment activities. The company also plans to pare back related costs not only by replacing STAR compensation with traditional options for the top 5 percent of its staff, but also by recalibrating STAR-based payouts, so that during years of spectacular stock performance the hit to the company's books is slightly mitigated.

But a potential problem remains. Analysts have traditionally accepted stock compensation, especially in the software industry, as an afterthought—extraordinary consideration that should be treated as a non-performance-related cost. In discussing the fourth-quarter 1999 results, a recent Deutsche Bank note stated, "if one strips out the STARs, EBIT rose by 60 percent. That's quite a recovery."[13] And that's quite a statement. The market seems more concerned with top-line growth. If this perspective changes and full staffing costs are someday recognized, then the growth status of some big high-techs may be seriously questioned.

But for now, these caveats do not alter the fact that SAP is a powerhouse of a company, with superb technical prowess and a dominant market share in an industry that will continue to expand rapidly as businesses adjust to the new global economy.

Charles Elliott of Goldman Sachs expects ERP will increasingly become the backbone of supply-chain management and business-to-business e-commerce, further propelling SAP's shares. And the stock can expect to maintain support by being one of the few industry-leading high-tech plays in Germany and Europe, with strong recurring revenue, an established growth record, and a February 2000 market cap of $80 billion. SAP now accounts for 8 percent of the DAX—Germany's main index—and this means for fund managers needing to track Germany or the eurozone, SAP has become a core investment.[14]

First-Half 2000 Highlights

➢ *Shares collapse and rebound*—Sell-off of Internet shares, weaker than expected first-quarter earnings, and a big STAR hit led to a sharp decline in SAP shares from a first-quarter (split-adjusted) peak of €350 to a second-quarter low of €176.33; the stock closed the first half at €193.50.

➢ *Continued growth*—Solid second-quarter numbers contributed to first-half revenue growth of 14.77 percent; still, net profit declined by 28 percent.

➢ *A more competitive stock price*—In June, the stock split 3 for 1.

➢ *Grand alliance*—SAP has teamed with Commerce One Inc., the global leader in e-commerce solutions for business, to create the next-generation e-business marketplace.

➢ *Web marketplace for retailers*—Danone Group and Nestlé set up Europe's first Internet marketplace for retailers to enhance logistics and cut purchase costs based on mySAP.com.

Suez Lyonnaise des Eaux

Ticker: SZE (Paris Stock Exchange)
Country: France
Industry: Utilities

" *Suez Lyonnaise is a new breed of defensive-growth utility with secure earnings that are increasing at a double-digit pace. The company is well positioned to exploit rapidly expanding global energy, water, and waste treatment markets as they are deregulated. At the same time, significant share appreciation should result from further restructuring that's refocusing strategic assets, substantially enhancing Suez's value, which the market has yet to recognize.* "

PARIBAS[1]

AT A TIME WHEN the most attractive stories seem to have a high-tech twist, the idea of venturing across the Atlantic to buy a utility stock may not appear all that ... well, venturesome. But Suez Lyonnaise is by no means your ordinary utility. This Paris-based multinational, with a market cap of nearly $32 billion, has operations in 120 countries. It's the world's largest international water provider, the third-largest independent power producer, and Europe's leading waste manager. Throw in being the biggest cable operator in France and Belgium and an additional €10 billion generated annually in financial, industrial, and construction services, and what you have is a very potent player capable of exploiting the world's rapidly expanding utility needs. If all this still doesn't impress, then consider Suez's shares, which appreciated by 25.31 percent annually in local currency terms over the five years through the first quarter of 2000.

Despite its historic roots, Suez Lyonnaise des Eaux is a new company, the product of a 1997 merger between two old French companies: Compagnie de Suez (which was involved in the construction of the Suez Canal) and Lyonnaise des Eaux (one of France's oldest water companies). By the 1990s, after more than a century of operations, Suez had become a near-bankrupt financial services and industrial conglomerate; Lyonnaise had diversified into an unfocused mix of utility, construction, and television services. However, together they pulled off what *The Wall Street Journal* regarded as "one of the more

Key Findings

➤ Suez Lyonnaise is a global multiutility superbly positioned to exploit increasingly deregulated energy, water, and waste management markets, which are expanding rapidly in both developed and emerging nations.

➤ Strength and stability of these markets are enabling Suez to define a new breed of defensive-growth utility stock, with EPS appreciating at an annual rate of 15 percent.

➤ Between the first quarter of 1995 and the first quarter of 2000, shares more than tripled in local currency terms.

➤ Already France's largest cable provider, Suez is pursuing fixed and mobile telecom licenses to help it become a significant telecom service provider, and this potential has yet to be factored into the stock's price.

➤ Likelihood of sustained growth coupled with shares selling at a discount to net assets suggests continued price appreciation.

radical overhauls in French corporate history."[2]

The new firm sold off operations worth billions of francs, including investment banking, mining, insurance, and other noncore activities. It unwound cross shareholdings with French insurance giant AXA and industrial concern Compagnie de Saint-Gobain and consolidated ownership of key positions, including the venerable Société Générale de Belgique, Belgium's dominant industrial and financial holding company.[3] The goal was to create a major multiutility operation with a strong Belgian connection, capable of building, financing, and operating energy, water, and waste management plants around the world.

The investment logic was simple. Deregulation is triggering tremendous demand for water, energy, and waste management services, accelerated by rapid urbanization, especially in developing nations, and by environmental initiatives in the United States and Europe. According to French bank BNP Paribas, whereas 80 percent of the world's population had access to clean water in 1980, by 1994 that proportion had dropped to 53 percent. In western Europe alone, the demand for water services will boom as the European Commission requires all cities with 5,000 or more residents to maintain their own water treatment facilities by 2005.[4]

Need for massive capital and technological investments, without encumbering taxpayers, has encouraged governments to turn to private operators for assistance. Opening up the markets is offering remarkable opportunities. For instance, in the United States, there are 55,000 water-related companies, and yet no more than 15 percent of all operations have been privatized—a number that will assuredly grow. In the wastewater market, the figure is closer to 5 percent.[5] So fragmented is the U.S. water industry that even the biggest operator is no more than one-fifth the size of Suez.[6]

Oddly, few private utilities in the United States appear to have recognized the potential for consolidation and expansion at home, much less abroad. This leaves Suez in a particularly formidable position, especially in the Americas, where it generated sales of €3.58 billion in 1999.[7] And Suez should reap further synergistic benefits by being able to offer cities and states one-stop shopping to address all of their essential services.

The success of Suez's restructuring was evident in the company's financial performance between 1997 and 1999.

➤ Annual sales grew 12.2 percent, from €24.98 billion to €31.42 billion, led by its energy division, which generated nearly 40 percent of 1999 revenues.[8]

➤ Consolidated net profits soared at annual pace of 30.9 percent, increasing from €1.59 billion to €2.73 billion.[9]

➤ The fastest-growing segment was water, with sales that expanded by 15.3 percent a year, to €6.29 billion.

➤ EBITDA from waste management soared 26.3 percent a year, to €680 million, with 1999 sales of €4.21 billion.[10]

The numbers are likely to significantly improve due to a series of market-consolidating moves in 1999 worth nearly $17 billion that further streamlined Suez's core functions.

In the first half of 1999, Suez acquired two U.S. water treatment operations: Calgon, for $425 million, and Nalco, the U.S. industry

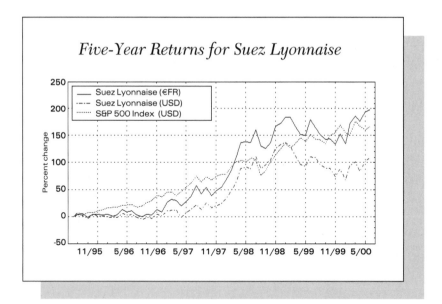

Five-Year Returns for Suez Lyonnaise

leader, for $4.1 billion. This effectively quadrupled sales in Suez's water treatment business to $2.4 billion globally.[11] By 2002, these two deals are expected to add $100 million annually to Suez's bottom line.[12]

Then in August, Suez Lyonnaise capped its water-related acquisitions by buying out the remaining two-thirds stake it didn't own of the second-largest private U.S. water utility, United Water Resources, for $1 billion.[13]

Also, in the middle of the summer, when many Belgian executives were caught off guard while on holiday, Suez put an end to contentious problems it had with its majority-owned position in Tractebel—a global power and waste services company with annual sales exceeding €11 billion—by buying out the remaining 49.7 percent of shares through a stock transfer worth $8 billion. This sets up the specter of Suez's acquiring Tractebel's subsidiary Electrabel, Belgium's primary energy utility—whose annual cash flow, in excess of $1 billion, could further drive international expansion.[14]

Then in the fall, Suez concluded a $900 million buyout of the remaining 29.5 percent of shares in Sita, Europe's leading waste services provider, with annual sales of €2.65 billion.[15] By eliminating minority interests and consolidating control of its core utilities, Suez can now better integrate its various operations. This will realize savings from units that were formerly competitors and gain Suez unimpeded access to their cash flows. Most important, increased unification will shift perception of the firm from a holding company of unrelated operations to an integrated industrial group.

What's so important about that? Most analysts feel this redesignation will lead to a multiple rerating that should help raise Suez's stock price and collapse the 31 percent discount to net asset value at which shares were trading as of the end of 1999.[16]

Collectively, these moves will help the company meet its earnings growth goal of 15 percent a year and double current EPS over a five-year span through 2002. J.P. Morgan projects return on equity over the same period will expand from 10.4 percent to 12.4 percent, and free cash flow will substantially increase. These improvements, the investment bank concludes, should "provide considerable protection against any downward risk."[17]

Also encouraging for investors is Suez's emphasis on shareholder value. The *Financial Times* observed that while "other French companies such as Banque Nationale de Paris are still focusing on building critical size, Suez is concentrating on improving its return on equity."[18]

Suez was one of the first major European utilities to offer equity-based compensation for top management. The company is encouraging greater employee shareholding. When divesting significant assets leads to excess capital, the company on occasion distributes special dividends. For several years it has maintained a share buyback program with the goal of reducing up to 10 percent of the company's capital shares.

The only significant concern investors should have is the company's strong reliance on shares to finance acquisitions, which could dilute EPS. By the end of 1999, the total number of outstanding shares rose to 198.3 million from 147.7 million in December 1998. However, according to company officials, the impact of share swapping on EPS is projected to add to earnings by 2001.[19]

Moreover, the company's overall financial health will allow it to continue to expand aggressively as foreign markets are deregulated. Suez's core businesses generate more than $4 billion in cash annually, giving it "one of Europe's largest war chests."[20] And subsequent divestment of its construction (Groupe GTM) and banking (Fortis) should generate an additional $8 billion.[21]

First-Half 2000 Highlights

➤ *Strong growth continues*—Sales rose 29 percent, to €19.1 billion, as earnings climbed 38 percent, to €1.27 billion, driven by acquisitions and increasing strength of core operations.

➤ *Increasing geographic diversification*—Percentage of sales generated outside of France increased 3.5 percentage points, to 44.5 percent of total revenue.

➤ *Telecom gains*—Already France's largest cable operator, Suez won a national wireless local loop license enabling it to offer broadband data transmission services to small and medium-sized corporations in France's largest 100 cities; partnering with Spain's Telefónica, Suez is also seeking a countrywide mobile license, a key step in becoming a serious telecom service provider.

➤ *Stock rises and discount diminishes*—Suez shares rose by more than 15 percent, helping to slice the year-end 1999 discount of 31 percent between net asset value per share and share price nearly in half.

Vodafone

Ticker: VOD (NYSE)
Country: United Kingdom
Industry: Telecommunications

> *❝ Vodafone AirTouch is the premiere wireless asset in the world, with superb management and significant stakes in leading mobile markets where cellular penetration is expected to double over the next five years. ❞*
>
> Credit Suisse First Boston[1]

VODAFONE IS A one-horse shop. It sells mobile phone service. Since it obtained Britain's first mobile license in 1983, it has become the world's largest mobile communications operator, with FY 2000 sales of nearly £7.9 billion, operating profits of nearly £800 million, 59 million customers, and a market cap of more than $300 billion—making it the largest company in Europe.[2]

Vodafone is the first telecom to create a Pan-European and nationwide U.S. network, further complemented by extensive holdings in the fast-growing Asia-Pacific region. Starting with the premise that mobile

Key Findings

➤ With its $62 billion acquisition of AirTouch, its $70 billion linkup with Bell Atlantic Mobile, and its $183 billion takeover of Mannesmann—the largest buyout in history—Vodafone has established the first transatlantic mobile network.

➤ The ability to identify fast-growing markets and to establish significant positions in them has enabled Vodafone to create one of the most valuable portfolios of regional mobile telecoms.

➤ The company is strongly positioned to exploit third-generation broadband technology, a major innovation in mobile telephony.

➤ Vodafone shares appreciated 68 percent annually over the five years through the first quarter of 2000, transforming it into Europe's largest company and an essential holding in all European portfolios.

➤ The major risks: the tremendous premium paid for Mannesmann and third-generation mobile licenses may weigh down near-term performance, while Vodafone's extraordinary market position will trigger aggressive responses by other major operators.

communications is the fastest-growing segment of the fastest-growing sector, Vodafone is positioned as one of the best investment stories around.

Performance of its shares more than confirms this sentiment. Over the twelve months through the first quarter of 2000, the stock was up 71.5 percent in local currency terms. And since the first quarter of 1995, shares of Vodafone have soared 68.02 percent annually.[3]

How did Vodafone generate such returns? Just as important, will the company continue to do so?

Vodafone sticks to a simple investment mantra: identify markets with the potential for strong growth, get into them early (even if it means initially overpaying for the mobile license), develop infrastructure that's compatible with the prevailing GSM technology, advertise and develop brand recognition, and most important, don't fight market sentiment.

This last point is no better illustrated than in the company's shift from contract sales to the prepaid phone market. The limited commitment to the latter has drawn vast numbers of new customers into the wireless age. This is proving to be the most effective means for mobile operators to capture the rapid growth in cellular penetration, which in developed markets is now expanding by 50 percent a year. At the end of 1999, there were 470 million mobile users; by the end of 2002, the figure is expected to reach 1 billion.[4] This level of penetration will essentially break the traditional hold fixed-line incumbents have had on customers through their control of "the last mile" of network connections, freeing customers to pursue the service and operator of their choice.

By 2000 Vodafone had established substantial positions in a wide range of expanding national markets—twenty-five countries in all. In Europe alone, Vodafone has stakes in thirteen countries, with majority positions in Austria, Germany, Italy, the Netherlands, Greece, Portugal, Hungary, and Sweden. It has stakes ranging from 23 percent to 27 percent in each of Japan's nine regional mobile operators, a 31.5 percent holding in South Africa, a 60 percent position in Egypt, and more than 90 percent of its Australian venture, and it wholly owns its New Zealand operation as well as its home-turf enterprise in the United Kingdom.[5]

Between 1999 and spring 2000, the following four deals—three of which were of blockbuster caliber—redefined Vodafone as the global telecom player:

First was its acquisition of the U.S.'s West Coast–based mobile operator AirTouch for $62 billion in January 1999—which was the world's largest cross-border deal.

What made this such a remarkable acquisition was AirTouch's substantial holdings in Europe. With its majority interests in Sweden and Portugal and its additional holdings in Germany, Belgium, Italy, Spain, Poland, Romania, Japan, Korea, India, and Egypt, AirTouch's assets complemented Vodafone's own European portfolio.

Together, the two companies created the Continent's largest mobile footprint, with 15.7 million European subscribers.[6] Besides consolidating a formidable European network, Vodafone also eliminated a competitor it frequently found itself running up against in bidding for European properties.

Acquisition of AirTouch's 12 percent share of the U.S. mobile market, the largest percent held by any single U.S. mobile operator, was the start of Vodafone's commitment to building a U.S. mobile network. European players see large untapped value in this affluent, fragmented market, which has been made inefficient by the following conditions.

First, U.S. mobile communications is hamstrung by the existence of four network standards; Europe has one. Second, mobile usage is restrained by the mobile user's being responsible for incoming charges. Third, the concept of prepaid (no contract) phones, which is now driving mobile usage in Europe and around the globe, has barely gotten started in the States.[7]

The next step Vodafone took toward U.S. consolidation was in June 1999, when it acquired the Colorado-based CommNet Cellular for $764 million.

This expanded its western U.S. mobile holdings from Montana to New Mexico.[8]

Then in September, Vodafone secured the last big piece of its U.S. puzzle by agreeing to a joint venture with Bell Atlantic Mobile—the major East Coast cellular operator.

Bell Atlantic, which Vodafone had beaten out in the bidding for AirTouch, had acquired GTE. Now operating collectively under the brand Verizon Wireless, this merger of mobile assets has created the largest mobile network in the United States, with 20 million customers. That's nearly twice the number of mobile subscribers of the nearest competitor, AT&T Wireless. The new network will generate $15.6 billion in annual revenues and cost savings of $330 million annually, leading to annual profits of $1.7 billion.[9] The estimated value of the joint venture: $70 to $80 billion, which could increase substantially with the issuance of an IPO or tracking stock.[10]

But all this seemed but prelude to the biggest deal yet: the $183 billion hostile takeover of the German conglomerate Mannesmann early in 2000.

Formerly an engineering, automotive, and steel-tube industrial group, Mannesmann had spent the 1990s sharply maneuvering into some of Europe's leading telecom operations: Italy's Omnitel, which services one-third of the Continent's largest mobile phone market; Infrastrada, Italy's second-largest fixed-line carrier; Mobilfunk, Germany's third-largest mobile carrier; and O.TEL.O, the joint venture of German utilities RWE and Veba (which turned Mannesmann into Germany's second-largest fixed-line operator). According to Merrill Lynch telecom analyst Christopher McFadden, "Mannesmann had assembled the most strategically important set of telecom assets in Europe," which had only been further enhanced with the company's minority holdings in France and Austria and its acquisition of the highly successful U.K. mobile telecom Orange.[11]

The benefits of creating a transcontinental network are simple. First, as *The Economist* reported, "the size and buying power of Vodafone AirTouch gives it unrivaled ability to set technical standards and to extract price reductions from handset and network equipment manufacturers. This will be especially useful over the next few years with the arrival of third-generation broadband mobile networks that will provide large data and Internet access to mobile customers."[12]

Then, by running such large networks, Vodafone cuts down on connect charges, which kick in when subscriber calls go beyond the network, requiring the assistance of external operators. This in turn enables Vodafone to cut its own tariffs. Lower prices bring in more customers, which leads to further economies and the creation of a virtuous cycle that generates not only further growth but also the ability to finance additional network improvements and acquisitions.

All of this, according to Salomon Smith Barney telecom analyst Thomas J. Lee, not only makes Vodafone the partner of choice for other telecoms requiring network access but also makes it the operator of choice for multinationals and for business and individual travelers seeking comprehensive service from a single carrier.[13]

With Vodafone's CEO, Chris Gent, expecting the company's customer base to almost double by 2003 (beyond 100 million),[14] and with cost synergies from its acquisitions expected to kick in well before that, Bear Stearns projects a 5-year annual growth rate of 20 percent.[15]

Vodafone shares should also continue to benefit from their rising positions in major equity indices, which fund managers often track. In

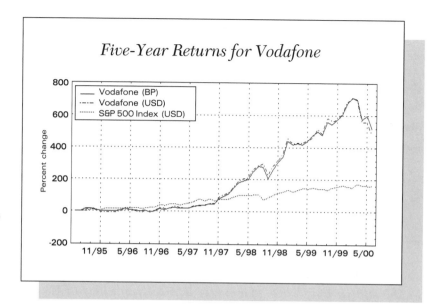

Five-Year Returns for Vodafone

Source: Bloomberg

the FTSE Eurotop 100, Vodafone has become the dominant position, representing 5.37 percent of the index. The company is the fourth-largest listing in the FTSE Global 100 index, accounting for more than 3 percent of the index.

Even more important was Dow Jones's adoption of Vodafone in September 1999 into its European blue-chip index, the STOXX 50. Vodafone became the index's second-most-weighted stock, representing 4.967 percent of the index. After the Mannesmann acquisition, in June 2000, Vodafone became the index's lead constituent, with a weight of 6.47 percent, making it an essential holding in any portfolio tracking Europe.

There are two general risks facing Vodafone. The most obvious is the price it paid for Mannesmann. At $12,400 per customer ($5,400 more than Mannesmann paid for Orange's purely mobile customers just two months earlier), how can Vodafone expect to make money from the deal?[16] The answer lies in the new expanded European coverage provided by Mannesmann's properties, improved economies, and anticipated explosive growth in mobile phone usage triggered by Internet access. With Vodafone shares selling at a triple-digit trailing P/E, the market is clearly expecting phenomenal things.

The second risk is Vodafone's success itself. Consolidating such dominant positions in both Europe and the United States is directly threatening competitors. The *Financial Times* expects a "fierce price and technology war" to ensue, which could bleed Vodafone as well as the likes of British Telecom, Cable & Wireless, Deutsche Telekom, and France Telecom in Europe and AT&T, MCI WorldCom, and Nextel in the States.[17] Odds are that in such a battle, the strongest-positioned player will be left on top. And from all vantages, that would appear to be Vodafone.

First-Half 2000 Highlights

➢ *Vizzavi*—VivendiNet and Vodafone have created a multiaccess Internet portal, Vizzavi, reaching more than 70 million customers throughout Europe, offering a consistent format via mobile phones, PCs, TVs, and personal digital equipment; Vivendi's subsequent acquisition of Seagram's Universal Studios significantly enhances content.

➢ *Divestiture and third-generation license acquisitions*—France Telecom paid Vodafone $40 billion for the U.K. mobile carrier Orange it acquired in the takeover of Mannesmann; and with additional Mannesmann non-telecom asset sales having raised €10.1 billion, Vodafone is able to finance all third-generation license acquisitions without debt.

➢ *Pan-European contract*—Seeking to consolidate its European mobile phone needs, Unilever signed the first global contract, for €20 million for two years.

➢ *Financials*—With its fiscal year ending March 31st and the company only reporting on a semiannual basis, no financial figures were available for FY 2001 before this book closed.

Chapter Ten

European Mutual Funds

F OR U.S.–BASED INVESTORS, there are relatively few mutual funds that focus exclusively on European equity markets. According to Morningstar, the Chicago-based fund tracking source, there were only eighty-seven European funds as of the beginning of 2000.[1]

However, that shouldn't deter investors from relying on mutual funds to profit from Europe's burgeoning equity markets. In fact, the limited number of offerings makes the selection process fairly easy.

European mutual funds fall into three basic categories: individual country funds, regional funds, and Pan-European funds. Although most are open-ended offerings, there are a dozen closed-end funds. These securities are exchange-traded, which means they can be sold short as well as long at a precise price—just like a stock.[2] But it also means that their market value fluctuates from their underlying net asset value—the collective worth of the securities in the portfolio.

There is also a group of hybrid funds originally called WEBS and since retitled iShares MSCI. Introduced in 1996, these funds track ten individual European countries. Their performance replicates the MSCI Index for each respective market.[3] Even though Morningstar classifies iShares as open-ended funds because their market values track exceedingly close to their net asset value, these two valuations are rarely identical—which is not the case with a true open-ended fund.

The creators of iShares wanted the funds to trade like stocks, offering instant liquidity and the ability to be shorted. They also wanted to avoid pitfalls that come with open-ended fund redemption—that is, when more investors want out than in, an open-ended fund would have to disburse its own cash or sell off pieces of its portfolio to repay exiting investors. Asset levels in closed-end funds are not directly affected by such fund investor activity because shares are not redeemed but are traded.

But to avoid the discount perils of closed-end funds, iShares had to be set up to enable arbitrageurs to trade large blocks of their underlying stocks. This ensures that when market value begins to vary from net asset value, arbitrageurs will quickly step in and net the difference, and in the process, close up any discount or premium.

Individual Country Funds

WITH THE ADVENT OF common currency, street sentiment has been moving away from the argument for individual country funds. Analysts instead are placing increasing emphasis on cross-border sector exposure, reflecting what many expect to be the new division of Europe.[4]

Before the euro, individual stock markets could be assured of substantial support from domestic pension and mutual funds; their managers were required to invest a majority of their assets in domestic companies because it restricted currency risks. But common currency has broken down these geographic barriers. Institutional investors are dispersing assets across the eurozone in response to changing investment benchmarks, which are expanding from local indices to more Pan-European performance measurements.

As a result, smaller peripheral countries like Portugal and Ireland have seen their stock markets slammed as domestic institutional support erodes in exchange for greater European exposure. And unfortunately for their domestic stocks, this outflow has not been offset by a corresponding inflow of foreign investment because of the limited weight these countries have in European indices. So after years of strong performance, the closed-end Irish Investment Fund lost 17 percent in 1999—despite a booming economy.[5]

Ironically, the fund's underlying net asset value actually held up during this time, down only 1.5 percent during the year. But because it's a closed-end fund, its actual market value is determined directly by demand for the fund itself. When a closed-end fund is highly desirable because of the quality of exposure it provides investors, its actual market value (the price investors are willing to pay for it) may exceed the collective value of its securities. When this occurs, the difference is called a premium. But declining desirability of Irish Investment's portfolio led to a discount that averaged 17.9 percent throughout 1999.

The existence of a discount is not necessarily indicative of a troubled fund. The majority of closed-end funds trade at some sort of discount. Despite racking up 5-year annualized market returns of over 18 percent from 1995 through 1999, Irish Investment has traditionally traded at a discount to its net asset value. But right now, with Ireland out of favor with the broad market, the fund is getting smacked not only by the diminishing value of its portfolio but also by an expanding discount, which hit a historic high of 24 percent in early 2000.

Germany makes the case for country-specific exposure. While euro-zone countries have been largely relieved of sovereign monetary policy, they still very much retain control over fiscal matters. At the end of 1999, German Chancellor Gerhard Schröder surprised the market by introducing legislation that would significantly revamp the country's tax code—especially as it applied to Germany's largest corporations. And the market roared in approval.

Significant amounts of capital in many large German corporations have been tied up for years in the form of cross-shareholdings in other major German companies. The purposes of this arrangement are enhanced corporate governance and, ultimately, protection of German interests from foreign competitors. But since privatization and deregulation have opened up markets, the value of this cross-ownership arrangement is diminishing rapidly. Still, companies have been reluctant to dispose of these shares because of the potential capital gains tax liability.

With the passage of tax reform in spring 2000, the government is preparing corporate Germany for a twin-engine burn. First, companies will be able to retain the huge profits they've racked up over the years. And then they will be able to more efficiently reallocate these resources to make their operations more valuable.

Looking at the 1999 performance of the closed-end Germany Fund shows the benefits gained through broad exposure to *Deutschland* at this time. After floundering for most of the year, the fund took off after Schröder's announcement, sending year-end market returns up 22.7 percent, outpacing net asset value appreciation by 3 percent. In fact, from

European Mutual Fund Survey

FUND	ANNUALIZED TOTAL RETURNS IN $U.S. AS OF DECEMBER 31, 1999		
	1-YEAR	3-YEAR	5-YEAR
COUNTRY FUNDS			
Austria Fund	40.94%	26.02%	17.96%
DFA United Kingdom Small Co.	41.83	9.26	13.4
Fidelity France	36.34	26.24	
Fidelity Germany	16.55	20.03	
Fidelity United Kingdom	14.74	13.54	
France Growth	37.11	34.74	26.57
Germany Fund	22.72	28.64	24.33
Growth Fund of Spain A	-5.24	19.3	22.16
Irish Investment	-17.11	9.91	18.25
iShares MSCI Austria	-10.36	-3.73	
iShares MSCI Belgium	-14.21	13.61	
iShares MSCI France	27.15	25.91	
iShares MSCI Germany	23.73	24.95	
iShares MSCI Italy	0.55	27.34	
iShares MSCI Netherlands	4.64	16.11	
iShares MSCI Spain	-2.1	20.42	
iShares MSCI Sweden	64.04	26.6	
iShares MSCI Switzerland	-3.23	15.9	
iShares MSCI United Kingdom	12.17	17.14	
Italy Fund	34.4	33.49	21.18
Kaminski Poland	23.62		
New Germany	3.64	14.28	14.62
Portugal Fund	-3.71	21	12.36
Spain Fund	17.49	38.75	30.6
Swiss Helvetia	-8.38	17.45	13.51
Wright EquiFund–Netherlands	-4.39	11.2	17.36
REGIONAL FUNDS			
Central European Equity	8.45	0.31	9.14
Central European Value	15.15	-0.18	4.15
Fidelity Nordic Fund	59.51	32.32	
Icon North Europe Region	20.74		

EXPENSE RATIO	1999 AVERAGE PREMIUM/DISCOUNT	3-YEAR TAX EFFICIENCY*	FRONT-END LOAD
1.68%			
0.72		55.6%	
2.12		95.41	3%
1.74		94.17	3
2.01		89.25	3
1.38	-16.4		
1.15	-10.4		
1.43		77.57	5.75
1.37	-17.9		
1.33			
1.04		70.56	
1.18		96.79	
1.08		96.23	
1.02		90.23	
1.12		85.12	
1.11		94.68	
1.17		90.94	
1.15		87.8	
1.03		90.35	
1.22	-16.6		
2.75			
0.98	-18.4		
1.5	-12.8		
1.44	-9.7		
1.09	-18.9		
1.88		84.66	
1.17	-21.5		
2.09	-16.7		
1.35		95.82	3
1.54			

*Tax Efficiency is a Morningstar calculation that indicates generally what percentage of a fund's earnings an investor can expect to keep. It is based on the specific nature of income and capital gains distribution, assumes no shares of the fund are sold, and takes into account the impact of federal taxes only

European Mutual Fund Survey (*continued*)

FUND	ANNUALIZED TOTAL RETURNS IN $U.S. AS OF DECEMBER 31, 1999		
	1-YEAR	3-YEAR	5-YEAR

REGIONAL FUNDS (*continued*)

Fund	1-Year	3-Year	5-Year
Icon South Europe Region	-4.67%		
Pictet Eastern European	35.63		
Regent Eastern European	29.7		
Vontobel Eastern Euro Equity	14.5	-12.73%	

PAN-EUROPEAN FUNDS

Fund	1-Year	3-Year	5-Year
AIM Euroland Growth A	35.14	20.57	18.15%
AIM European Development A	66.62		
Alliance New Europe A	26.12	22.58	21.38
Chase Vista European A	36.06	28.4	
Deutsche European Equity	45.43	27.34	
Deutsche European Mid-Cap A	28.83		
Deutsche Top 50 Europe A	20.55		
DFA Continental Small Company	-2.67	9.13	8.25
Dresdner RCM Europe N	43.5	35.24	23.12
European Warrant	27.52	49.04	42.07
Europe Fund	15.9	20.56	24.53
Excelsior Pan-European	24.6	20.1	20.02
Federated European Growth A	27.59	22.35	
Fidelity Adv Europe Cp App A	20.94		
Fidelity Adv Europe Cp App I	21.15		
Fidelity Europe	18.69	20.77	21.33
Fidelity Europe Capital Appreciation	23.76	23.45	22.13
59 Wall Street European Equity	21.98	20.41	19.48
First Eagle International Y	16.78	12.96	13.28
GAM Europe A	16.21	17.95	18.36
GE Europe Equity A			
GE Instl Europe Equity			
Goldman Sachs Euro Equity A	26.26		
Guinness Flight New Europe	19.79		
Hancock European Equity A	17.51		
ICAP Euro Select Equity	22.03		
ING European Equity A	18.59		

EXPENSE RATIO	1999 AVERAGE PREMIUM/DISCOUNT	3-YEAR TAX EFFICIENCY*	FRONT-END LOAD
1.56%			
2			
4.36			
2.41			
1.75		91.13%	5.5%
1.98			5.5
1.78		86.51	4.25
1.74		91.24	4.75
0.9		85.66	
1.6			5.5
1.6			5.5
0.7		66.71	
1.6		84.31	
1.77	-19.8		
1.27	-11.3		
1.43		89.72	
1.85		93.19	5.5
			5.75
1.09		89.88	3
1.08		90.13	3
1.19		80.79	
2.4		85.41	
2.06		78.92	5
1.79			5.5
1.98			
			5
1			
			5.75

*Tax Efficiency is a Morningstar calculation that indicates generally what percentage of a fund's earnings an investor can expect to keep. It is based on the specific nature of income and capital gains distribution, assumes no shares of the fund are sold, and takes into account the impact of federal taxes only

European Mutual Fund Survey *(continued)*

FUND	ANNUALIZED TOTAL RETURNS IN $U.S.AS OF DECEMBER 31, 1999		
	1-YEAR	3-YEAR	5-YEAR
PAN-EUROPEAN FUNDS *(continued)*			
Invesco European	37.99%	28.31%	26.7%
iShares MSCI EMU			
Ivy Pan-Europe A	18.29		
J.P. Morgan Instl European Equity	20.44	21.39	
Kemper New Europe M	51.01	32.49	30.02
Legg Mason Europe A	25.41	27.83	26.7
Lipper Prime Europe Equity PremA	15.7	22.07	
LKCM International	42.71		
Mercury Pan-European Growth A	16.23		
Merrill Lynch EuroFund B	14.11	20.39	19.36
MSDW European Growth B	27.7	21.43	23.52
MSDW Instl Euro Equity A	9.68	11.8	13.82
Mutual European Z	46.81	23.72	
Nuveen European Value A	25.38		
Oppenheimer Europe A			
Payden & Rygel Euro Gr&Inc R	10.53		
Pioneer Europe A	25.16	22.43	23.13
Prudential Europe Growth A	27.26	23.66	22.45
Prudential Europe Index Z	15.84		
Putnam Europe Growth A	23.15	22.88	22.52
Scudder Greater Europe Growth	34.58	29.19	28.39
Smith Barney European A	33.37	19.06	20.64
TCW Galileo Euro Equities I	34.08		
T. Rowe Price European Stock	19.7	20.79	22
Vanguard European Stock Index	16.66	23.15	22.59
Van Kampen European Equity A	10.1		
Warburg Pincus European Equity			
European Stock Fund Average	**24.93**	**20.26**	**20.7**
Standard & Poor's 500	**21.04**	**27.55**	**28.54**

EXPENSE RATIO	1999 AVERAGE PREMIUM/DISCOUNT	3-YEAR TAX EFFICIENCY*	FRONT-END LOAD
1.56%		87.65%	
0.84			
2.49			5.75%
1		90.82	
1.41		87.46	
1.81		81.18	4.75
1.54		88.23	
1.2			
			5.25
2.03		68.16	
2.1		87.81	
1		68.88	
1.05		85.88	
			5.75
			-5.75
0.69			
1.54		95	5.75
1.43		90.49	5
0.6			
1.23		92.82	5.75
1.48		96.52	
1.56		96.62	5
1.06			
1.05		88.35	
0.29		95.34	
			5.75
1.78			**1.25**

*Tax Efficiency is a Morningstar calculation that indicates generally what percentage of a fund's earnings an investor can expect to keep. It is based on the specific nature of income and capital gains distribution, assumes no shares of the fund are sold, and takes into account the impact of federal taxes only

August 1998 through the end of 1999, shareholders realized a 14 percent gain just from the decline in the fund's discount from 24.1 to 10 percent.

With market sentiment shunning country-specific funds in preference for sector or Pan-European funds, has the euro generally undermined the value of country fund investing? Not really.

One reason is that there are no European sector funds open to U.S. investors at this time. But more to the point, certain domestic equity markets are still attractive. Germany, France, and the United Kingdom are Europe's largest economies, hosting a proportional amount of the region's strongest and most profitable companies. While Europe's weaker markets, such as Spain, Portugal, and Italy, excelled in the years leading up to common currency, Europe's three core markets paced the way in 1999.

France enjoyed an exceptional year as corporate restructuring and mergers and acquisitions boosted Gallic stocks well above Europe's average. The MSCI France Index was up more than 27 percent. Germany gained 24 percent, while the United Kingdom appreciated by a more modest 12 percent.

Does this suggest a trend from which investors can profit? That's hard to say. Toward the end of 1998, most experts would have expected peripheral markets to continue their ascent in 1999 as the actual benefits of common currency kicked in. These markets in fact lost ground in 1999. Taking note of systemic change occurring in France and Germany may have clued in some investors. But most would not have projected this reversal in fortunes, except for anticipating the impact portfolio rebalancing was to have on smaller national markets.

The only certain lesson: observe where the most significant fundamental changes are taking place. Remember, markets primarily react to anticipated improvements, not to their ultimate realization.

Another caveat in specific country fund investing: know the corporate composition of an individual country before jumping in. In 1999, the Swedish and Finnish markets soared 87 and 194 percent, respectively.[6] But in each case, an individual telecom drove the rise in their respective market-cap-weighted indices. Ericsson makes up more than 44 percent of the Swedish market; Nokia, nearly two-thirds of the Finnish market.[7] When adding in the effects of other domestic companies booming on their coattails, investors should realize that country fund investments in either of these states have become telecom proxies, offering limited diversity.[8]

As long as the telecom sector remains strong, this region should continue to outperform the rest of Europe. The Fidelity Nordic fund, which provides exposure across Scandinavia with a bias toward telecom stocks (close to 30 percent of the portfolio), soared 64 percent in 1999. Though the fund is getting a boost from other hot stocks, including life insurer Skandia and fashion retailer Hennes & Mauritz, if telecom shares begin to falter, so will the fund.

A final thought on country funds takes us back to Ireland and the additional risk and potential offered by closed-end funds.

As mentioned earlier, the Irish Investment Fund was trading at a nearly 24 percent discount to net asset value in January 2000. Quality stocks in its portfolio, such as Allied Irish Banks, were hammered unmercifully in 1999. Now that asset rebalancing across the region has been pretty much completed, investors will look to places like Ireland where strong, profitable companies are trading for a song. When selective movement of capital returns to the Dublin Exchange, the Irish Investment Fund should receive a double boost from rising value of its individual holdings as well as a closing of its discount as investors move in to profit from stocks that have been oversold.

The lesson from Ireland: watch when countries in Europe are hurt explicitly by the outflow of cash triggered by administrative changes, especially as they relate to European union—not in response to corporate performance. In time, demand for their premium equities will likely return.

Regional Funds

THE CASE FOR regionally focused investment in Europe is rooted in the argument for individual country investment: states, or regions, excel in different industries that in a particular time may be exceedingly profitable. We've already seen an example with the Fidelity Nordic Fund and the boost it's been receiving from the region's strong hold on the mobile phone industry.

But the reality is that there are very few regional European funds. Morningstar tracks eight. More than half are locked in on central and eastern Europe, because the countries in those regions are unified by their common emerging-market status.

In theory, what these funds are hoping for is an explosion in these nascent equity markets to generate eye-popping returns. In reality, they are discovering that mining value in the former Soviet bloc is hampered by lack of transparency, affecting fund managers' ability to anticipate corporate performance and governments' commitment to change.

The region's performance is further handicapped by its perceived exposure to Russia. When the bear sneezes, markets in central Europe catch cold. Further, the region's emerging-market status also exposes the local economies to infections contracted anywhere else in the world's emerging markets. So when Russia defaulted on its massive foreign debt or when the Brazilian *real* collapsed, the region's markets tumbled.

These funds are also hurt by the region's inherent volatility. Closed-end offerings suffer from hefty discounts; open-ended funds are exposed to capital flight. The latter normally occurs when stocks are tanking, which means that fund managers are often forced to sell out of positions at the worst possible time.

Despite these caveats, if one is determined to gain exposure to this region, the Central European Equity Fund appears to be the best equipped to control risk. Its $160 million asset base is by far the largest. Its five-year annualized return of 9.14 percent is also tops in the region. Deutsche Bank manages the fund. While more than half of the portfolio is invested in the promising markets of Poland, Hungary, and the Czech Republic, the fund maintains nearly 36 percent of its assets in German companies for ballast. And trading at a huge 27 percent discount may suggest future performance will largely be driven by actual net asset value. But with exposure to a whole flock of weak currencies, U.S. investors must be mindful that returns are likely to be compromised when translated back to dollars—which has no doubt contributed to the fat discount.

Icon offers two unique regional funds that divide western Europe in half: north and south. While distinguishing Europe's older rich industrial core from its rapidly rejuvenating Mediterranean countries sounds intriguing, the fund's results have been less than captivating since it started up in 1997.

The North Europe Region fund turned in unexceptional returns in 1998 and 1999, averaging 18 percent a year—despite access to some of the best-performing stocks and countries. More than three-quarters of its assets were invested in Sweden, the United Kingdom, and Norway—a rather high degree of concentration. But even stranger was its virtual lack of exposure to France and Finland—two of the hottest markets in northern Europe.

The South Europe Region fund is even more of an enigma. Not only did it decide that Switzerland is a southern European country, by spring of 1999, it had dumped more than half its assets into this sluggish equity market. It was little surprise that by the end of the year, the fund had declined in lockstep with Switzerland, down by nearly 5 percent.

This move is even more perplexing considering that Switzerland is outside the eurozone. For a fund focused on southern Europe, gaining exposure to some of the region's smaller economies that continue to substantially restructure as they ascend into a common currency that will be stronger than their own would seem to be the fund's essential appeal. By the beginning of 2000, Italy had replaced Switzerland as the fund's top domestic exposure. But until it refocuses a larger chunk of its portfolio on the region's strongest growth prospects—the markets from Spain to Greece—the fund will remain a far more ordinary play than its name suggests.

So where does all this leave investors?

Pan-European Funds

THE EASIEST WAY to profit from Europe is through funds invested across the Continent. Because they are able to shift assets freely from one end of Europe to the other, gaining exposure to the full offering of various industries, these funds have notched the best long-term returns. And for all but the most aggressive fund investors, who believe they can uncover the next great growth story tucked away somewhere within a particular corner, these funds are the best way to invest in Europe. This is not just because of a record of strong returns; these fund managers have proven their ability to navigate effectively through Europe's evolving equity culture.

According to Morningstar, of the sixteen European funds that outperformed the S&P 500's total annualized gains of 22.87 percent over the three years from February 1998 through February 2000, thirteen were Pan-European funds.[9] Over a five-year period, four European funds exceeded the S&P 500's extraordinary annualized return of 26.57

percent. And all four were Pan-European: Dresdner RCM Europe N, Invesco European, Scudder Greater Europe Growth, and Legg Mason Europe A. Collectively, they averaged gains of 28.76 percent a year from February 1995 through February 2000.

As of March 2000, the funds shared some common characteristics:

➤ All are open-ended funds that are easy to buy and sell;

➤ At the end of 1999, all four were heavily invested in stocks—no bonds, holding little cash, primarily focused on large-cap growth companies; and

➤ Europe's core economies—the United Kingdom, France, and Germany—comprised about half of these funds' portfolios.

Despite being far from the top performers in 1999, U.K. companies were fund managers' clear favorites. They represented on average 25 percent of the portfolios, followed by French and then German equities. Sweden and the Netherlands were the next most popular countries, followed closely by Finland, Italy, and Spain.

It's little surprise that telecom was the most popular sector, with a focus on manufacturers and service providers. Nokia and Mannesmann were among the top holdings. The degree of exposure to these stocks tells us something about the varying level of risk each fund manager is willing to take.

For instance, Bärbel Lenz, of Dresdner RCM Europe, appears to be the most aggressive fund manager of the group, locking in more than 8 percent of her assets in Nokia and 6 percent in Mannesmann. These two plays have paid off in spades. But as a general rule, it seems that the other managers limit their top bets to no more than 4 to 5 percent of assets. Invesco's Steven Chamberlain's total exposure to Nokia and Mannesmann, his second- and fourth-largest plays, amounted to 7.5 percent of assets. And some managers make a point of topping off their lead holdings to no more than 2 percent of assets.

But when judging portfolio holdings, investors should keep in mind that a stock's performance can distort portfolio weighting. During the last quarter of 1999, both Nokia and Mannesmann more than doubled in value. Where some fund managers may take some profits off the table and reallocate assets to maintain balance, others may decide they are still in the best possible investments and continue to ride these shares' momentum.

Another fundamental difference between the funds is the size of their assets. Dresdner RCM Europe is the smallest among the four funds discussed here, with 1999 year-end holdings of $68 million. Scudder Greater Europe comes in on the high end, with more than $1.3 billion in assets.

Fund size can influence performance. A larger asset base can reduce expense ratios as costs are diluted over more clients. Whereas Scudder's annual expense ratio of 1.48 (for every $1,000 invested, a shareholder will pay the fund $14.80 to manage it) comes in well below the average for European funds (1.74 percent), Legg Mason's costs come in at the high end, 1.81 percent.[10]

There is often a connection between mutual fund costs and trading strategy. For instance, Vanguard's European Stock Index fund, which has the lowest turnover ratio, less than 10 percent (the fund will trade less than 10 percent of its portfolio every year), has an expense ratio that's under 0.3 percent.

Over the past several years, Scudder's turnover ratio has been creeping up toward 100 percent. Dresdner's turnover in 1999, when its expense ratio was 1.97, was over 200 percent, indicating a very active investment style that limits the average duration of holdings. This suggests a manager's desire to catch fire, continuously attempting to shift assets into the hottest stocks to generate top returns that will in turn attract more investors and assets. Funds with large secure asset bases (over $1 billion) may feel less compelled to chase after the quick kill. Dresdner's aggressive style seems to explain its extensive exposure to its two largest holdings, Nokia and Mannesmann, as well as the limited number of stocks in its portfolio: fifty-two issues in all.

Scudder, on the other hand, is more diversified. Its top holdings rarely exceed 2 percent of assets, and the fund maintains nearly 100 stocks in its portfolio.

The bottom line: Whereas both funds have generated superb returns, earning Morningstar's elite five-star rating, Scudder has done so by taking what the fund-rating company deems "below average" risks. Dresdner's performance required "above average" risk-taking.[11] However, these, like all ratings, are but rough guideposts. Toward the end of 1999, when Dresdner's top holding was everyone's favorite, Nokia, the lead post in Scudder's portfolio was the little-known upstart Italian bank BIPOP, trading at a triple-digit trailing P/E.[12]

A final concern in fund investing is trading costs. Three of the four funds, the exception being the Legg Mason Europe A fund, have no front-end or back-end sales charges. That means you will not pay an asset-related fee to get into or out of them. You may, however, pay a small flat trading fee, depending on your broker.

The Legg Mason fund charges an up-front sales commission of 4.75 percent of the investment. The world of no-load funds is expanding, but it's still not unusual to find funds that charge a load, especially when offering access to less-than-common investments—such as European stocks. The loads are a way for funds to compensate full-service brokers for distributing their securities.

Sometimes it's possible to find various share classes of the same fund that offer different load and fee structures. Generally, A shares are front-end loaded, with comparatively low expenses. B shares offer a declining back-end fee that disappears after six years. C shares levy an annual 1 percent fee that never goes away.

Legg Mason offers A and C classes of shares. If you are intent on buying a European fund through a full-service broker, then also consider Chase Vista European B shares. The fund's 3-year annualized performance is 2 points greater than Legg Mason's, and it has a slightly lower expense ratio: 1.74 versus 1.81 percent.

So why then was Chase Vista not featured here? Because for many investors, it simply hasn't been around long enough.

It's normally hard to make a case for a load fund that can take nearly 5 percent off the top before you start, accompanied by well-above-average expense fees. However, both Legg Mason and Chase Vista have far outperformed the bulk of European funds, making their charges simply the price one pays to gain access to some very talented fund managers. Just keep in mind that the returns of the lower-cost load-free funds are just as good—if not better.

For investors looking for alternatives to traditional mutual funds, the European Warrant Fund and Lehman Brothers' unit investment trust known as 10 Uncommon Euro Values are two unique products that offer high-stakes exposure to European equity markets.

Although its inherently risky nature may move it off most investors' radar screens, the European Warrant Fund has been an extraordinary play. It's a closed-end fund that trades on the New York Stock Exchange. As its name suggests, it's an option fund that gets high-octane results—both up and down—through leveraged bets on the long-term growth prospects of Europe.

How does it work? Warrants, like calls, cost just several percentage points of the value of the total investment. They can capture all the gains a stock makes several times over during the lifetime of the option, which currently averages two and one-half years. This is what provides the fund with leverage. Management can control risk by varying the degree of leverage based on the sentiment of the market, exploiting bullish times and pulling back exposure during downturns in the market. But unlike a long position in a stock that goes south, the value of a warrant or a call is worthless after it expires.

All this makes EWF the most volatile European fund available to the U.S. investor. And this is highlighted by the average discount at which the fund has been trading.

By the end of 1999, more than two-thirds of the fund's assets were invested in warrants tracking the top U.K., eurozone, and European stocks, as well as baskets of Scandinavian telecom and European information technology shares.

Being exchange listed, the fund's trading costs are the same as a stock. Its annual expense ratio is slightly high at 1.77. But considering the greater managerial care the fund requires and the success its managers have achieved, this expense seems modest.

In 1999, the European Warrant Fund was up 27.52 percent. Over the preceding three years, the fund racked up gains of more than 49 percent a year. Since 1995, annualized returns were 42 percent—the best Europe had to offer. But due to the fund's volatility, short- and medium-term returns are significantly affected by the timing of an investment.

The Lehman Brothers' 10 Uncommon Euro Values is less than two years old, too new for me to recommend it, but intriguing enough to tell investors to keep an eye on it. This unit investment trust is an offspring of Lehman's celebrated U.S. version, which has outperformed the market more than 70 percent of the time over the last half a century.[13] In its 1999 debut year, the euro version soared by more than 52 percent in dollar terms, nearly quadrupling the MSCI Europe Index.

Some basics: Uncommon Euro Values is a concentrated bet on only ten equally weighted European stocks that may include equities from outside the eurozone. It's designed for institutional investors, but

Select European Mutual Funds

| FUND | ANNUALIZED TOTAL RETURNS IN $U.S. AS OF DECEMBER 31, 1999 * | | | | |
	1-YEAR	3-YEAR	5-YEAR	NET ASSETS	EXPENSES
Dresdner RCM European N Ticker: DRENX	43.5%	35.24%	23.12%	$68 M	1.60%
Scudder Greater Europe Growth Ticker: SCGEX	35.58	29.19	28.39	$1.66 B	1.48%
Invesco European Ticker: FEURX	37.99	28.31	26.7	$758 M	1.56%
Legg Mason European A † Ticker: LMEFX	1 7.15	25.89	25.91	$73 M	1.81%
European Warrant Fund Ticker: EWF: NYSE	27.52	49.04	42.07	$305M	1.77%
Lehman Brothers 10 Uncommon Euro Values §	52.5	NA	NA	NA	0.25%
S&P 500	21.04	27.56	28.56		
European Fund Average #	24.93	20.26	20.7		

* Portfolio information is as of 31 December 1999, except for Lehman Brothers' 10 Uncommon Eurovalues, which is recreated each January.
† Dollar-based returns are inclusive of the initial sales load.
‡ These percentages are based on the portfolio's fully leveraged value of $442 million. This exceeds the fund's actual asset value of $305 million, reflecting the gearing of the portfolio.

LOADS	COUNTRY EXPOSURE*	TOP FIVE STOCKS
None	Germany 20.4% U.K. 18% France 17.2% Finland 14.8% Italy 6.9%	Nokia 8.2% Mannesmann 6% STMicroelectronics 4.9% Sonera 4.8% ASM Lithography 3.8%
None	U.K. 26% France 20% Germany 15% Netherlands 12% Italy 9%	Editoriale L'Espresso Publicis 3.4% Nokia 2.9% BIPOP 2.8% Siemens 2.8% Telefónica 2.5%
None	U.K. 23% France 17.33% Sweden 8.46% Spain 8.17%	Mannesmann 3.98% Nokia 3.83% Ericsson 3.08% STMicroelectronics 3.03%
4.75%	U.K. 27.09% France 17.97% Germany 14.86% Netherlands 8.8% Sweden 6.44%	Nokia 3.97% Mannesmann 3.84% BP Amoco 3.79% British Telecom 3.39% SAP 3.29%
None	U.K. 32% France 14% Germany 11.5% Scandinavia 11% Benelux 8.5%	FTSE 100 Warrants 25% ‡ Euroland 11 Indices Warrants 19.2% Scandinavia Telecom Basket Warrants 12.5% Eurotop 100 Warrants 11.2% Information Technology Basket Warrants 10.7%
2%	Netherlands 40% U.K. 20% Germany 10% France 10% Sweden 10%	Mannesmann 10% °° Ericsson 10% TOTAL FINA ELF 10% ABB 10% AstraZeneca 10%

Source: Morningstar

§ This security is a unit investment trust whose portfolio is thoroughly reconfigured each year in January.
°° The trust's ten holdings for 2000 are equally weighted in the portfolio. The order of holdings here is based on each stock's overall market capitalization, starting with the largest.

Lehman does sell the $10 units in lots of 1,000 and permits a host of brokerage firms to resell the product in even smaller $1,000 increments.

Unlike a mutual fund, a unit investment trust has a limited life span—in this instance, only one year. Lehman charges a 2 percent sales commission; brokerage firms reselling the units may charge a higher load. The annual management fee is a modest 25 basis points.

Although there isn't a formal secondary market for this product, units may be sold back to Lehman at any time up through the official date of redemption. Investors are permitted to roll over assets into the next year's offering, but they are subject to an additional 1.5 percent sales charge as well as capital gains taxes based on the previous year's performance.

The appeal of the trust is that unlike a mutual fund, whose manager can play hunches and consistently shift assets in and out of stocks, this security reflects a leading international investment bank's commitment to ten specific stocks over a limited period of time. There is absolutely no uncertainty about what investors are buying, no hidden investment strategies, none of the exotic bets that distinctly color returns of some mutual funds. And unlike individual stock plays based on recommendations of a single analyst, broker, or fund manager, 10 Uncommon Euro Values is the distillation of several levels of institutional review that involves strong, overt support for each of the underlying investments— the same selection process upon which the U.S. version has relied. Finding an investment backed by such explicit endorsement is unique.

However, there is one caveat. If something goes wrong with any one of the ten stocks, you're stuck with it. The trust can't trade out of dogs poised to turn into real hounds. But you can always redeem your holdings.

While the 1999 trust was a well-diversified portfolio that won big on Finnish telecom manufacturer Nokia, German industrial giant Siemens, and French media leader Canal Plus, the 2000 portfolio had a greater concentration on telecoms. This included a shift from Nokia to its Swedish rival Ericsson and a bet that German industrial-turned-telecom-service-provider Mannesmann would succumb to Vodafone's hostile bid. Other investment changes included exposure to the oil sector (TOTAL FINA ELF) and a shift from one industrial turnaround story that already paid off handsomely, Siemens, into another, ABB of Switzerland.

Chapter Eleven

Nuts and Bolts

Accounting and Financial Reporting

I N 1993, GERMAN AUTOMAKER Daimler-Benz was listed on the New York Stock Exchange, an act that would subsequently provide it the currency for the acquisition of Chrysler. As required of all foreign corporations trading on major U.S. stock exchanges, Daimler reconciled its financial statements according to U.S. Generally Accepted Accounting Principles (GAAP). Daimler was the first German corporation to have its financials restated, and the company's experience reveals why other foreign firms were reluctant to list in the States.

One can only imagine that back in the Daimler boardroom in Stuttgart jaws dropped in disbelief when company officials discovered its 1993 German GAAP–reported profits of DM 615 million translated into a U.S. GAAP–reported loss of DM 1.84 billion.

Had this paragon of German engineering been pulling the wool over its investors' eyes?

Hardly. But the event did give investors pause and illustrated some of the substantial differences that exist between accounting standards within the world's major equity markets.

"Cultural, institutional, political, and tax differences," observes Bruno Solnik, professor of finance at the HEC School of Management in Paris, "can make cross-border comparisons of accounting numbers hazardous and misleading." For example, treatment of depreciation and extraordinary items may vary so significantly that "an analyst," Solnik concludes, "would probably have to double the net income of some Swedish or German firms to make a meaningful comparison with the corresponding figures for British or U.S. firms."[1]

In Daimler's case, the biggest restatement involved Retained Earnings pertaining to provisions, reserves, and valuation differences, which knocked off more than DM 4.2 billion from the company's profits.

How could accounting practices of two highly industrialized countries vary so widely?

Well, it begins with the Continental European practice of relying on only one set of financials for both shareholders and the government. In the United States, companies prepare two distinct financial reports, one that accurately gauges a company's economic performance, the other designed to exploit legitimate tax benefits. The Continent's single-book approach produces a more conservative set of numbers, reflecting a traditional reliance on debt rather than equity financing.

Understating earnings and allowing for generous provisions protects the interests of both lenders and the corporations themselves, especially through the creation of substantial hidden reserves. "In good times," Solnik reports, "German firms will build provisions to reduce earnings growth; in bad times, German firms will draw on these provisions to boost earnings." The latter is exactly what Daimler did in the wake of the recession that hit Germany in 1993, which resulted in a huge restatement.[2]

Daimler's net income took another hit—DM 624 million—in the way it recorded pensions and other retirement benefits, which at the time were accrued but not fully funded as required in the United States.

On the positive side, Daimler received a boost of DM 2.6 billion in deferred taxes, largely due to significant tax benefits related to net operating losses recognized by U.S. GAAP but not by German GAAP. But at the end of the day, U.S. GAAP converted Daimler's EPS of DM 12.92 into a loss of DM 39.47. And this difference filtered through every financial ratio.

This reported loss did not mean Daimler was in particular trouble. Often restatement simply reflects cultural differences in the way each country measures performance rather than the existence of loopholes that distort true financial health. As BMW's chief financial officer, Volker Doppelfeld, observed at the time of his competitor's listing on the NYSE, "the quarterly reporting requirements of the exchange would undermine long-term corporate planning by emphasizing short-term profits."[3]

Moreover, restatement may also involve the reshuffling of numbers. Although reconciling Daimler's financials turned a gain into a loss, it also ended up boosting the company's net worth, from DM 18.15 billion to DM 23.92 billion.[4] By 1994, as Germany began to pull out of recession and with the company being more sensitive to the implications of U.S. restatement, Daimler's numbers were back on track, reporting a U.S. GAAP net income of DM 1.05 billion, or earnings of DM 21.53 per share.[5]

An exchange-listed ADR produces line-by-line reconciliation, enabling bona fide comparisons with a company's American competitors. But the real challenge for investors going abroad is in relying on statements that haven't been reconciled with U.S. GAAP. This uncertainty makes a good case for sticking with only those European shares that are listed on major U.S. stock exchanges. Several hundred trade on the NYSE, Nasdaq, and AMEX, including six of the ten stocks featured in this book.

However, it would be myopic to ignore some of Europe's industry-leading operations, such as Sweden's retail powerhouse Hennes & Mauritz and France's global utility leader Suez Lyonnaise des Eaux, simply because they do not trade in the States. So then, how can investors avoid getting hurt by financials that may be materially deficient to U.S. GAAP—a reporting standard considered to be among the most investor-oriented around?

First, investors should contact companies' shareholder relations departments and inquire about major differences between their statements and U.S. GAAP–reported numbers.

At the same time, consult various publications that review accounting standards by nations. Although such texts tend to be hard to decipher for nonprofessionals, they will provide important guideposts.[6] And see if brokerage reports identify accounting differences that affect comparisons with U.S. competitors. If they don't, call the analysts directly to make sure accounting is a nonissue.

As a starting point, review the following line items that are frequently restated when foreign enterprises come to the States. They are identified and defined in the annual reports of ADRs under the section called "Significant Accounting Differences with U.S. GAAP." This list, comprised from a review of Nokia, SAP, British Airways, Daimler-Chrysler, and Vodafone, is by no means a comprehensive guide to how foreign financial statements differ from their U.S. counterparts. However, it will help orient investors to some of the key issues affecting the measurement of a company's profitability.

Deferred Income Taxes

In FY 1999, Vodafone's net income was restated downward by £126 million, to £510.4 million. Of that change, 20 percent involved an increase in deferred income taxes. This line item refers to an estimated amount of taxes that a company will likely have to pay on an annual basis—beyond the current reporting period—once certain tax advantages expire. Variations in the treatment of depreciation of capital expenditures, revenue recognition, and goodwill account for a large portion of the differences in deferred income taxes between U.S. and European companies.

Development Costs

Nokia's 1999 restated net income of €2.54 billion was virtually identical with the number derived from the use of International Accounting Standards. However, the largest line difference involved development costs. While IAS capitalizes R&D and then depreciates it over a two- to five-year period, U.S. GAAP requires this cost to be expensed directly off the income statement, immediately cutting into profitability. In 1999, an increase in recognized development costs reduced Nokia's U.S. GAAP–reported earnings by €47 million.

Goodwill

More than 80 percent of the reduction in Vodafone's restated net income was due to a readjustment in goodwill. Goodwill is the surplus paid for a company in excess of its fair market value, a matter of particular relevance to the highly acquisitive Vodafone. Downward adjustment by more than £99 million in the company's 1999 U.S. GAAP income statement was largely due to a former U.K. accounting rule that permitted goodwill to be written off against shareholders' funds in the year of acquisition. Now, like the States, the United Kingdom requires goodwill to be capitalized and amortized over the asset's useful life. However, reconciling past goodwill generates larger expenses and smaller profits.

Depreciation

British Airways' 1999 profit of $332 million was cut in half after being restated. However, treatment of depreciation kept the reconciliation from actually slicing deeper into net income. Europe tends to depreciate assets at a faster rate than the United States prescribes. With its jets being a substantial component of its operations, British Airways' net income was enhanced by more than $94 million due to a slower rate of depreciation.

Marketable Securities

In 1998 and 1999, the second-largest line adjustment to Nokia's restated income statement was marketable securities. In 1998, U.S. GAAP added €29 million to restated profits; in 1999, it deducted €15 million. In Finland, where management has designated certain marketable securities as "intended to be sold," the company keeps their value marked to market, with unrealized profits or losses reported on the income statement. In the United States, the value of securities "available for sale" is reported as a separate component of shareholders' equity and shifted to the income statement only when they are actually traded. Therefore, the company's 1998 unrealized losses—recognized in Finland—are put back into the reconciled statement, just as Nokia's 1999 gains are taken away.

Pensions

Pensions are funded in the United States, the Netherlands, Switzerland, and the United Kingdom. However, this is still not the case in much of Europe, especially in Italy and France, which depend on a pay-as-you-go approach. Reconciling this difference can have a significant impact on the bottom line. Back in 1993, as stated earlier, when German pension costs were mostly accrued but not funded, Daimler's pensions and other postretirement benefits were reduced by DM 624 million—more than Daimler's entire German GAAP–stated profit. While German companies have since been required to fund their pensions, underlying methodology and economic assumptions are still less than conservative, resulting in understated liabilities.[7] Restated pension provisions reduced SAP's 1998 net income by DM 5.4 million.

Revenue Recognition

Overall, restatement of SAP's net income of DM 1.05 billion was reduced by only 2 percent in 1998—the year the company listed on the NYSE. But differences in the way in which revenue is recognized in Germany versus the manner in which it's done in the States reduced the company's U.S. GAAP net income by more than DM 49 million. In 1997, the impact of restated revenue was even greater, DM 77.5 million, which cut net income by 9 percent. At the heart of the matter, German GAAP permits SAP to recognize revenue from software license agreements when customers are authorized to access the system. U.S. GAAP recognizes revenue over a longer period of time, in accordance with actual usage.

In dealing with the problems of financial reconciliation, investors should ultimately keep in mind that restating financial data does not address the issues of the quality of information disclosed, its timeliness, nor a firm's prospects for the future—the keys behind a solid investment.[8]

Toward that end, Professor Frederick D. S. Choi, Dean of the undergraduate Stern School of Business at New York University, recommends moving onto a different set of financials. "Cash flow statements," Choi observes, "offer better insight into the economics of what's really going on inside a business by tracking the direct affect of sales and expenses, sidestepping the pitfalls attached to differences in domestic accounting regimes."[9]

Although restating foreign financials according to U.S. GAAP may occasionally reveal hidden operational weaknesses and no doubt promotes more accurate cross-border industry comparisons, generally the impact of these differences on a stock's price may be limited. Virtually all ADRs represent only a small fraction of their respective companies' free float. Foreign shares are most affected by trading activity in their home markets. There, domestic investors rely on original financial statements, making these numbers the most influential.

In the long run, financial reconciliation may become a matter of decreasing importance. European union is encouraging the movement toward common reporting practice. Many large companies are adopting rules—to a large degree comparable to U.S. GAAP—set out by the International Accounting Standards Committee. In addition, early in 2000, the U.S. Securities and Exchange Commission indicated that it may be in favor of accepting IAS for companies wishing to trade on U.S. stock exchanges. This could conceivably trigger a huge expansion in foreign share listings in the States, making it easier for U.S. investors to venture abroad.

Foreign Exchange and Bonds

IN 1999, THE MSCI EUROZONE index soared 37.47 percent in local currency terms. However, during the year, the value of the euro—the currency in which the entire index is based—declined by nearly 18 percent against the dollar. This cut a U.S.-based investor's return in half.

How exactly does foreign exchange affect an investment?

Take a European stock that began 1999 trading at €100. At that time, one euro was worth $1.16. So in dollar terms, the stock was worth $116 a share. If over the year the stock appreciated in local currency terms by 10 percent, it closed 1999 at €110. But for the dollar-based investor, with the euro having depreciated to near parity by year's end, the value of his investment actually declined from $116 to $110. This explains why on any given day a stock reported to have gone up in the local exchange-rate quotes of the *Financial Times* could show a decline in its corresponding ADR listed in *The Wall Street Journal*.

When investors venture abroad, foreign exchange can involve as much risk as security selection itself. And while the advent of common currency has collapsed the exchange risk of investing in eleven western European countries into just one currency, the euro has been as volatile as any of the former European currencies it replaced. By early September 2000, it was trading at less than $0.87, a decline of 25 percent since its introduction twenty months earlier.

Why has the euro collapsed?

That's not an easy question. Here are some basic explanations.

A number of the Continent's weaker currencies—the Italian lira, the Spanish peseta, and the Portuguese escudo—appreciated substantially upon gaining charter membership in the euro. Qualifying for the euro and then handing over future monetary policy to the European Central Bank, whose leadership would be dominated by the fiscal conservatives, gave these peripheral currencies instant integrity. It perhaps made investors overly enthusiastic and likely led to overvaluation of these currencies. With the exchange rate of the euro a composite of all eleven countries participating in the new currency through 2000, a correction of some kind was therefore likely.

Another factor contributing to the momentum against the euro is a lack of a trading history. Whereas technical analysts can suggest at what price a slumping stock is likely to attract buyers, the new currency is only now establishing its trading patterns and thus lacks tangible support levels to help stem a slide. And in this context, as currency traders will tell you, momentum becomes a dominant force against a currency.

A third issue: the European Central Bank, the caretaker of the euro, also lacks a track record. How well it will be able to balance economic growth, inflation, and currency valuation, as well as the disparate concerns of its member nations, are big unknowns. And markets inherently distrust central banks until they've distinguished themselves. Case in point: When Greenspan talks, people listen. Not the case so far with the ECB.

While traditional explanations of currency movements lie in such things as purchasing-power parity, current account balances, and inflation rate differentials, the easiest way for individual investors to understand the euro's decline (and foreign exchange in general) is to think of currency as a commodity: the more it's in demand for the purchase of a country's goods, services, and securities, the more it's worth.[1]

Accordingly, it has been the strength of the U.S. economy that has been driving down the value of the euro. Faster corporate growth, a protracted bull market, and considerably higher interest rates than Europe's have worked together to generate a huge net cash flow out of the Continent and into the States.[2]

Mary Ann Bartels, senior international quantitative strategist at Merrill Lynch in New York City, reports net cash flow from the eurozone into the United States was about $196 billion in 1999. That's nearly $50 billion more than what it was in 1997. So despite an increasingly more healthy eurozone economy that's moving in the right direction on many fronts, greater demand for U.S. assets has meant less demand for European assets and ergo for the euros needed to buy them with.[3]

What, then, will stabilize the euro and cause it to rebound?

The European Central Bank can continue to push up interest rates to attract greater demand for the euro. But that risks slowing growth. The ECB can also encourage major central banks to start buying euros. The first such global intervention did in fact occur in September 2000, which immediately boosted the euro's value. But the benefits of intervention are generally short-lived when running against broad market sentiment. Relying instead on a more pure market response will likely generate a more sustained rebound in the euro's value.

A cheap euro reduces the price of European exports, which should boost corporate sales and bottom lines. As demand for European goods and services increases, so must demand for the euros needed to pay for them. Further, for European companies doing extensive business in the States, like AEGON, Vodafone, and DaimlerChrysler, repatriating these sales back into euro-denominated financials will further boost their bottom lines.[4] As these companies' shares look more attractive, demand for them should increase as well, further increasing the demand for the euro. At some point, all of this will trigger a run-up in the euro's value. The question is when.

While the euro has dominated European foreign exchange headlines, there are more than a half-dozen separate currencies still actively traded in Europe. Vodafone is quoted in British pounds, Hennes & Mauritz in Swedish kronor, and Adecco in Swiss francs. Although the central European countries of Poland, Hungary, and the Czech Republic may soon join the European Union, citizens of these nations are still a long way from turning in their zlotys, forints, and korunas for euros.

In 1999 the most stable of these other European currencies vis-à-vis the dollar was the British pound, which depreciated only 2.7 percent against the greenback. Investments in Sweden and Norway also held up fairly well in 1999, with their currencies having declined by only 6.1 and 7.2 percent, respectively.

However, all the other noneuro currencies performed as miserably as the euro. The two hardest-hit in developed western Europe were the Swiss franc, down 16.8 percent, and the Danish krone, down 17.4 percent. The central European currencies—the Czech koruna, Polish zloty, and Hungarian forint—all depreciated similarly, off an average of 20 percent. And as it prepared to join the euro, the Greek drachma lost 18.7 percent against the dollar.[5]

Although recent currency performance offers little guidance to future exchange rates, this brief survey does reveal the substantial risks of investing abroad.

There is a way to mitigate currency risk when purchasing foreign stocks.[6] Large investors regularly employ hedging techniques that involve the purchase of futures contracts and options against the currency in which an investor is exposed. The cost of this protection usually runs several percent of the entire investment and is affected by the duration of the hedge and volatility of the currency. However, due to high minimum costs and the intricacy of the play, most European analysts discourage individual investors from hedging their investments.

But there is a positive side to all this. Foreign exchange rate movement can be as much opportunity as risk. Many funds specialize in profiting from currency fluctuation, relying on complicated derivatives and options. Small-time investors can exploit currency weakness as well by simply purchasing securities when a weak exchange rate makes them ostensibly cheap.[7]

The investment logic for locking into a cheap currency is the precise inverse of the example presented in the beginning of this section. If the euro has indeed bottomed out at or around $0.85 and over the next year it appreciates modestly to $0.94, then any investment in a euro-denominated security will be boosted by 10 percent. So a stock that rises from €100 to €125 would actually return a dollar-based investor 35 percent.

Most foreign investment advisers would discourage the purchase of foreign bonds for income because currency risk far outweighs any interest premium over bond yields in an investor's home market. But certain bonds do furnish an effective means to bet on a weak currency.

According to currency specialist Neil Rackoff, president of the Friedberg Mercantile Group in New York City, "if an investor wants to be long a major currency such as the euro and believes interest rates will remain relatively stable, then short-term sovereign debt offers relative price stability compared to stocks plus an interest payment." Further, Rackoff observes that investors may also realize capital gains when a currency appreciates. How so? Greater investor confidence in a currency often produces increased support for securities denominated in that currency.

So with government and investment-grade bond yields in the eurozone running between 5 and 7 percent, a 10 percent rise in the euro over a twelve-month period would more than double a dollar-based investor's return. But is a 15 percent or even 20 percent return adequate compensation for the risk of this play?

Eurozone junk bonds and investment-grade debt issued in central Europe by financial services companies and by supranationals, respectively, do offer higher coupons. For instance, Atlantic Telecom, a fixed-access and mobile service provider based in the United Kingdom, is paying investors 13 percent interest on a B3-rated euro-denominated bond selling at par and due in January 2010. However, that's only 100 to 150 basis points above what comparable U.S. junk bonds are paying, and only 5 percentage points above domestic investment-grade yields. A small decline in the euro would wipe out this difference in this credit-risky play.

In March 2000, an AAA-rated International Bank Reconstruction and Development bond, issued in Polish zlotys, was yielding 16 percent, trading below par at 95, and due in September 2001. Although there is virtually no credit risk, the bonds expose investors to substantial currency risk. With the zloty depreciating at more than 10 percent a year versus the dollar, the total return once repatriated hardly seems worthwhile.

However, there may be a small window of opportunity for investing in central European debt once Poland, Hungary, and the Czech Republic join the European Union and presumably prepare for membership in common currency. For the latter to happen, these countries must achieve substantial macroeconomic gains that would cut current account deficits, inflation, and interest rates, thus effectively stabilizing their currencies. This then creates the conditions for what the market regards as a convergence play. Several examples: In the late 1990s, high-coupon southern European bonds from Portugal to Italy and more recently in Greece soared in value as these once troubled economies reformed in preparation for EMU.

If Poland, Hungary, and the Czech Republic follow the same scenario and if the stringent conditions for euro membership do not change, there is little reason why a similar play in their bonds won't prove equally profitable.

There are three keys to making a successful convergence play. First and most important, an investor must be right about a country's willingness to adopt the tough policies necessary to qualify for euro membership. Remember, qualification is not about growth rates; it's about the ability to demonstrate monetary and fiscal restraint. The second key: buying bonds just before interest rates begin their descent toward convergence with the eurozone. And the third essential: selling out before approaching maturity begins to exert a gravitational pull on prices.

Getting in too early—especially if a government subsequently finds itself unwilling to maintain its monetary and fiscal vigilance—will expose investors to capital erosion due to currency depreciation that may well exceed even the rich interest being earned. On the other side, investors who hesitate too long—uncertain about whether these nations will actually qualify for euro membership—will end up paying a high premium for bonds with limited capital appreciation potential and an interest rate differential that would hardly make the play worthwhile.

Equity Indices, Benchmarks, and Performance Discrepancies

AN INVESTOR WHO WANTS to know how the U.S. market is doing inquires about the Dow Jones Industrials, the S&P 500, or maybe the Nasdaq composite. But how does an investor gauge returns in Europe?

Open up the *Financial Times* and it's little surprise to find the FTSE Eurotop 300 prominently displayed. It's among Europe's most widely followed indices, comprised of western Europe's 300 largest companies. The *Financial Times* also reports the FTSE Europe, an index of 677 western European companies, and the FTSE Eurobloc, a composite of 306 companies headquartered within the eurozone.

Go to *The Wall Street Journal* and, again, it's no surprise to see its parent Dow Jones's STOXX and Euro STOXX indices featured. Like their FTSE cousins, these two benchmarks track 600 European and 300 eurozone-based companies, respectively. But whereas the FTSE indices track the largest companies, Dow Jones's STOXX is comprised of a proportional number of large-, mid-, and small-cap stocks, with the Euro STOXX index extracted from it.

For those investors who prefer more concise benchmarks, FTSE and Dow Jones also maintain smaller, more concentrated versions that track Europe's and the eurozone's fifty largest companies.

MSCI and Standard & Poor's also weigh in with their own European indices. All told, these four tracking agencies—along with a host of major brokerage houses—slice up Europe in every way imaginable, generating hundreds of regional, national, sector, industry, market-cap-specific, and even growth and value indices.

Why the explosion in tracking devices? Part of the answer lies in the development of a European equity culture, something relatively new. A number of these indices have become key investment benchmarks. Moreover, many are generating substantial licensing fees from management companies, brokers, and exchanges who have created funds, futures, and options that precisely track their performance.

EMU has driven this index boom. Before the euro, European investors analyzed the market in national terms. Where U.S. investors would look to the Dow, German investors turned to the DAX 30, French investors to the CAC 40, Italian investors to the MIB-tel 30. Common currency has begun to change all this, erasing the barriers that required many mutual and pension funds to invest primarily within their own borders to minimize currency risk. With thousands of companies now all quoted in euros, fund managers have seen their investment horizons expand. And with them, so does the need to develop benchmarks to gauge performance.

Which index best serves the needs of investors moving into Europe? Well, that would depend on what an investor is buying. Whereas American brokerage firms and the financial press are in the habit of gauging the performance of any domestic stock against the S&P 500, investing in Europe perhaps should make us rethink this approach. Should one judge the performance of Nokia against a collection of 300 mid-to-large-cap eurozone or Pan-European stocks? Or would comparison with a telecom sector index mean more?

Taking the argument a step further, one might wonder if a U.S. investor seeking to improve upon his domestic returns should simply gauge any foreign investment against the broad American market.

Despite the growing belief in the global marketplace, analysts still rely on local benchmarks to gain a sense of geographical context. Since most foreign investors would likely be focused on mid-to-large-cap

Performance of European Indices

(Through December 31, 1999 in U.S. Dollars*)

INDEX	NUMBER OF COUNTRIES	NUMBER OF COMPANIES
FTSE Europe	16	677
FTSE Eurotop 300	16	300
FTSE Eurotop 100†	9	100
FTSE Eurobloc 300	10	147
FTSE Eurobloc 100†	6	100
DJGI Europe	16	613
DJ STOXX	16	600
DJ STOXX 50	9	50
DJ Euro STOXX	10	309
DJ Euro STOXX 50	7	50
Dow Jones Ind. Ave.	1	30
MSCI Europe	15	542
MSCI EMU	10	309
S&P Euro	10	160
S&P Europe 350°	15	350
S&P 500	1	500

* Annualized returns with dividends reinvested.
† FTSE changed the manner in which it tracked and calculated returns for its Eurotop 100 and Eurobloc 100 indexes in 1998, preventing presentation of true historic returns.

stocks, using any of the major indices would prove worthwhile. If one wanted to rely on a particular index for an investment, the historic synthetic returns listed below may help sort out which way to go.

Index performance varies significantly for several reasons. Selection criteria and constituent weighting are by no means the same. Some indices, like the FTSE, track the very largest companies based on market capitalization, then adjusted by actual free float. Others seek a cross-section of the market. DJ proportionally weights STOXX between small-, mid-, and large-cap stocks. MSCI replicates 60 percent of the broad market based on industry weighting and proportional national market-cap representation.

With the release of fast-growing IPOs and tremendous merger and acquisition activity, the composition of European stock markets

1-YEAR RETURNS*	3-YEAR RETURNS*	5-YEAR RETURNS	WEB SITE
16.14%	22.39%	22.55%	www.ftse.com
16.82	23.53	23.86	
17.51	NA	NA	
19.72	26.01	24.27	
20.88	NA	NA	
17.06	22.16	21.72	indexes.dowjones.com
18.20	23.49	23.05	
24.04	29.46	27.55	
21.11	28.01	24.67	
27.30	30.90	27.94	
25.22	21.26	24.56	
16.23	23.02	22.53	www.msci.com
19.25	26.72	23.61	
21.72	34.43	21.97	www.spglobal.com
16.93	32.08	21.29	
28.58	28.23	24.06	

is changing rapidly. Not all of the indices capture these changes at the same time, leading to further performance discrepancies. Vodafone's acquisition of Mannesmann highlights a potential problem for some tracking funds when a constituent stock exceeds the legal weight limit.

Then there is the issue of dividends and reinvestment—which investors should note also distorts, from source to source, the reported performance of individual stock returns. It's common for indices to calculate a daily average dividend contribution for each stock. But things begin to get messy with some countries requiring companies to withhold taxes while others don't. Each index may treat this issue differently. The precise time when indices reinvest dividends may also vary. And then there is the matter of the extraordinary dividends and warrants that some companies occasionally issue, which may further distort comparison among indices. Finally, treatment of currency also generates performance discrepancy, especially when generating historic returns.

Before January 1999, the euro didn't exist, but the European Currency Unit (ecu) did. The ecu is a weighted basket of EU currencies. So to determine pre-1999 returns, most indices recalibrated their numbers in ecus. The problem is the ecu is not an accurate substitute for the euro for the simple reason that the British pound weighed in at 13 percent of the ecu's value and has no part in the euro.

FTSE solved this discrepancy by generating a synthetic euro for its historical analysis. But one may argue that the euro's unpredictably volatile behavior would not have been captured by simple integration of the former underlying currencies. Still, it's an improvement over the ecu in helping investors gauge past returns.

Resources

CERTAINLY BEFORE THE AGE of the Internet, investing in Europe was a challenging proposition. Analyzing prospective investments, much less tracking prices, was virtually impossible for individual investors. Even brokerage houses offered limited coverage of foreign securities.

But today following a European equity is about as easy as watching an American stock, thanks to expanded coverage by business magazines, news services, nongovernment organizations, and investment firms—with the Internet bringing everything home.

STOCKS

COMPANY	TELEPHONE	FEATURED PRODUCT / WEB ADDRESS
Bank of New York	212.815.2084	http://www.bankofny.com/adr
Financial Times	011.44.207.873.3000	*European Company Performance Survey*
Financial Times/Paribas	011.44.207.873.3000	Financial Times *Guide to the FTSE Eurotop 300* http://www.ftse.com
Goldman Sachs	212.357.1772	*Inside the FT/S&P Actuaries World Indices*
IBES International	800.438.4237 212.437.8500	http://www.trapeze.net
J.P. Morgan		http://www.adr.com
Multex.com	800.721.2225 212.607.2490	http://www.multex.com
Value Line	800.654.0508 212.907.1500	*Value Line Investment Survey* http://www.valueline.com

Below is a select list of organizations, publications, and Web sites that offer extraordinary access to national, sector, and corporate information. Each company has a remarkable range of free and paid products that go well beyond the items listed here. And collectively their Web links prove the concept of six degrees of separation, where virtually any piece of financial information may be brought to a desktop with no more than a few clicks of a mouse. And for those who prefer hard copy, major university and public business libraries offer free access to a large portion of the paid material described below.

DESCRIPTION

A fairly decent look at many of the world's American Depositary Receipts provided by one of the leading sponsors of ADRs.

An invaluable annual that appears sometime in June as an insert in the *FT*, providing extraordinary statistical review of the European marketplace, organized by sector.

Annual review of Europe's largest 300 public companies, with in-depth focus on the top 100.

A monthly publication that provides current and historic corporate, national, regional, and sectoral performance.

An invaluable resource for analyzing all stocks. Subscription isn't cheap, but what you get is access to a myriad of current domestic and foreign brokerage reports on virtually every public company around. Besides offering superb financial coverage, these reports offer an inside look at what Wall Street is thinking.

Newly created site that should turn into a superb resource for investors, focusing on American Depositary Receipts.

Another online research service, providing access to a wide range of analyst reports tracking companies around the world. Offers products at various fee schedules.

The classic tightly distilled one-page equity reports are now online, full of financials and 300-word analyses.

COMPANY	TELEPHONE	FEATURED PRODUCT / WEB ADDRESS

STOCKS (continued)

Winthrop Corporation	203.330.5343	http://www.corporateinformation.com
Yahoo		http://finance.uk.yahoo.com

MUTUAL FUNDS

Morningstar	800.735.0700 312.69.6000	*Morningstar Mutual Funds Survey* http://www.morningstar.com
Value Line	800.654.0508 212.907.1500	*Value Line Mutual Fund Survey* http://www.valueline.com

COUNTRIES

Business Central Europe	011.43.1.713.3363; 011.44.207.830.7000	Business Central Europe http://www.bcemag.com
The Economist	011.44.207.830.7000 800.938.4685 212.554.0600	*The Economist* http://www.economist.com; Economist Intelligence Unit Quarterly and Annual Country Reports http://www.eiu.com; EIU Viewswire http://www.viewswire.com
Euromoney	011.44.207.779.8888	*Euromoney; Euromoney Research Guides* http://www.euromoney.com
Financial Times	800.628.8088 212.641.6500	Country Surveys http://www.ft.com
International Finance Corporation	202.473.7411	Monthly Review of Emerging Stock Markets http://www.spglobal.com
International Monetary Fund	202.623.7430	Article IV Country Consultations; International Financial Statistics http://www.imf.org

DESCRIPTION

A truly remarkable free data source, providing descriptive and financial data and analysis, translatable into all currencies, along with stock quotes. Offers far-reaching site linkage, including access to every company's Web site.

Source for international stock quotes and a whole lot more, especially via Web links.

Superb comprehensive survey of all significant mutual funds, including performance, portfolio, risk and cost analysis. Its Web site is terrific.

Another useful print and online mutual fund review of domestic and European mutual funds.

One of the best linked Web sites servicing the region, offering country-by-country review and a lot more.

The leading global financial weekly offers periodic country surveys.

Comprehensive macroeconomic studies with reference to significant corporate events.

A paid online site, prepared by the Economist Intelligence Unit, providing well-organized access to a continuous flow of articles organized by country.

This glossy in-depth monthly has a superb Web site that offers free access to its archives of articles organized by country. Also periodically publishes helpful country research guides.

A periodic insert into the daily paper, these annual national surveys are comprised of a series of brief articles on key macroeconomic and corporate issues.

Provides a current review of central and eastern European stock markets, including historic data and analysis, presented in both local currency and dollar terms.

Article IV studies are succinct periodic macroeconomic reviews of every nation; IFS is a thick monthly compilation of current and historic national macroeconomic statistics covering everything from exchange rates and money supply to national accounts.

COMPANY	TELEPHONE	FEATURED PRODUCT / WEB ADDRESS

COUNTRIES *(continued)*

COMPANY	TELEPHONE	FEATURED PRODUCT / WEB ADDRESS
OECD	011.33.145.24.13.91	Country Surveys http://www.oecd.org
Olsen & Associates		http://www.oanda.com
Standard & Poor's/ DRI	800.933.3374 781.860.6527	International Financial Bulletin; Global Risk Services http://www.dri.standardandpoors.com

GENERAL

COMPANY	TELEPHONE	FEATURED PRODUCT / WEB ADDRESS
Bloomberg L.P.	800.388.2749	*BLOOMBERG® MARKETS* http://www.bloomberg.com
Business Week	212.512.2000	*Business Week* http://www.businessweek.com
Dow Jones & Co.	212.416.2000	*The Wall Street Journal* http://www.wsj.com
The Economist	011.44.207.830.7000	*The Economist* http://www.economist.com
Euromoney	011.44.207.779.888	*Euromoney* http://www.euromoney.com
European Investor		http://www.europeaninvestor.com
Financial Times	800.628.8088 212.641.6500	*Financial Times* http://www.ft.com http://ftmarketwatch.com
Institutional Investor	212.224.3300	*Institutional Investor* http://www.iimagazine.com

DESCRIPTION

Comprehensive periodic national surveys providing extensive macroeconomic data, including focus on key country-specific issues. Superb access to all government economic ministries via <oecd.org/daf/corporate-affairs/privatisation/other-links.htm>.

This Swiss econometric research firm maintains a remarkable currency-related Internet site offering historical review of exchange rates between every combination of currencies for any day.

Two monthly reviews of national financial markets, currencies, macroeconomic conditions, and government policy, with historical financial data.

A wide range of European corporate and country stories are available in print and online.

Through its International and Corporate departments, this American business weekly runs frequent stories on Europe, all of which are archived on its Web site.

The daily American guide to business offers an expanding focus on European corporate and macroeconomic news and analysis.

This British weekly publication is the most comprehensive periodical review of European business and finance available anywhere.

An in-depth monthly publication that's tilted toward the financial professional, with a very useful Web site. Also periodically publishes country-specific research guides.

A multipurpose news and investment guide to European markets, stocks, and currencies.

Financial Times is a London-based but internationally distributed daily bible for all investors interested in Europe. Provides the most comprehensive published European stock listing by country quoted in local currency terms. Watch for periodic inserts surveying a wide range of sector, regional, national, and global topics. Its Web site offers free access to its vast article archives.

This U.S.-based monthly investment publication focuses regularly on Europe.

Notes

Chapter 1

1. Developed Markets Price Index. <http://www.msci.com>.

2. The BLOOMBERG PROFESSIONAL™ service.

3. Developed Markets Price Index. <http://www.msci.com>.

4. Ibid.

5. Mark L. Yockey, interview with author, 7 November 1997.

6. IBES International, New York.

7. G. Pascal Zachary, "For France's Gemplus, the Secret of Success is Made in the USA," *The Wall Street Journal*, 8 June 1998.

8. "Swisscom Sets Price of Initial Price Offer at About $25 and ADR," *The Wall Street Journal*, 5 October 1998.

9. "Skoda Thrives Under Foreign Ownership," *Financial Times*, 12 January 1999.

10. Robert Anderson, "VW in Skoda Deal," *Financial Times*, 23 May 2000, 19.

11. Developed Markets Price Index. <http://www.msci.com>.

12. "Austria Country Profile: 1998-1999," Economist Intelligence Unit, 1998, 1-4.

13. Clifford Stevens, "Attracting Attention at an Explosive Rate," *Financial Times*, 11 December 1998, III.

14. "The End of Privatization," *The Economist*, 13 June 1998 <http://www.economist.com>.

15. Stefan Wagstyl, "Comment and Analysis: Mergers a la Mode," *Financial Times of London*, 14 October 1997.

16. Ibid.

17. Stanley Reed and Carol Matlack, "The Big Grab," *Business Week*, 24 January 2000, 130-131; and Alex Skorecki, "M&A Bandwagon Swerves on Regardless," *Financial Times*, 12 May 2000, 35.

18. Suzanne McGee, "Europe's Industrial Firms Reinvent Themselves to Reap Big Multiples as 'Growth' Companies," *The Wall Street Journal*, 6 May 1999.

19. Eric Bleines, interview with author, 16 September 1997.

20. Antony Currie, "European Equities," *Euromoney*, April 1997.

21. Tess Read, "Learning to Love Shareholders," *Euromoney*, February 1998.

22. Janet Guyon, "Europe's New Capitalists," *Fortune*, 15 February 1999, 105.

23. Ibid.

24. "Bidding for the Future," *The Economist*, 12 February 2000, 71-74.

25. Haig Simonian, "The Monoliths Stir," *Financial Times,* 28 September 1999, 17.

26. Antony Currie, "Wising Up to Shareholder Value," *Euromoney,* March 1998.

27. Ibid.

28. Scott Clemons, interview with author, 17 July 2000.

29. David Woodruff, "The German Worker Is Making a Sacrifice," *Business Week,* 28 July 1997, 47.

30. "Germany's Economy: The Sick Man of the Euro," *The Economist,* 5 June 1999, 23.

31. "Union's Unions," Survey: European Business, *The Economist,* 29 April 2000, 16.

32. "Germany's Economy: The Sick Man of the Euro," 23.

33. "IG Metall and German Wages," *Financial Times,* 24 March 2000, 12.

34. Charles Fleming, "Pechiney Plant Plays a Heavy-Metal Tune of Change," *The Wall Street Journal,* 28 July 1998, B4.

35. James Blitz, "Italian Industry Fears Relegation within Europe," *Financial Times,* 20 June 2000, 16.

36. Gordon Cramb, "Incentives Allow Deep Cuts in Company Tax," *Financial Times,* 28 April 1999, 3.

37. Bertrand Benoit, "The Devil Is in the Detail of Tax Reform," *Financial Times,* 19 July 2000, 18.

38. "Bidding for the Future," *The Economist,* 12 February 2000.

39. Jack Ewing *et al,* "Tax-Cut Fever," *Business Week,* 6 March 2000, 56-57.

40. Cramb, 3.

41. Simon Targett, "Retirement at 69 Would Defuse Pension Time Bomb," *Financial Times,* 14 October 1999, 2.

42. Ellen Schultz, "Fund Track: Going, Going ... Global: 401(k) Plans," *The Wall Street Journal,* 26 November 1996, C1.

43. Mark Griffen, "The Global Pension Time Bomb and Its Capital Market Impact," Goldman Sachs, 28 May 1997, 17-19.

44. Debbie Harrison, "Brussels Set to Publish Reform Plan," *Financial Times* Survey of Pension Fund Investment, 12 May 2000, V.

45. Jo Wrighton, "The Stalled Promise of European Pension Reform," *Institutional Investor,* February 2000.

46. "The Transatlantic Productivity Race," *Financial Times,* 3 June 2000, 6.

47. Mary Ann Bartels, Merrill Lynch & Company, interview with author, 5 June 2000.

48. "New Economy, Old Problems," European Business Survey, *The Economist,* 29 April 2000, 17.

49. Ibid., 18.

50. Jeremy Kahn, "Europe's 25 Hottest Tech Stocks," *Fortune,* 20 March 2000, 149.

51. Ibid, 153.

Chapter 3

France

1. G. Pascal Zachary, "For France's Gemplus, The Secret of Success Is Made in the USA," *The Wall Street Journal,* 8 June 1998, A1.

2. Charles Fleming, "Pechiney Plant Plays a Heavy-Metal Tune of Change," *The Wall Street Journal,* 28 July 1998, B4.

3. Richard Evans, "Inside AXA," *Barron's,* 23 November 1998, 25-26; and <http://www.axa.com>.

4. Gail Edmonson, "A Quiet Revolution," *Business Week,* 28 June 1999, 46.

5. "France," Inside the FT/S&P Actuaries World Indices, Goldman Sachs, January 2000, 86.

6. Ibid., 88-89.

7. Samer Iskander, "Powerful Magnet for Foreigners," *Financial Times,* 14 October 1998, II.

8. Source of all macroeconomic data: "IMF Concludes Article IV Consultation with France," Public Information Notice No. 99/100, International Monetary Fund, 22 October 1999; and "France: 2Q2000 Country Report," Economist Intelligence Unit, 5, 21.

9. Marie Owens Thomsen, "The French Economy," Merrill Lynch, 20 October 1998, 8.

10. "Growing Shareholder Value in France," Paribas, July 1998, 1.

11. "France's Industrial Revolution," *Euroweek,* May 1998.

12. "Growing Shareholder Value in France," 3.

13. Tess Read, "Learning to Love Shareholders," *Euromoney,* February 1998.

Germany

1. Bertrand Benoit, "Tradition Is Put on the Sidelines," *Financial Times Survey of the FT 500,* 4 May 2000, 21.

2. "Germany's Economy: The Sick Man of the Euro," *The Economist,* 5 June 1999 <http://www.economist.com>.

3. Developed Markets Price Index <http://www.msci.com> and "Inside the FTSE Actuaries World Indices," Goldman Sachs, January 2000, 94-95.

4. Graham Bowley, "A Sector Transformed," *Financial Times,* 10 November 1998, VIII.

5. "Linde to Seek Approval for Share Buyback," *Financial Times,* 24 March 1999.

6. "Germany: Fourth Quarter 1998 Country Report," Economist Intelligence Unit, October 1998.

7. Ibid., 28.

8. International Institute for Management Development, as cited in "A Survey of Germany," *The Economist,* 6 February 1999, 8.

9. Matt Marshall and Brandon Mitchener, "German Union's Consent to Wage Cuts Signals New Erosion of Labor's Power," *The Wall Street Journal,* 6 June 1997.

10. David Woodruff, "The German Worker Is Making a Sacrifice," *Business Week,* 28 July 1997, 47.

11. "A Survey of Germany," *The Economist,* 6 February 1999, 8.

12. "Germany: May 2000 Country Report," Economist Intelligence Unit, 4 May 2000, 11, 28.

13. Ibid., 5, 12, 27, 29, 30.

14. William Drozdiak, "To German Industry, US Is New World of Opportunity," *The Washington Post,* 7 May 1998.

15. "A Survey of Germany," 7.

16. Tony Barber, "East German Economy Feeling Chill Winds," *Financial Times,* 11 February 1999, 2.

17. Haig Simonian, "Tax Move a Spur to Growth," *Financial Times Survey of the Eurozone,* 25 February 2000, 8.

18. "A Survey of Germany," 7.

19. Ibid., 8.

Italy

1. "Inside the FTSE Actuaries World Indices," Goldman Sachs, January 2000, 100.

2. "Inside the FT/S&P Actuaries World Indices," Goldman Sachs, January 1999, 110.

3. "Inside the FTSE Actuaries World Indices," Goldman Sachs, January 2000, 102.

4. "Italy," Monthly Equity Report, Merrill Lynch, 14 December 1998.

5. David Lane, "Everything Must Go," *Financial Times,* 16 December 1998, IV.

6. Deborah Ball, "Italy, Despite Growth Slowdown, Meets Its Target Deficit for 1998," *The Wall Street Journal,* 5 January 1999.

7. James Blitz, "Wanted: A Strong Governing Executive," *Financial Times Survey of Italy,* 19 June 2000, I.

8. Michael Hartnett, "Global Economic Review," Merrill Lynch, 21 January 1999.

9. James Blitz, "Struggle to Keep in Step Continues," *Financial Times,* 30 October 1998.

10. "Italy—Country Profile," and "Italy—Fourth Quarter 1999 Country Report," Economist Intelligence Unit, 1999.

11. "Italy—Fourth Quarter 1998 Country Report," Economist Intelligence Unit, 1998.

12. David Lane, "Foreign Business Looks Beyond Tuscany and Tenors," *Financial Times,* 16 December 1998, VI.

13. "Italy," *Economic Surveys,* OECD, December 1998, 13.

14. Paul Betts, "Facade Weakened by Structural Problems," *Financial Times,* 16 December 1998, I.

Switzerland

1. "Inside the FTSE Actuaries World Indices," Goldman Sachs, January 2000, 66.

2. William Hall, "Secrecy Giving Way to Practicalities," *Financial Times Survey of Switzerland,* 22 March 1999, II.

3. _____, "Tunnels Will Ease Pressure on Alps," *Financial Times Survey of Switzerland,* 22 March 1999, IV.

4. _____, "'Old Giants Still Have Domination," *Financial Times Survey of Switzerland,* 17 May 2000, IV.

5. _____, "Advertisement for Corporate Eminence," *Financial Times,* 28 January 1999.

6. _____, "ABB and Alstom Join Forces," *Financial Times,* 24 March 1999.

7. "Stratec Shares Surge on Merger," *Financial Times,* 27 February 1999.

8. "Swisscom Sets Price of Initial Price Offer at About $25 an ADR," *The Wall Street Journal,* 5 October 1998.

9. Gautam Naik, "Swisscom IPO Promises to Be a Crucial Test," *The Wall Street Journal,* 22 July 1998.

10. "Swisscom Sells Its Fibre Optics Activities," *L'Agefi Suisse,* 30 November 1998.

11. William Hall, "Swisscom Withdraws from Overseas Venture," *Financial Times,* 19 March 1999.

12. "Swisscom Expands in Italy," *Finanz Und Wirtschaft,* 16 December 1998.

13. "Switzerland: 1998-1999 Country Profile," Economist Intelligence Unit, 1998.

14. Hall, "'Old Giants," IV.

15. Ibid.

16. Ibid.

17. "Economic Survey of Switzerland," OECD, July 1999, 175.

18. Frances Williams, "Asia Is Blamed for Slowdown," *Financial Times Country Survey: Switzerland,* 22 March 1999, II.

19. "Inside the FT/S&P Actuaries World Indices," Goldman Sachs, 1999, 72.

20. Developed Markets Price Index <http://www.msci.com>.

21. Hall, "'Old Giants," IV.

22. Developed Markets Price Index <http://www.msci.com>.

23. Margaret Studer, "Swiss Embrace Stocks to Buoy Social Security," *The Wall Street Journal,* 25 January 1999.

24. Vincent Boland and Samer Tskander, "Swiss and French in Market Alliance," *Financial Times,* 29 January 1999.

25. William Hall, "Switzerland Ponders Relations with EU Trade Partners," *Financial Times*, 29 January 1999, 2.

26. Hall, "Secrecy Giving Way," II.

27. Hall, "Switzerland Ponders Relations," 2.

28. Ibid.

29. Williams, "Asia Is Blamed for Slowdown," II.

United Kingdom

1. Developed Markets Price Index <http://www.msci.com>.

2. "UK: Best Business Location After Netherlands," Economist Intelligence Unit, 30 November 1998.

3. Tony Blair, "Dawn of the Euro: An Opportunity, Not a Threat," *The Wall Street Journal*, 4 January 1999.

4. "IMF Concludes Article IV Consultation with the United Kingdom," International Monetary Fund, 6 March 2000, 6.

5. "The British Disease Revisited," *The Economist*, 31 October 1998 <http://www.economist.com>.

6. "Relative Economic Performance—A British Miracle," *The Economist*, 25 March 2000 <http://www.economist.com>.

7. "The End of Privatization," *The Economist*, 13 June 1998 <http://www.economist.com>.

8. Brian Groom, "Regeneration Needs to Come from Within," *Financial Times,* 11 June 1998, l.

9. Stanley Reed, "Britain: Colonized and Loving It," *Business Week*, 17 November 1998, 136.

10. "United Kingdom Country Profile: 1989-1999," Economist Intelligence Unit, 29.

11. Ibid., 34.

12. Kevin Brown, "European Connection Lifts Trade," *Financial Times Survey of Inward Investment into the UK,* 14 October 1999, I; and Kevin Brown *et al,* "Blow for Euro Camp as Inward Funds Soar," *Financial Times*, 6 July 2000, 10.

13. The BLOOMBERG PROFESSIONAL™ service.

14. Kevin Brown *et al,* "Blow for Euro Camp as Inward Funds Soar," *Financial Times,* 6 July 2000, 10.

15. Ibid.

16. Ibid.

17. "Riding the Merger Wave," *The Economist*, 23 January 1999, 53-54.

18. "Inside the FTSE Actuaries World Indices," Goldman Sachs, January 2000 40, 43.

19. Ibid., 39.

Chapter 4

Ireland

1. "The Euro-Zone's Hot Periphery," *Financial Times,* 24 June 2000, 8.
2. "Ireland: Country Profile 2000," Economist Intelligence Unit, April 2000, 53, 55, 56.
3. "IMF Concludes Article IV Consultation with Ireland," International Monetary Fund, 20 August 1999, 5.
4. David Poutney and Inigo Edsberg, "Bankers' Paradise—Review of Irish Banks," Panmure Gordon (London), May 1998 p.4.
5. Ibid.
6. John Murray Brown, "Irish Economy 'Shows Signs of Overheating,'" *Financial Times,* 26 May 2000, 2.
7. "Ireland: Country Profile 2000," 54.
8. Poutney, "Bankers' Paradise," 3.
9. Poutney, "Bankers' Paradise," 2.
10. John Murray Brown, "Advocate of Pragmatic Privatization," *Financial Times,* 22 September 1998, III.
11. "Irish Economy: An Emerald Glow But an Isle No More," *The ADR Investor,* Bank of New York, October 1998.
12. Nuala Moran, "Information Technology—The Pulling Power of a President," *Financial Times,* 22 September 1998, III.
13. Ibid. and John Murray Brown, "Sins of the Past Overshadow New Triumphs," *Financial Times Country Survey: Ireland,* 4 November 1999, I.
14. "Inside the FTSE World Indices," Goldman Sachs, January 2000, 98.
15. John Murray Brown, "Ireland Struggles to Settle in the Euro-zone," *Financial Times,* 26 May 2000, 26.
16. _____, "Ireland the Greatest Loser from Euro's Weakness," *Financial Times,* 28 April 2000, 2.

Netherlands

1. "International Financial Statistics Yearbook," International Monetary Fund, 1996.
2. "Netherlands: Quarterly Economic Review," Economist Intelligence Unit, 1985.
3. "Netherlands: Country Profile: 1998-1999," Economist Intelligence Unit, 1998.
4. Jeremy Gray, "The Netherlands: The One-Time Sick Man Is Now Thriving Again," *Financial Times,* 2 October 1998, XIII.
5. "Economic Survey of the Netherlands, 2000," OECD, March 2000, 4.
6. "Dutch Economic Indicators," *Statistics Netherlands,* April 2000.

7. "Netherlands: First Quarter 2000 Country Report," Economist Intelligence Unit, 7 March 2000, 5.

8. Ibid.

9. Ibid.

10. "The Netherlands: 1998-1999 Country Profile," Economist Intelligence Unit, 1998,12.

11. The BLOOMBERG PROFESSIONAL™ service.

12. Tom Hyam, "Netherlands Leads Continental Boom," *Corporate Finance,* August 1998.

13. Developed Markets Price Index <htpp:://www.msci.com>.

14. Ibid.

15. "Inside the FTSE Actuaries World Indices," Goldman Sachs, January 2000, 104-106.

16. "Netherlands Risk Report," *Standard and Poor's/DRI*, 3rd Quarter 1998.

17. "Netherlands: First Quarter 2000 Country Report," Economist Intelligence Unit, 7 March 2000, 16-17.

Portugal

1. Barry Hatton, "Portugal: Moving Into the EU Limelight," *Institutional Investor,* December 1997 and "Portugal: April 2000 Country Report," Economist Intelligence Unit, 17 April 2000.

2. "Portugal: Third Quarter 1998 Country Report," Economist Intelligence Unit, London, 1998; and "Portugal," OECD Economic Outlook, OECD, May 2000, 173.

3. Hatton, "Portugal: Moving Into the EU Limelight."

4. "Portugal: Public Information Notice 98/82." International Monetary Fund, 26 October 1998, and "Portugal: April 2000 Country Report," Economist Intelligence Unit, 17 April 2000.

5. Peter Wise, "Economy: Success Based on Change and Stability," *Financial Times,* 28 October 1998, II.

6. "Recent Privatization Trends," *Financial Market Trends*, OECD, No. 76, June 2000, 46.

7. Hatton, *Institutional Investor*.

8. Peter Wise, "Artful Dodgers Are the Principal Target," *Financial Times,* 28 October 1998, III.

9. Hatton, "Portugal: Moving Into the EU Limelight," and "Portugal," *Euromoney,* September/October 1998.

10. "Inside the FTSE World Indices," Goldman Sachs, January 2000, 110, and Developed Markets Price Index <http://www.msci.com>.

11. Peter Wise, "Enjoying Life in the Euro Zone," *Financial Times* Survey of Portuguese Banking and Finance, 17 April 2000, I.

12. Ibid., II.

Spain

1. Gail Edmonson, "Spain's Surge" *Business Week,* 22 May 2000, 73-80.
2. Spain: Country Profile 1992-93, Economist Intelligence Unit, 1993.
3. Gail Edmondson, "Spain's Success," *Business Week,* 3 August 1998, 54.
4. "Spain: Second Quarter 2000 Country Report," Economist Intelligence Unit, 4 April 2000, 5.
5. Ibid.
6. Christophe Duval-Keiffer and Giovanni Zanni, "Spain: The Productivity Mystery," *U.K. and Europe Investment Perspective,* Morgan Stanley Dean Witter, 12 August 1998, 18. "Spain: Second Quarter 2000 Country Report," Economist Intelligence Unit, 4 April 2000, 5.
7. "Spain: Third Quarter 1998 Country Report," Economist Intelligence Unit, 1998.
8. Edmonson, "Spain's Success," 54.
9. "World Economic Analysis: Spain," *Euromoney,* September 1997.
10. Tom Burns, "Home Truths: Overseas Opportunities," *Financial Times,* 8 June 1998.
11. Edmondson, "Spain's Success," 54.
12. Geoff Dyer, "Telefónica Plans $3.8 Billion for Brazil," *Financial Times,* 27 November 1998, 17.
13. Edmonson, "Spain's Surge," 73-80.
14. Burns, "Home Truths."
15. "Inside the FTSE Actuaries World Indices," Goldman Sachs *& Co.,* January 2000, 112.
16. Ibid., 112.
17. Ibid., 115.

Chapter 5

Denmark

1. The figure represents the total amount raised through public offerings between 1993 and 1998. "Denmark: First Quarter 1999 Report," Economist Intelligence Unit, 1999.
2. "Denmark: Economic Survey,"OECD, 1999, 1-9.
3. "Denmark: 1998-1999 Country Profile," Economist Intelligence Unit, 1998.
4. "Inside the FTSE Actuaries World Indices," Goldman Sachs, January 2000, 50.
5. Ibid., 52.
6. Peter Bradshaw *et al,* "Nordic Monthly Strategy Report," Merrill Lynch, 21 January 1999, 16.
7. "Denmark: First Quarter 1999 Report," Economist Intelligence Unit,

1999, 18.

8. Clare MacCarthy, "Quality Is Incentive Enough," *Financial Times*, 30 November 1998, II; and press release: "IMD Announces the World Competitiveness Yearbook 2000 Results," International Institute for Management Development, 19 April 2000.

9. "OECD Economic Outlook," OECD, December 1999, 220.

10. "A Global War Against Bribery," *The Economist*, 16 January 1999, 22-24.

Finland

1. Developed Markets Price Index <http://www.msci.com>.

2. "Inside the FTSE World Indices," Goldman Sachs, January 2000, 84.

3. Greg McIvor, "Finland: Happy State of Affairs Due to Continue," *Financial Times*, 30 October 1998, 18.

4. "Finland: 2000-01 Country Profile," Economist Intelligence Unit, 10 December 1999, 42, and "Finland: First Quarter 2000 Country Report," Economist Intelligence Unit, 18 February 2000, 5, 10.

5. "Finland: First Quarter 2000 Country Report," 5.

6. "Finland: Country Risk Report," *Standard & Poor's/DRI*, 1998.

7. "Finland to Pay Off Debt," *Financial Times*, 15 October 1999.

8. "Finland Economy: Privatization Update," Economist Intelligence Unit, 8 September 1998.

9. Christopher Brown-Humes, "High Optimism, High Technology," *Financial Times Survey of Finland*, 10 July 2000, 2.

Norway

1. Economist Intelligence Unit, International Monetary Fund, and OECD.

2. "Norway: Economic Trends and Outlook," Foreign Commercial Service and U.S. Department of State, 1998.

3. "Norway: 1998-1999 Country Profile," Economist Intelligence Unit, 1998.

4. Tim Burt, "Calming Down the Economic Squalls," *Financial Times* Annual Country Review: Norway, 11 November 1998, I.

5. "Well-Oiled Independence," *The Economist Nordic Countries Survey*, 23 January 1999, 13.

6. Ibid, 14.

7. Tim Burt, "Cooling an Overheated Strategy," *Financial Times Annual Country Review: Norway*, 11 November 1998, II.

8. "Medium-Term Projects for the Norwegian Economy to 2002," *Economic Bulletin*, Norges Bank, December 1998.

9. Richard H. Woodworth, "Norway: Strategy," *Nordic Monthly Strategy Report*, Merrill Lynch, 21 January 1999, 12.

10. Tim Burt, "Calming Down the Economic Squalls," *Financial Times* Annual Country Review: Norway, 11 November 1998, I.

11. Mark Atkinson, "Norway's Black Monday Tarnished Sliding Crown," *The Guardian*, 25 August 1998.

12. "Inside the FT/S&P Actuaries World Indices," Goldman Sachs, January 1999, 60.

13. "Inside the FTSE Actuaries World Indices," Goldman Sachs, January 2000, 60-61.

14. Valeria Sköld, "Statoil Profit Slump Forces Revamp," *Financial Times*, 20 February 1999.

15. _____, "Statoil Wants End to State Ownership," *Financial Times*, 23 January 1999.

16. _____, "Profits Dip at Norsk Hydro," *Financial Times*, 16 February 1999.

17. _____, "Aker RGI Changes Strategy," *Financial Times*, 4 March 1999.

18. _____, "Nordic Shipping Groups in Link-up," *Financial Times*, 26 March 1999.

19. _____, "Teekay to Buy Bona and Create Giant Fleet," *Financial Times*, 30 March 1999.

20. _____, "Kraerner Unveils Tough Restructuring Plans," *Financial Times*, 24 February 1999.

21. _____, "DnB to Buy Postbanken for NKr 4.5bn," *Financial Times*, 24 March 1999.

22. _____, "Den Danske Bank Secures 93 Percent of Fokus' Capital," *Financial Times*, 11 December 1998.

23. Nicholas George and Valeria Sköld, "Storebrand and Skandia in Non-Life Link," *Financial Times*, 23 February 1999.

24. _____, "Oslo Sells 16 Percent Christiania Stake," *Financial Times*, 4 March 1999.

25. "Reactions to Wider Choice for Pension Investments," International Insurance Monitor, Third Quarter 1998.

26. Valeria Sköld, "Oslo Stock Exchange Launches Remote Trading," *Financial Times*, 5 February 1999.

Sweden

1. "Inside the FTSE Actuaries World Indices," Goldman Sachs, January 2000, 34, 62.

2. "Sweden: 2000 Country Profile," Economist Intelligence Unit, 3 March 2000, 24, 44.

3. "Sweden: 1998-1999 Country Profile," Economist Intelligence Unit, 24 April 1998, 23.

4. Ibid.

5. Philip Swinden, "Where Money Gets Wired," *Corporate Location*, November/December 1998.

6. Almar Latour and Greg Steinmetz, "Swedish Giant: Barnevik Sets About Task of Preserving Wallenburg Empire," *The Wall Street Journal*, 18 May 1998.

7. "Too Good to Be True," Survey of Nordic Countries, *The Economist*, 23

January 1999, 9.

8. Greg McIvor, "Competitiveness: Tax Burden May Prompt an Exodus," *Financial Times,* 14 April 1998.

9. "Sweden: 1998-1999 Country Profile," Economist Intelligence Unit, 1998, p. 17.

10. "Sweden: 1998-1999 Country Profile," 33.

11. Stanley Reed, "Busting Up Sweden, Inc.," *Business Week,* 22 February 1999, 52-54.

12. "Inside the FTSE World Indices," 64.

13. Anne Swardson, "In Sweden, a Step Ahead on Funding Retirement," *The Washington Post,* 30 January 1999.

14. Ibid.

15. Nicholas George, "Sweden's Listed Companies Flex Their Capital," *Financial Times,* 16 June 2000, 25.

16. _____, "Consolidating Will Be a Reality in May," *Financial Times* Stock and Derivatives Survey, 23 March 1999, IX.

17. "IMF Concludes Article IV Consultation with Sweden," International Monetary Fund, 1-4 September 1998.

18. Philip Swinden, "Sweden: Baltic Brain Center," *Corporate Location,* November/December 1998.

Chapter 6

Austria

1. "IMF Concludes Article IV Consultation with Austria," Press Information Notice 98/43, International Monetary Fund, 24 June 1998; "Financial Times Survey: Austria," *Financial Times,* 11 December 1998, 7; "Austria—First Quarter 2000 Country Report," Economist Intelligence Unit, 2000; "Economic Indicators," *The Economist,* 6 February 1999, 108.

2. "Austria—First Quarter 2000 Country Report."

3. "Inside the FT/S&P Actuaries World Indices," Goldman Sachs, January 1999, 34, 82.

4. Mark Breedon, interview with author, 5 February 1999.

5. William Hall, "Missing Entrepreneurial Elements," *Financial Times* Survey of Austria, 16 November 1999, IV.

6. "Austria: Looking East and West," *Euromoney,* September 1997.

7. William Hall, "Missing Entrepreneurial Elements," IV.

8. Ibid.

9. "Austria" Country Profile: 1989-1999, Economist Intelligence Unit, 1998, 1-4.

10. Clifford Stevens, "Attracting Attention at an Explosive Rate," *Financial Times,* 11 December 1998, III.

11. "Austria," Country Profile 1998-1999, 15.

12. William Hall, "Ready for Take-off," *Financial Times,* 11 December 1998, V.; and Mark Breedon, Austria Fund, London.

Belgium

1. "Belgium: Third Quarter 1998 Report," Country Risk Report, *Standard and Poor's/DRI.*

2. While twice the mandated limit dictated by EMU, Belgium's huge debt-to-GDP ratio didn't disqualify the country from joining the euro because the ratio was trending in the right direction.

3. "IMF Concludes Article IV Consultation with Belgium," International Monetary Fund, 23 February 1998.

4. Kevin Brown, "European Connection Lifts Trade," *Financial Times Survey of Inward Investment in the U.K.,* 14 October 1999, I.

5. "Belgium: First Quarter 2000 Country Report," Economist Intelligence Unit, 8 February 2000, 8.

6. Neil Buckley, "Old Hands at Being Adaptable," *Financial Times,* 3 November 1998, IV.

7. "Belgium: Third Quarter 1998 Report," 22.

8. Neil Buckley, "Old Hands at Being Adaptable," *Financial Times,* 3 November 1998, IV.

9. "Belgium: Country Profile: 1998-1999," Economist Intelligence Unit, 17.

10. Developed Markets Price Index <http:www.msci.com>.

11. Ibid.

12. "Inside the FTSE World Indices," Goldman Sachs, January 2000, 80.

13. IMF Concludes Article IV "Consultation with Belgium," International Monetary Fund, 3 March 2000, 2.

Chapter 7

Czech Republic

1. "Czech Republic," Economic Survey, OECD, May 1998 <http://www.oecd.org/publications>.

2. "Skoda Thrives Under Foreign Ownership," *Financial Times,* 12 January 1999.

3. "Czech Republic," Survey.

4. James Rutter, "Cleaning Up the Stock Market," *Euromoney,* September 1998.

5. "Czech Republic," Survey.

6. "Czech Republic: 1999-2000 Country Profile," Economist Intelligence Unit, 1999.

7. Stefan Wagstyl, "Urgency of Reform Reflects Problems Within the Sector," *Financial Times,* 19 January 1999, 27.

8. "Czech Republic," Survey.

9. "Czech Republic: First Quarter 1999 Country Report," and "Czech Republic: April 2000 Country Report," Economist Intelligence Unit; "Czech Republic," Economic Survey, OECD, May 1998; and "IMF Concludes Article IV Consultation with the Czech Republic, *IMF,* 6 March 1998.

10. "Czech Republic: First Quarter 1999 Country Report."

11. Stefan Wagstyl and Robert Anderson, "Novice Government Still Needs to Show its Mettle," *Financial Times,* 19 January 1999, 25.

12. "Czech Republic," Survey.

13. Wagstyl, "Urgency of Reform Reflects Problems," 27.

14. Miroslav Nosal, Czech Republic analyst, Merrill Lynch, interview with author, 26 April 1999.

15. David Aserkoff and Petra Lapkova, "Czech Market Commentary," Credit Suisse First Boston, 2 May 2000, 4.

16. CzechInvest press release.

Greece

1. Emerging Markets Price Index <http://www.msci.com>.

2. "Ionian Sale Flop Casts a Cloud," *Euroweek,* September 1998.

3. "Economic Overview," Bank of Greece, Guide to Greece, *Euromoney,* 1998, 2.

4. Ibid., and "Greece: Country Profile 2000," Economist Intelligence Unit, 21 March 2000, 20.

5. "Euro Worries," *The Economist,* 3 October 1998.

6. Helene Cooper, "Greece Gets Serious about Joining EMU," *The Wall Street Journal,* 7 October 1998.

7. "Opportunities and Challenges," *Institutional Investor,* October 1998.

8. "Inside the FTSE World Indices," Goldman Sachs, January 2000, 56-57.

9. "Privatization," Bank of Attica S.A., Guide to Greece, *Euromoney,* 1998,

Hungary

1. Anna Willard, "Matav's Bold Move Pays Off Despite Turmoil in Markets," *Central European,* December/January 1998.

2. Nigel Dudley, "Banks with a Confident Air," *Euromoney,* April 1998.

3. "Hungary Country Profile: 1998-1999," Economist Intelligence Unit, 28 September 1998.

4. Business Central Europe Web site and "Hungary," Economic Survey, OECD, 11 January 1999, 78.

5. "113.5B Forints APV Rt. Closes a Successful Year," Hungarian Privatisation and State Holding Company, 13 December 1999.

6. "Hungary: First Quarter 1999 Report," Economist Intelligence Unit, 1 March 1999, 76.

7. Kevin Done and Kester Eddy, "Convergence on Course," *Financial Times*

Survey: Hungary, 7 December 1998, II.; and David Holley, "Hungary's Economy Setting the Pace in Eastern Europe," *Los Angeles Times,* 2 April 2000.

8. "Hungary," Economic Survey, OECD, 11 January 1999, 74.

9. "Hungary Country Profile: 1998-1999," Economist Intelligence Unit.

10. "IMF Concludes Article IV Consultation with Hungary," International Monetary Fund, 8 March 2000, 3-4.

11. "OECD Economic Oulook—Preliminary Edition," OECD, May 2000, 144.

12. Kevin Done, "Millennium Promises Many Happy Returns," *Financial Times* Survey: Hungary, 7 December 1998, I.

13. "Banks Jostle for Hungary Euro as Croatia Mandates CSFB/Dresdner," *Euroweek,* 15 January 1999.

14. Charles Olivier, "Investors Converge on Hungary," *Euromoney,* March 1999.

15. Sathnay Sanghera, "Hungary Maintains Momentum," *Financial Times,* 22 December 1999, 24.

16. Emerging Markets Price Index <http://www.msci.com>.

17. "Hungary," Country Risk Survey, *Standard and Poor's/DRI,* First Quarter 1999, 73.

18. "Hungary Country Profile: 1998-1999," Economist Intelligence Unit.

19. "Hungary," OECD, 71.

20. "Hungary: First Quarter 1999 Report," Economist Intelligence Unit, 1 March 1999.

21. "High-Tech Prospects," *Business Central Europe.*

22. "Hungary," OECD, 1999.

23. "High-Tech Prospects."

24. Michael Kapoor, "Forget the Past," *Business Central Europe,* April 1999.

Poland

1. "The Right Partner at the Right Time," Global Review, *Apisa International,* 20 April 1999.

2. Ibid.

3. OECD, IMF, EIU, and *Business Central Europe.*

4. "Poland: First Quarter 1999 Country Report," Economist Intelligence Unit, 15 February 1999.

5. Daniel Michaels, "Russian Crisis May Help Polish Poland's Image," *The Wall Street Journal,* 14 September 1998.

6. Stefan Wagstyl and Christopher Bobinski, "Braced for a Difficult Year," *Financial Times Annual Country Survey: Poland,* 30 March 1999, I.

7. Lucian Kim, "World's Busiest Shopping Street? Think Warsaw," *Christian Science Monitor,* 24 December 1998.

8. "Poland: 1998-1999 Country Profile," Economist Intelligence Unit, 10 November 1998, 38.

9. *Business Central Europe,* <http://www.bce.com>.

10. Vincent Koen, "Poland: Privatization as the Key to Efficiency," *The OECD Observer,* August-September 1998, and Ladan Mahboobi, "Trends in Privatization," Financial Market Trends 76, OECD, June 2000.

11. CDM Pekao Securities, "The Polish Equity Market," *Central European,* June 1998.

12. Stefan Wagstyl, "Floats Steer Course Overseas," *Financial Times Finance and Investment Survey of Poland,* 27 October 1998, IV.

13. Kim, "World's Busiest Shopping Street? Think Warsaw."

14. Christopher Bobinski, "Daewoo Is Close to Leading a Market Dominated by Westerners Who Negotiated Promises of High Tariffs on Imports," *Financial Times,* 1 March 1999.

15. "Poland: 1998-1999 Country Profile," Economist Intelligence Unit, 10 November 1998, 35.

16. Christopher Bobinski, "Fund Managers Jostle for Position," *Financial Times Annual Country Survey: Poland,* 30 March 1999, 5.

17. Stefan Wagstyl, "Wrong Perception and Harsh Reality," *Financial Times Finance and Investment Survey of Poland,* 27 October 1998, 4.

18. *Fact Book 2000,* Polish Stock Exchange, 2000, 17.

Chapter 8

Banking

1. "European Company Performance Survey," *Financial Times Survey of the European Performance League,* 23 June 2000, III.

2. David Ibison, "An Irresistible Urge to Meddle," *Financial Times Survey of Banking in Europe,* 26 May 2000, VII.

3. "A Quagmire in Europe," *The Economist,* 17 April 1999 <http://www.economist.com>.

4. For a brief analysis of strong peripheral banks, see the descriptions that appear below of Unicredito, Allied Irish Banks, and National Bank of Greece.

5. Andrew Garfield, "CSFB's Exposure on Russia put at $2.2 Billion," *The Independent,* 10 September 1998.

6. "A Quagmire in Europe," <http://www.economist.com>.

7. Karen Lowry Miller, "Fixing Deutsche Bank," *Business Week,* 19 July 1999, 57.

8. Suzanne McGee, "European Firms Try to Retake Investment Banking Turf," *The Wall Street Journal,* 27 November 1998.

9. Juliana Ratner, "Global Ambitions Fuel a Takeover Boom," *Financial Times Survey of Banking,* 30 June 2000, IV.

10. Charles Pretzlik, "Euro Gives a Boost to Bond Markets," *Financial*

Times Survey of Banking, 26 May 2000, VI.

11. Carlos Pertejo, J.P. Morgan Securities, interview with author, 9 July 1999.

12. "European Company Performance Survey," III.

13. "Allied Irish Banks," Warburg Dillon Read, 16 November 1998, 2.

14. "Bankers' Paradise: A Review of the Irish Banks," PanmureGordon, May 1998, 15, 26.

15. "Greek Banking Sector Review: 1998," Intersec International Securities, 1999, 2.

16. Farid Ahmed Khan, "National Bank of Greece: A Franchise to Hold," Crédit Lyonnaise Securities Asia, 7 June 2000, 6, 9.

17. "National Bank of Greece," ING Barings, 15 March 1999, 2.

18. "A Quagmire in Europe," <http://www.economist.com>.

19. James Sproule, "Europe's Cozy Banking Ties," *The Wall Street Journal Europe,* 31 December 1998.

Insurance

1. "European Company Performance Survey" *Financial Times Survey of the European Performance League,* 23 June 2000, IV.

2. "European Insurance," Schroders Securities, 23 February 1999, 494.

3. Tim Dawson, interview with author, 24 August 1999.

4. Ibid.

5. Excess capital accrued from the rise in their stock market exposure has also enabled insurers to take on additional policies and risk, which has led to pricing wars and uneconomic premiums.

6. Dawson, interview.

7. "Insurance Review," Credit Suisse First Boston, July 1999, 3.

8. Dawson, interview.

9. Richard Urwick, Director, Schroders Securities, London, interview with author, 13 August 1999.

10. "European Insurance," 23 February 1999, 382, 410; Schroders Securities, "European Company Performance Survey," IV.

11. "European Company Performance Survey," IV.

12. Ibid and The BLOOMBERG PROFESSIONAL™ service.

13. "Insurance 1999: Issues and Outlook," Goldman Sachs, December 1999.

14. "Insurance Review," Credit Suisse First Boston, July 1999, 33, 36, 47, and 67.

15. "European Company Performance Survey," IV.

16. The BLOOMBERG PROFESSIONAL™ service.

17. Jo Wrighton, "The Stalled Promise of European Pension Reform," *Institutional Investor,* February 2000.

18. Urwick, interview.

19. Richard Burden, interview with author, 16 August 1999.

Retail

1. "European Company Performance Survey," *Financial Times Survey of the European Performance League,* 23 June 2000, III and IV.

2. Clive Vaughan, Retail Intelligence, London, interview with author, 7 October 1999.

3. Ibid.

4. "Retailer Selling Power," *The Economist,* 10 April 1999.

5. Michèle Wolff *et al,* "Ahold: US Foodservice Increases Rerating Potential," Merrill Lynch, 19 June 2000, 4.

6. Ibid.

7. "European Company Performance Survey," III.

8. "Kingfisher," Williams de Broë, May 1999, 40.

9. "European Company Performance Survey," III.

10. Ian MacDougall, "Dixons: Out in Front," Williams de Broë, 31 August 1999, 2.

11. Julie Ramshaw *et al,* "Dixons: Time to Revisit Retail Fundamental," Morgan Stanley Dean Witter, 20 July 1999, 1.

12. Clive Vaughan, Retail Intelligence, interview with author.

13. "Hennes & Mauritz," *Financial Times,* 22 September 1999, 14.

14. "European Company Performance," *Financial Times Survey,* 18 June 1999, 6.

15. "Hennes & Mauritz," *Financial Times,* 22 September 1999, 14.

16. Anna-Karin Olsson *et al,* "Hennes & Mauritz: Still Too Early to Accumulate," Handelsbanken Markets, 22 June 2000, 1.

17. Ibid., 2.

18. Christian Guyot and Murial D'Ambrosio, "Metro-Add," Credit Lyonnaise Securities Europe, 12 June 2000, 1-2.

19. "European Company Performance Survey," *Financial Times Survey of the European Performance League,* 23 June 1999, 3.

20. Eric Biassette, "Pinault Printemps Redoute," ING Barings, 19 July 1999.

21. Victoria Maxwell-Snape, HSBC Securities, London, interview with author, 29 September 1999.

22. Fay Dodd, Merrill Lynch, interview with author, 7 October 1999.

23. Nick Hawkins, "Stores: Counterpoints No. 70," Merrill Lynch, 10 September 1999, 18.

24. "European Company Performance Survey," *Financial Times Survey of the European Performance League,* 23 June 1999, 3.

25. Richard Edwards *et al,* "Kingfisher: World in Motion," Salomon Smith Barney, 15 September 1999, 5.

26. Gilles Goldenberg, "Euro: Costs and the Retail Changeover Challenge," EuroCommerce and Deloitte Consulting Group, November 1997.

27. Keith Wills *et al,* "Internet Threat to European Retailers," Goldman Sachs, 28 April 1999, 5.

28. Ibid.

29. Ibid.

Telecommunication Services

1. "European Company Performance Survey," *Financial Times Survey of the European Performance League,* 23 June 2000, III.

2. Charles Olivier, "Financing the Global Telecoms Boom," *Euroweek,* 30 April 1999.

3. Ibid.

4. Janey Guyon, "Dialing for Euros," *Fortune,* 10 May 1999.

5. David Pringle, Yankee Group Europe, interview with author, 28 June 1999.

6. Gautam Naik, "English Lesson: Telecom Deregulation in Britain Delivered a Nice Surprise," *The Wall Street Journal,* 5 March 1998.

7. "Surviving the Telecoms Jungle," *The Economist,* 4 April 1999 <http://www.economist.com>.

8. *Financial Times Telecom Survey of European Company Performance,* 18 June 1999, 9.

9. "European Company Performance Survey," III.

10. "Surviving the Telecoms Jungle," <http://www.economist.com>.

11. Paul Betts, "Mother of All Takeovers Reflects Powerful Changes" *Financial Times Telecom Survey,* 18 March 1999, XVI.

12. Ibid.

13. Alan Cane, "Olivetti Opens the Floodgates," *Financial Times,* 26 May 1999, 20.

14. William Boston, "Germany's Mannesmann May Win from Successful Bid by Olivetti," *The Wall Street Journal,* 24 February 1999.

15. Charles Olivier, "Financing the Global Telecoms Boom," *Euroweek,* 30 April 1999.

16. Peter Purton, "Is This Finally the End of Regulation as We Know It?" *Financial Times Telecom Survey,* 18 March 1999, XIV.

17. Michelle DeBlasi, "Telecom Grows, World Shrinks," *BLOOMBERG® MARKETS,* March 1999, 56.

18. Stanley Reed, "Ready to Take On the World," *Business Week,* 12 June 2000, 70-71.

19. Stephen Baker and Kerry Capell, "How Vodafone Aims to Rule the World," *Business Week,* 25 January 1999, 56.

20. Stephen Baker and Kerry Capell, "The Race to Rule Mobile," *Business Week,* 21 February 2000, 59.

21. "European Company Performance Survey," *Financial Times Survey of the European Performance League,* 23 June 2000, III.

Utilities

1. "European Company Performance Survey," *Financial Times Survey of the European Performance League*, 23 June 2000, III-IV.

2. "European Company Performance," *Financial Times Survey*, 18 June 1999; 5, and Wright Investors Services, Inc.

3. Chris Rowland, Merrill Lynch utility analyst, interview with author, 4 August 1999.

4. Khalid Beydown, HSBC utility analyst, interview with author, 26 July 1999.

5. Ian Graham, utility analyst at Merrill Lynch, interview with author, 6 August 1999.

6. Rowland, interview.

7. "Electricity Market Opens Up," *The Economist*, 29 February 1999.

8. The book went to press as Vivendi was prepararing the spin-off of Vivendi Environnement.

9. Pierre Coiffet, Paribas utility analyst, interview with author, 29 July 1999.

10. Marc Loneux, "Vivendi," Dresdner Kleinwort Benson, 25 June 1999, 91.

11. "European Company Performance Survey," III.

12. Sam Brothwell, Merrill Lynch utility analyst, interview with author, 28 July 1999.

13. Simon Flowers, "Scottish Power," Merrill Lynch, 6 May 1999.

14. Bruce Barnard, "Electricity Markets Light Up," *Europe*, April 1999.

15. Daniel Fisher, "Waiting Game," *Forbes,* 9 August 1999, 88.

16. Angus McPhail, "Gas Natural," Banca D'Intermediazione Mobiliare, 20 August 1998, 20-21.

17. Carol Bowers, "Europe Embraces Energy Deregulation," *Utility Business,* January 1999.

18. "European Company Performance Survey," *Financial Times Survey of the European Performance League*, 23 June 2000, III.

19. Steve Turner, HSBC Securities utility analyst, interview with author, 27 July 1999.

20. "Natural Gas in the Energy Market in 1998," Ruhrgas AG, 1999.

21. "European Company Performance Survey," III.

22. Nick Antrill, interview with author, 29 July 1999.

23. Shawn Tully, "Water, Water Everywhere," *Fortune,* 15 May 2000, 343-354.

24. "European Company Performance Survey," IV.

25. Laurence Boisseau, "Vivendi: A Fresh Start," Wargny Group, April 2000.

26. Pierre Coiffet, "Vivendi," Paribas, May 1998.

27. James Grant, BNP Paribas utility analyst, interview with author, 28 June 2000.

28. Teri Yue Jones, "Water, Water Everywhere," *Forbes,* 20 November 1998.

29. "European Company Performance Survey," IV.

30. Michael Cohen, Schroders utility analyst, interview with author, 30 July 1999.

Chapter 9

Adecco

1. Marc van't Sant and Nick Williamson, "European Outsourcing," Dresdner Kleinwort Benson Research, 2 November 1999, 1, 6.

2. Gail Edmondson *et al*, "A Tidal Wave of Temps," *Business Week* [International Edition], 24 November 1997.

3. David Allchurch *et al*, "Adecco: The Strong Get Stronger," Morgan Stanley Dean Witter, 1 December 1999, 3.

4. Jan Stuifbergen, industry analyst, HSBC, interview with author, 24 January 2000.

5. Ibid.

6. "The Great American Jobs Machine," *The Economist*, 15 January 2000, 25-26 <http://www.economist.com>.

7. John Browner and Feliz A. Weber, "Press and Analyst Conference: Results 1999," Adecco, 27 January 2000.

8. David Allchurch *et al*, "Adecco: The Strong Get Stronger," Morgan Stanley Dean Witter, 1 December 1999, 51.

9. Adecco did not reveal the price of this acquisition.

10. Marc van't Sant and Nick Williamson, "European Outsourcing," Dresdner Kleinwort Benson Research, 2 November 1999, 6.

11. Ibid.

12. Allchurch *et al*, "Adecco: The Strong Get Stronger," 5.

13. Allchurch *et al*, "Adecco: The Strong Get Stronger," 10.

14. Paul Ginocchio *et al*, "Adecco SA: Reaching a Swiss Peak," Deutsche Bank, January 2000, 2.

15. Konrad Zomer *et al*, "European Staffing Services," Credit Suisse First Boston, 13 January 2000, 14-20.

16. Simon Marshall-Lockyer, "Adecco: Growth with a Solid Performance Record," Cheuvreux, March 2000, 35.

17. Jan Stuifbergen, "European Staffing: Breaking the Cycle," HSBC, May 1999.

18. Paul Ginocchio *et al*, 2.

19. Allchurch *et al*, "Adecco: The Strong Get Stronger," 19.

AEGON

1. Michael Huttner, Susan Holiday, and Angus Runciman, "European Insurance: Profiting from the Apocalypse," J.P. Morgan, 11 October 1999, 16 and 19.

2. Jason B. Zucker, "AEGON Insurance Group," Banc of America Securities, 5 May 2000, 8.

3. Tabitha Rendall, InterSec Research Corp., interview with author, 13

January 2000.

4. "European Company Performance Survey," *Financial Times Survey of the European Performance League,* 23 June 2000, IV.

5. Zucker, "AEGON Insurance Group," 12.

6. Zucker, "AEGON Insurance Group," 10-11.

7. Zucker, "AEGON Insurance Group," 8.

8. Angus Runciman, J.P. Morgan insurance analyst, interview with author, 9 December 1999.

9. Nicholas Byrne, Merrill Lynch insurance analyst, interview with author, 8 December 1999.

10. Philippe Foulquier and Natacha Roussett, "AEGON," Credit Lyonnaise Securities Europe, 8 October 1999, 13.

11. Jason B. Zucker, "AEGON," Bear Stearns, 5 April 1999, 6. Zucker made these comments while he was working at Bear Stearns.

12. "AEGON," Stephens, Inc., 12 November 1999, 1.

13. Huttner, Holiday, and Runciman, "European Insurance Profiting," 20.

14. Foulquier and Rousett, "AEGON," 3.

15. Zucker, "AEGON Insurance Group," 8.

BIPOP-Carire

1. Leonardo Rubattu and Duncan Farr, "BIPOP: Trade on Me, Trade Me On ... Line!", Morgan Stanley Dean Witter, 23 July 1999, 3.

2. Vincenza Colucci *et al*, "Italian Banks: Bit B@nks Beat Big Banks," ABN AMRO, 28 January 2000, 23.

3. Colucci *et al*, "Italian Banks," 19.

4. Colucci *et al*, "Italian Banks," 56.

5. For the record, the share price of Italian banks is on average 16 times 2000 earnings and 2.1 times 1999 book value. Neil D. Crowder *et al*, "BIPOP-Carire: Does Valuation Matter?" Goldman Sachs, 17 January 2000, p 2.

6. Colucci *et al*, "Italian Banks," 5.

7. Neil D. Crowder *et al*, "BIPOP-Carire: Does Valuation Matter?" 1 and 15.

8. Leonardo Rubattu and Duncan Farr, "BIPOP: Take.A.Break.Com," Morgan Stanley Dean Witter, 9 December 1999, 1.

9. Alberto Gaddi, "When at a Feast, Don't Give Up Your Seat at the Table," *SG Equity Research*, January 2000, 1.

10. Colucci *et al*, "Italian Banks," 54.

11. Gaddi, "When at a Feast," 3.

12. Laura Spotorno, "BIPOP-Carire: Cool Company," J.P. Morgan, 3 August 1999, 24.

13. Rubattu and Farr, "BIPOP: Take.A.Break.Com," 2.

14. Crowder *et al*, "BIPOP-Carire: Does Valuation Matter?" 8.

15. Spotorno, "BIPOP-Carire: Cool Company," 28.

16. Simone Concetti, "BIPOP: Potential Speaks Louder Than Numbers," Merrill Lynch, 25 November 1999, 1, 3.

17. Crowder *et al*, "BIPOP-Carire: Does Valuation Matter?" 6.
18. Sara Calian, "Road to Rome: Fund Firms Covet Hot Italian Market," *The Wall Street Journal*, 15 July 1999.
19. Correspondence from Cristina Finocchi, head of European Investor Relations, BIPOP, 2 February 2000.
20. Ibid.
21. Spotorno, "BIPOP-Carire: Cool Company," 18.
22. Spotorno, "BIPOP-Carire: Cool Company," 2.
23. Luca Caollo and Vincenza Colucci, "EuroBIPOP," ABN-AMRO, 7 July 2000, 3.

Carrefour

1. Alberto Montagne, "Carrefour + Promodès," Lehman Brothers, 7 October 1999, 1.
2. While the deal was technically regarded as a merger, Carrefour is clearly in charge of the new enterprise.
3. Nicholas HJ Jones *et al*, "Carrefour: French Deal, Global Consequences," Goldman Sachs, 11 November 1999.
4. Dutch food retailer Ahold was my initial choice before unanimous analyst support for Carrefour swayed my decision. Still, keep an eye on Ahold. It's a very strong player, especially in the States, where it earns nearly two-thirds of its profits.
5. Michèle Wolff *et al*, "Carrefour-Promodès: An Excellent Fit," Merrill Lynch, 21 September 1999, 9.
6. Jaime Vasquez and Liz Staples, "Carrefour: ... And All the World Its Oyster," Salomon Smith Barney, 19 March 1999, 3.
7. Wolff *et al.*, "Carrefour-Promodès: An Excellent Fit," 5.
8. Montagne, "Carrefour + Promodès," 24.
9. Jaime Vasquez *et al*, "Promodès: Capitalizing on European Integration," Salomon Smith Barney, 16 August 1999, 1.
10. Montagne, "Carrefour + Promodès," 1.
11. Ibid.
12. Vasquez *et al*, "Promodès: Capitalizing on European Integration," 3.
13. "European Company Performance," *Financial Times Survey*, 18 June 1999, 6.
14. Jaime Vasquez, "Carrefour: A Bigger Fish in the Global Pond," Salomon Smith Barney, 13 September 1999, 4.
15. Amita Gulati *et al*, "Carrefour: A Global Brand," Morgan Stanley Dean Witter, 15 November 1999, 3.
16. While this total figure is on the high end of estimates, nearly all analysts project earnings to grow by no less than 27 percent a year between 2000 and 2002. Amita Gulati *et al*, "Carrefour: A Global Brand," *Morgan Stanley Dean Witter*, 15 November 1999, 3.
17. Montagne, "Carrefour + Promodès," 9.

Hennes & Mauritz

1. Victoria Maxwell-Snape, "Hennes & Mauritz," HSBC Securities, 23 September 1999.

2. Hennes & Mauritz Annual Report 1998, 30.

3. "European Company Performance Survey," *Financial Times Survey of the European Performance League,* 23 June 2000, III.

4. Nicholas George, "H&M Leaps as Expansion Looms," *Financial Times*, 22 September 1999, 17.

5. Monika Elling, "Hennes & Mauritz," Enskilda Securities, 4 May 1999, 3.

6. "Knickers to the Market," *The Economist*, 28 February 1998 <http://www.economist.com>.

7. Ake Heden and Gunnar Widhagen, "Hennes & Mauritz," WorldVest Base Inc., 1998.

8. "Hennes & Mauritz," *Financial Times*, 22 September 1999, 14.

9. Monika Elling and Cecilia Parsmann, "Hennes & Mauritz: Short-Term Pain, Long-Term Gain," Enskilda Securities, 6 July 2000, 4.

10. As of 20 October 1999.

11. John Baille and Mike Tattersall, "Hennes & Mauritz," Cazenove & Co., 23 June 2000, 5.

12. Mal Patel, "Hennes & Mauritz: No End in Sight," Merrill Lynch, 22 September 1999, 1.

13. Louise von Blixen *et al*, "Hennes & Mauritz: Ain't No Stopping Them," SG Securities, 23 September 1999, 3.

14. *Hennes & Mauritz Annual Report 1998,* 30.

15. Nicholas George, "Fashioning a Store of Value," European Company Performance, *Financial Times Survey*, 18 June 1999, 4.

16. Monika Elling, Enskilda Securities, 4 May 1999.

Nokia

1. "A Broken Record of the Nicest Sort," Goldman, Sachs & Co., 23 July 1999, 1.

2. Robert Heller, "In Search of European Excellence," Harper Collins Business, 1998, 222.

3. "Nokia: Icy Hot," Goldman, Sachs & Co., 27 April 1999, 3.

4. Nokia's 1999 Financial Statements, 35.

5. Inventory turnover is measured by the number of days units are warehoused before being sold.

6. Jan Dworsky and Sasu Ristamaki, "Nokia," Crédit Agricole Indosuez Cheuvreux, 25 August 1999.

7. Ibid.

8. Jorma Ollila, "Nokia: Fourth Quarter 1998 and Full-Year 1998 Review," *Nokia*, 1999.

9. Interview with Nokia Investor Relations, 14 and 22 September 1999.

10. "Nokia: Icy Hot," 10.

Ryanair

1. Andrew Light, "Ryanair: Leading the European Low-Fares Travel Crusade," Salomon Smith Barney, 24 August 1999, 3.

2. Michael Skapinker, "Carrying the No-Frills Flag," *Financial Times*, 8 December 1998, 14.

3. Light, "Ryanair: Leading," 27.

4. John Murray Brown, "BA's Focus on Business Travelers May Boost Ryanair," *Financial Times*, 29 May 1999, 22.

5. Andrew Light, "Ryanair: Reinstating Buy Rating After FY00 Results," Schroder Salomon Smith Barney, 30 June 2000, 7.

6. Jonathan Wober *et al*, "Ryanair: Fair Value," Deutsche Bank, 6 July 2000, p. 16.

7. Light, "Ryanair: Leading," 8.

8. Light, "Ryanair: Leading," 16.

9. Light, "Ryanair: Leading," 17.

10. "Avoiding Peanuts," *The Economist*, 13 November 1999, 72.

11. Light, "Ryanair: Leading," 24.

12. *Ryanair: 1999 Annual Report and Financial Statements*, 10.

SAP

1. Marc Rode *et al*, "SAP," Warburg Dillon Read, 3 January 2000, 3.

2. Matthew Rose, "With American Hasso, Plattner Leads Europe's Tech Revival," *The Wall Street Journal*, 2 July 1998, A1, 14.

3. Geoffrey Nairn, "SAP: A Puzzle for the Enterprise Industry," IT Review, *Financial Times*, 2 February 2000, IV.

4. Coleen Kaiser, "SAP: Six More Months of Cloudy Weather," Merrill Lynch, 13 August 1999, 11.

5. Kaiser, "SAP: Six More Months," 12.

6. Charles Elliott, "SAP: Transitioning to E-Business," Goldman Sachs, 2 February 2000, 4.

7. Elliott, "SAP: Transitioning to E-Business," 5.

8. Jeremy Grant, "SAP: Success Built on the Back of Business Management," Baden-Württemberg Survey, *Financial Times*, 29 September 1999, III.

9. Marc Rode, Warburg Dillon Read technology analyst, interview with author, 16 February 2000.

10. Kevin Ashton *et al*, "SAP: 4Q99 Results—Positive Surprises," Deutsche Bank, January 2000, 2, 5.

11. Alla Gorelova, "SAP: When the End of the World Did Not Happen," Oppenheim Finanzanalyzse, 26 January 2000, 3.

12. Gorelova, "SAP: When the End of the World Did Not Happen," 4.

13. Kevin Ashton *et al*, "SAP: 4Q99 Results—Positive Surprises," Deutsche Bank, 24 January 2000, 3.

14. Charles Elliott *et al*, "SAP: Crossing the Rubicon?" Goldman Sachs, 21

July 1999, 1. Note that SAP's market capitalization dramatically increased in just two months after the end of 1999, when it broke past $56 million.

Suez Lyonnaise des Eaux

1. Pierre Coiffet, *Paribas*, interview with author, 28 October 1999.

2. Martin du Boise and Thomas Kamm, "Suez Lyonnaise Chief Strips Down Conglomerate in Ambitious Bid to Focus the Global Concern," *The Wall Street Journal*, 21 July 1998.

3. Dick Leonard, "Suez to Buy SGB," *Europe*, June 1998.

4. Pierre Coiffet, "Suez Lyonnaise," Paribas, November 1998.

5. Nikki Tait, "Water: An Industry in Flux," *Financial Times*, 3 September 1999, 25.

6. "Making Money from Water," *Institutional Investor*, July 1998.

7. *1999 Annual Report, Suez Lyonnaise des Eaux,* 12.

8. Financial services was excluded from this calculation because during this period Suez was divesting itself of this operation.

9. Adam Dickens *et al*, "Suez Lyonnaise des Eaux: Scale of Electricity and Communications Divisions to be Boosted," HSBC, 3 May 2000, 9.

10. Dickens *et al*, "Suez Lyonnaise des Eaux." 8.

11. Samer Iskander and Nikki Tait, "Suez Moves to Own Whole of UWR," *Financial Times*, 24 August 1999, 26.

12. Kerri Walsh, "Suez Buys Nalco, Claims Top Spot," *Chemical Week*, 7-14 July 1999.

13. Andrew Taylor, "TransAtlantic Investment Is a Two-Way Street," *Financial Times*, 1 September 1999, 22.

14. Neil Buckley and Samer Iskander, "Takeover Leads Tractebel to Merger Crossroads," *Financial Times*, 20 August 1999, 20.

15. Samer Iskander, "Suez Group Absorbs Sita Waste Division," *Financial Times*, 8 October 1999, 30.

16. Pierre Coiffet, "Suez Lyonnaise des Eaux," Paribas, October 1999, 1.

17. Pierre Stiennon and Jyrki Korhonen, "Suez Lyonnaise des Eaux: Becoming a Focused Growth Utility," J.P. Morgan, 21 April 1999, 15, 22.

18. Samer Iskander, "Utilities Group Has Crystal Clear Aims," *Financial Times*, 16 June 1999, 37.

19. Patrick Ayoub, Investor Relations, Suez Lyonnaise des Eaux, interview with author, 4 November 1999.

20. Samer Iskander and Nikki Tait, "Suez Moves to Own Whole of UWR," *Financial Times*, 24 August 1999, 26.

21. *Suez Lyonnaise des Eaux en 1998 Annual Report,* 11.

Vodafone

1. Robert Mocatta, "Vodafone AirTouch," Credit Suisse First Boston, 26 March 1999, 2.

2. *Vodafone 2000 Annual Report,* 35.

3. "European Company Performance," *Financial Times Survey,* 18 June 1999, 9.

4. *2000 Annual Report,* 3.

5. *2000 Annual Report,* 44.

6. This number is composed of Vodafone's home market and the company's equity proportion of subscribers in local telecoms in which the company has a stake.

7. Kevin Condon, "Vodafone AirTouch," Warburg Dillon Read, 1 October 1999.

8. Gautam Naik, "Vodafone AirTouch Agrees to Acquire CommNet Cellular for $764 million," *The Wall Street Journal,* 20 July 1999.

9. Stephanie N. Mehta, "Bell Atlantic Joins Vodafone to Form Cellular Venture," *The Wall Street Journal,* 22 September 1999.

10. Andrew Hill, "Bell and Vodafone Agree to Merge Assets," *Financial Times,* 22 September 1999, 17.

11. William Boston, "Germany's Mannesmann May Win from Successful Bid by Olivetti," *The Wall Street Journal,* 24 February 1999.

12. "Look, No Wires," *The Economist,* 23 January 1999 <http://www.economist.com>.

13. Thomas J. Lee, "AirTouch Communications," Salomon Smith Barney, 29 January 1999.

14. Richard Evans, "Tomorrow the World," *Barron's;* 6 March 2000.

15. Stuart J. Birdt, "Vodafone AirTouch," *Bear Sterns Focus List,* October 1999, 10.

16. Stephen Baker, "What's a Cell-Phone User Worth?" *Business Week,* 21 February 2000.

17. Alan Cane, "Mobile Revolution," *Financial Times,* 19 January 1999, 24.

Chapter 10

1. There are actually thousands of European mutual funds offered in Europe. But securities regulations limit U.S.-based investor access to only those funds registered in the States. As a result, the funds most available to U.S. investors are those affiliated with large U.S. fund families, e.g., Scudder, Fidelity, and Invesco. For investors eligible to own European-based funds, see the daily listing of managed funds in the *Financial Times* for a sample range of offerings.

2. Orders to sell or buy open-ended funds can only be executed at the end of the trading day, after their underlying value is tallied. Unlike trading a stock or a closed-end fund, investors cannot execute an order at a set price.

3. The MSCI Indices are a product of Morgan Stanley Capital International, recognized as one of the leading guides to national, regional, and global markets.

4. As of the beginning of 2000, no European sector funds were available to U.S. investors.

5. Morningstar provided nearly all fund performance data cited in this chapter. Portfolios and current performance can change dramatically. Consult specific funds and <http://www.morningstar.com> for the most up-to-date information.

6. Returns are based in local currency and are derived from the MSCI Indices.

7. Alex Skorecki, "Unfortunate Few Caught in the Steps of Giants," *Financial Times*, 17 February 2000, 29.

8. As of the end of 1999, U.S. investors had access to only a Swedish country fund: iShares MSCI Sweden, traded on the American Stock Exchange.

9. The three non–Pan-European funds that also exceeded the Standard and Poor's 500 during this time were Fidelity France, Fidelity Germany, and Fidelity Nordic. Note the time frame cited here is different than the period on which the table is based. This accounts for the difference in performance figures.

10. Source: Data from Morningstar. Note that all performance data are net of expenses.

11. These "Risk Ratings" are a trademark product of Morningstar.

12. BIPOP is one my featured stocks. (See Chapter 9.)

13. Between 1995 and 1999, while the Standard and Poor's 500 churned out returns of more than 25 percent a year, Lehman's 10 Uncommon (U.S.) Values averaged gains of more than 35 percent a year.

Chapter 11

Accounting and Financial Reporting

1. Bruno Solnik, "International Investments," *Addison-Wesley Publishing Company*, 1996, 214.

2. Ibid., 217.

3. Ibid., 190.

4. Ibid., 217.

5. Today, DaimlerChrysler prepares its financials only in accordance with U.S. GAAP.

6. Two superb sources are Fredrick D. S. Choi, *International Accounting and Finance Handbook*, John Wiley & Sons, 2nd Edition, (1997); and the periodic reports of Merrill Lynch analyst Gary S. Schieneman that appear under the title "Global Accounting and Valuation."

7. Gary S. Schieneman, "Global Accounting and Valuation: European and U.K. Accounting Differences," Merrill Lynch, 24 February 1999, 12.

8. Solnik, "International Investments," 221.

9. Frederick D. S. Choi, Dean of the Undergraduate Stern School of Business, New York University, interview with author, 28 February 2000.

Foreign Exchange and Bonds

1. For those not familiar with the basics of international trade, when an American firm wants to buy British goods, it doesn't just write a check in dollars; it must first convert dollars into British pounds and then cable the proceeds. It's little wonder that the global foreign exchange market trades more than a trillion dollars' worth of currencies each day.

2. Some analysts have blamed the euro's continuous fall on the need for further European structural reforms to trigger increased productivity. But these changes have been going on for quite some time across nearly all of Europe and show no signs of abating.

3. Mary Ann Bartels, Merrill Lynch, interview with author, 5 June 2000.

4. U.S. investors can mitigate their foreign exchange exposure when buying European equities by investing in companies like AEGON, Vodafone, and DaimlerChrysler, who own major operations in the States. Because these companies generate a substantial portion of sales in dollars, their profits are enhanced by a strengthening dollar.

5. All currency calculations were based on historic exchange rates provided by the Swiss econometric group Olsen & Associates through its Web site, <http://oanda.com>.

6. Currency hedging wouldn't work for bond investors because the cost of the hedge virtually amounts to the difference in interest payments, therefore negating the purpose of the investment.

7. Guidance to forecasting currency movement is intentionally relegated to a footnote because even for seasoned professionals, these prognostications are far from a sure thing. The essence of one general strategy involves tracking the trading range of a given currency against the dollar over the past five or ten years, noting reasons for all extraordinary movements. If an investor finds a currency is trading near its historic low without substantial cause and the near-term macroeconomic outlook appears positive, then one may see a rebound in the currency over the next twelve months. Remember, exchange rate fluctuations of 10 to 20 percent over a year are common, even between currencies of developed economies.

But without a significant history of its own, the euro is still in the process of forging its initial trading pattern. Further, its existence may be skewing the performance of other European currencies. In the past, the highly respected German Bundesbank was credited for sustaining much of western Europe's monetary integrity, which in turn supported many of Europe's currencies. But the European Central Bank, which is now in charge of the eurozone's monetary policy, has not been in power long enough to have earned the market's trust to anywhere near the same degree.

Index

About Bloomberg

Bloomberg L.P., founded in 1981, is a global information services, news, and media company. Headquartered in New York, the company has nine sales offices, two data centers, and 80 news bureaus worldwide.

Bloomberg, serving customers in 100 countries around the world, holds a unique position within the financial services industry by providing an unparalleled combination of news, information, and analytic tools in a single package known as the BLOOMBERG PROFESSIONAL™ service. Corporations, banks, money management firms, financial exchanges, insurance companies, and many other entities and organizations rely on Bloomberg as their primary source of information.

BLOOMBERG NEWS℠, founded in 1990, offers worldwide coverage of economies, companies, industries, governments, financial markets, politics, and sports. The news service is the main content provider for Bloomberg's broadcast media, which include BLOOMBERG TELEVISION®—the 24-hour cable and satellite television network available in ten languages worldwide—and BLOOMBERG RADIO™—an international radio network anchored by flagship station BLOOMBERG® WBBR AM1130 in New York.

In addition to the BLOOMBERG PRESS® line of books, Bloomberg publishes *BLOOMBERG® MARKETS, BLOOMBERG PERSONAL FINANCE™*, and *BLOOMBERG® WEALTH MANAGER*. To learn more about Bloomberg, call a sales representative at:

Frankfurt:	49-69-920-410	San Francisco:	1-415-912-2960
Hong Kong:	852-977-6000	São Paulo:	5511-3048-4500
London:	44-171-330-7500	Singapore:	65-438-8585
New York:	1-212-318-2000	Sydney:	61-29-777-8686
Princeton:	1-609-279-3000	Tokyo:	81-3-3201-8900

For in-depth market information and news, visit **BLOOMBERG.COM**®, which draws proprietary content from the BLOOMBERG PROFESSIONAL™ service and Bloomberg's host of media products to provide high-quality news and information in multiple languages on stocks, bonds, currencies, and commodities, at **www.bloomberg.com.**

About the Author

Eric Uhlfelder has been covering international markets as a writer and analyst for more than ten years. His work is featured in *Business Week, Euromoney's Global Investor, Individual Investor, Mutual Funds,* and *Fidelity Focus* magazines. Uhlfelder's articles have focused on Europe's evolving equity culture, foreign exchange and the euro, bonds, technology, and the area's regional and emerging markets. He has been an editorial consultant for PaineWebber, Gerard Klauer Mattison, the Friedberg Mercantile Group, the Gartner Group, and Advest. In addition, he has published various studies on municipal finance, including articles on New York City's fiscal crisis of the 1970s, privatization, and innovative methods for funding urban redevelopment.